500
HORRIBLE
WAYS
TO DIE IN
GEORGIA

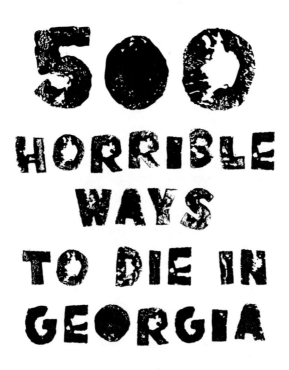

500 HORRIBLE WAYS TO DIE IN GEORGIA

A Collection of
Grim, Grisly, Gruesome, Ghastly, Gory, Grotesque,
Lurid, Terrible, Tragic, Bizarre, and Sensational Deaths
Reported in Georgia Newspapers
Between 1820 and 1920

A. STEPHEN JOHNSON

BOOKLOGIX˙
Alpharetta, GA

ISBN: 978-1-6653-0274-6

Library of Congress Control Number: 2021924460

Printed in the United States of America   1 2 2 3 2 1

⊚This paper meets the requirements of ANSI/NISO Z39.48-1992 (Permanence of Paper)

This book is dedicated to my good friend,
Charles Dudley Salley, PhD,
scholar, Germanophile, opera patron,
and a real southern gentleman.
The title of this book was his idea.

Contents

Foreword

I first became interested in reading old newspapers when I was serving as Historic Preservation Chairman for a small town in Georgia. It was necessary to determine the date various buildings were constructed, and old newspapers were the only source of information.

Old newspapers are fascinating. They give us eyewitness accounts of national and world events which are now history. They give us insight into the daily lives of our ancestors. And newspapers are an important resource for genealogical research. Many marriage and death notices in old newspapers cannot be found anywhere else, since Georgia has lost many records in courthouse fires. Also, before 1900, many people were buried in unmarked graves, and many did not leave a will or estate papers.

Newspapers of the early 1800s contain mostly political editorials, news of national and world events, legal notices, and advertising. The few marriage and death notices are minimal and succinct. As the century progressed, news of ordinary people occupied more and more space in newspapers, particularly in small towns. Death notices, particularly, contained a great deal of detail, and especially so in accidental deaths.

I have chosen the period 1820 to 1920 for this book because that hundred-year period saw a great increase in technological advances. Stagecoaches as a means of transportation were replaced by steamboats and railroads. The steam engine, originally invented to pump water out of English coal mines, found new applications in factories, sawmills, and cotton gins. The development of the petroleum industry in 1859 provided new (and flammable) fuels. Electricity found new applications at the end of the century, and automobiles appeared in the early 1900s. During that time, narcotics, other drugs, and liquor were readily available, and it seems that every person, young and old, had ready access to a shotgun, rifle, or pistol. All of these elements provided an environment rife with a multitude of accidental deaths, which were described in newspapers in detailed, graphic, gruesome language which would not be considered appropriate today.

I suspect that readers of nineteenth century newspapers probably actually enjoyed reading the most sensational language editors could muster in describing all the details of how the unfortunate victim met his or her sudden end, just as readers of today's tabloids enjoy reading about the latest scandals in the entertainment world or the British royal family.

The deaths reported in this book fall roughly into six categories:
1. murders
2. suicides
3. natural deaths under unusual or bizarre circumstances
4. carelessness or unfamiliarity with moving vehicles,

machinery, animals, firearms, explosives, drugs, fires, electricity, or the like

5. bad luck/freak accident or being in the wrong place at the wrong time and
6. just plain stupidity.

Suicides were far more common than I had expected, and it was unbelievable how many men got drunk and then laid themselves down on the railroad tracks to sleep it off, with consequent dissociation of body parts. However, some of them may have been murdered first, and then placed there.

Some of the deaths in this book took place outside of Georgia, but they all were reported in Georgia newspapers. Those which occurred in other states are so unique and sensational that I felt that they deserved inclusion in this book.

I must apologize for the language used in these reports to refer to slaves and free black persons. I have simply reprinted all the reports exactly as they appeared in the newspaper, and the language reflects the language and attitudes of the time. We can all be thankful that our society has progressed to allow persons of color equal status and equal opportunities under the law.

Finally, I expect that this book will be of greatest appeal to teenage boys and others of an equally perverse mind. If you are the squeamish sort who can't stand the sight of blood, better not read it. It might give you nightmares.

A. S. J.

Sources

The following newspapers were used as sources for items in this book:

AB: *Athens Banner*

AbC: *Abbeville Chronicle*

AP: *Albany Patriot*

AtC: *Atlanta Constitution*

AWI: *Atlanta Weekly Intelligencer*

BD: *Bainbridge Democrat*

BWD: *Bainbridge Weekly Democrat*

CA: *Cuthbert Appeal*

CCG: *Coffee County Gazette* (Pearson, GA)

CE: *Columbus Enquirer*

CG: *Central Georgian* (Sandersville and Sparta, GA)

CI: *Christian Index and South-Western Baptist*

CS: *Chronicle and Sentinel* (Augusta, GA)

CT: *Calhoun (GA) Times*

DB: *Douglas (GA) Breeze*

DCJ: *Dodge County Journal*

DE: *Douglas (GA) Enterprise*

DJ: *Dawson (GA) Journal*

DTJ: *Dodge Times-Journal*

DWJ: *Dawson (GA) Weekly Journal*

ECN: *Early County News*

ET: *Eastman Times*

GH: *Greensboro Herald*

GJ: *Georgia Journal* (Milledgeville, GA)

GJM: *Georgia Journal and Messenger* (Macon, GA)

GM: *Georgia Messenger* (Fort Hawkins & Macon, GA)

GMF: *Georgia Mirror* (Florence, Stewart County, GA)

GT: *Georgia Telegraph* (Macon, GA)

GWT: *Georgia Weekly Telegraph* (Macon, GA)

HD: *Hawkinsville Dispatch*

HDN: *Hawkinsville Dispatch and News*

HHJ: *Houston Home Journal*

HJ: *Hamilton Journal*

HV: *Hamilton Visitor*

HWV: *Hamilton Weekly Visitor*

LH: *LaGrange Herald*

LR: *LaGrange Reporter*

MCC: *Macon* (County) *Citizen*

MoM: *Montgomery Monitor*

MT: *Macon* (GA) *Telegraph*

NN: *Newnan News*

QB: *Quitman* (GA) *Banner*

QI: *Quitman* (GA) *Independent*

SMN: *Savannah Morning News*

SR: *Southern Recorder* (Milledgeville, GA)

TG: *Tifton Gazette*

TR: *Republic* (Macon, GA)

TSR: *Times and States Rights Advocate* (Milledgeville, GA)

TT: *Thomasville Times*

VN: *Vienna News*

WGR: *WireGrass Reporter* (Thomasville, GA)

WGT: *Weekly Georgia Telegraph* (Macon, GA)

WS: *Weekly Sun* (Columbus, GA)

WTS: *Weekly Times & Sentinel* (Columbus, GA)

Terms and Definitions

Some definitions and explanations which may be necessary in understanding these accounts:

Melancholy: used as an adjective implied tragic rather than merely sad or depressing.

Intelligence: news or information.

Esq. or Esquire: a title used to denote a person of influence or considerable wealth, such as a public official, large land-owner, lawyer, etc.

(sic): means that the word is reproduced exactly as it was printed, even though incorrect.

(. . .) indicates that an unimportant part of the newspaper account has been omitted.

These terms were often used after dates:

Ult. or **ultimo**: the previous month.

Inst. or **instant**: the present month. (If the article is taken from another newspaper and refers to an incident in the previous month, the term inst., may be used since it was worded that way in the original article.)

Prox. or **proximo**: the next month. (Rarely used in death notices.)

500 Horrible Ways to Die in Georgia

BRUTAL AFFAIR. In Wayne County, on the 13th inst. RICHARD HOPS, was murdered, by stabs in several parts of his body, and being cut open with a knife, so that his entrails were exposed to view, by James Yates, who immediately escaped but has, we are glad to state, been apprehended through the vigilance of the sheriff of that county, and one or two other persons. On his being arrested, he stated, as we are informed, that he had been aided by Henry Summerville (in whose house it occurred) in executing the above horrible deed.

Summerville, we understand, has also been arrested and committed to the gaol in Camden County - where they both are to remain to stand their trial at the next Superior Court for Wayne County.

–Darien Gaz, 24th inst.

June 19, 1821 (SR)

DIED at his residence in Baldwin County, Mr. Cary Curry, Sen., in his 62d year. He was afflicted with a cancer on his face twenty-five years, was confined to his house eighteen months, and survived several months after being deprived of sight, and nose, and all the bones comprising the upper jaw on one side of his face up to the eye-brows. His nutriment for three months previous to his death, was composed of spirits, honey and water . . . He was a soldier of the revolution, and was in the Florida expedition in '78 . . .

May 19, 1823 (GM)

MR. JAMES S. RICHARDSON was killed in Sparta on Tuesday evening last by a fall from the window of his apartment, in the second story of the Eagle tavern. He was not discovered till a late hour in the evening – when found, the vital spark was extinct. He was a native of England, and a teacher of music.

April 18, 1829 (GM)

On Friday of last week Joseph Williams was executed in Marion (Twiggs County) for the murder of Nimrod Phillips. After his trial he exhibited the most hardened indifference to his fate. When taken from the jail, and on his way to the place of execution, he continued to hum a frivolous song, and while under the gallows took several drinks of whiskey. Up to the last moment he behaved with the utmost recklessness and hardihood. He observed to the byestanders (*sic*) that he did wish to go into another world with a broken neck, and his head on his shoulder, and being aware of the moment at which he was to be suspended, drew up his legs before the sheriff had let go the drop and accordingly suspended himself, without breaking his neck. A few days previous he made an attempt to destroy himself by taking two ounces of laudanum, but the dose being too large, he was unable to retain it upon his stomach.

April 9, 1831 — (MT)

MELANCHOLY CASUALTY. On Monday afternoon last, Mr. Alexander Smith, of Jasper County, was drowned in attempting to ford a small creek, on his way home from the village of Monticello. It appears that Mr. S. had been in the village most of the day, indulging freely in intoxicating liquors, and it is presumed that he fell from his horse into the creek (which was unusually swollen by the rains of that day,) and was unable to extricate himself. The creek at the ford was wide but scarcely knee deep. A coroner's inquest was held over the body verdict accidental death by drowning. Mr. Smith was between 50 and 60 years of age.

March 7, 1833 — (GJ)

STAGE ACCIDENT AND LOSS OF LIFE. – The Mail Stage in fording Walnut Creek, last Friday night, 2 or 3 miles from Macon, on the road from Clinton, was swept by the current from the rockey (*sic*) ford into deep water, where it capsized, and we lament to say, Mr. Charles W. Washington, of Macon, one of the passengers, being unable to swim, was drowned. Two other passengers, a white and a black man, escaped by swimming. The driver swam out on one of the horses, but the other three could not be extricated from the harness, and perished.

April 10, 1833 ——————————————— (TSR)

DIED. . . . Also, on the same (Sunday) evening, an interesting child of Dr. Tomlinson Fort, who came to its death from swallowing a large number of percussion caps.

July 19, 1834 ——————————————— (CE)

It is with feelings of the deepest lamentation that the community of Harris county, learn the death of the Rev. John M. Gray. This melancholy event occurred on the night of the 14th inst. in Alabama, where he had been two or three days preaching the gospel of Christ. Being at the house of a steam Doctor, he was induced to take a dose of Lobelia, not so much for the benefit of his health as to experience the operation, as he sometimes administered that medicine himself, but had never taken it. Seeming not to do well after taking it, the doctor endeavored to relieve him, but he expired about 11 o'clock at night . . .

Thus one of the most useful men in the Western part of Georgia, has fallen victim to the system of steam quackery.

March 31, 1835 ——————————————— (GJ)

SUICIDE. A stage driver on the Florida route, Walter Jones by name, in a fit of insanity, put an end to his existence lately in Laurens County, by taking the backlog from a good fire, and laying himself down in the place of it.

August 16, 1836 (GJ)

MURDER AND SUICIDE. We have just learned that a most shocking murder was committed in Forsyth County, on the Chestatee River, on the 30th ult. Hiram Norton, heretofore considered a sober, honest and respectable citizen, without any apparent cause, struck his wife on the head with an axe, causing her death instantly. He immediately directed his little son to go to the nearest neighbor's and inform them what had happened, and then went to the river, threw himself in and was drowned. He had been for some time laboring under deep religious impressions, and it is supposed had become partially deranged.

–Athens Banner, August 6.

May 8, 1838 (CS)

MELANCHOLY DEATH. We learn from the *Darien Telegraph,* that a man by the name of William McBride Lewis, was burned to death not far from that city. It appears that he had been attending Court as a Bailiff, and camped out on his return home, with some other friends, all of whom were intoxicated and while lying in that state near a fire the clothes of the unfortunate Lewis caught, and he was so badly burnt that he expired a short time afterwards.

May 7, 1839 ———————————— (GMF)

Tallahassee, April 10. **MRS. PERRINE KILLED BY THE INDIANS!** This day, one week ago, a party of Indians, consisting of ten or fifteen, attacked the dwelling of Capt. James Scott, who lives about two miles from Bailey's mills in Jefferson county; at the first fire Mrs. P. was killed, a lad, a nephew of Col. Bailey, shot in the arm, and a negro woman very dangerously wounded.

It is stated that Capt. Scott and his overseer, Mr. Skipper, defended the house with great courage, killed one of the Indians, and put to flight the remainder.

Mrs. Perrine, we learn, was an amiable and accomplished lady, whose husband is absent on a tour of civil Engineering.

October 12, 1839 ———————————— (GMF)

From the *Georgia Jeffersonian*. **MELANCHOLY OCCURRENCE.** An occurrence, which resulted in the death of four men, citizens of the adjoining county of Chambers, in the State of Alabama, was detailed to us yesterday, and from the respectability of its source we have no doubt of its truth. We have not been able to obtain the names of the sufferers.

It appears that a well, in the neighborhood of Standing Rock, in the county above mentioned, having failed to yield its usual supply of water, the owner of the premises determined to have it cleared out. A person was let down by the well bucket and rope, but showed no signs of action at the bottom – he was called to, but did not answer. A second proposed to go down and ascertain what was the matter, and he also as soon as he arrived at the bottom, became supine and silent. A third proposed to go down, but it was only to join his unfortunate companions. When he got nearly to the foot of the well he called to be drawn up; but when about half way up, he fell from the bucket! A fourth then proposed that he should be lashed fast, and he would descend with the understanding also that he should be hauled as soon as he called out. He had descended but little more than half way when he gave the word, they drew him up quickly, but had barely time to unlash him before he was extinct. The other three were then taken out of the well with grapples, but none of them showed the least signs of life - the vital spark was forever extinguished! This melancholy catastrophe happened on Thursday, and the bodies of the unfortunate sufferers were consigned to the grave on Friday last.

Thus has (*sic*) four human lives been destroyed, and their spirits hastened to eternity; for the want of a small share of caution. A well should not be descended, when there is the least haze or appearance of vapor within it, without first trying it by introducing therein a candle or torch; if the light will continue to burn there is no danger, but if it is extinguished in its descent or as soon as it arrives at the bottom, the utmost caution should be observed in descending.

September 7, 1843 ——————————— (LH)

MELANCHOLY ACCIDENT. We are informed that on Tuesday, 29th ult., while returning from the Harris Campmeeting; the mules of Mr. Wm. Walker, took fright, and ran away with the carriage, which contained his wife, son, two young ladies, and a servant woman. The mules striking the bridge, which is over Mulberry Creek, breaking the railings, and one falling over, caused the driver to spring from his seat, and open the carriage door, from which the two young ladies sprang out upon the bridge: Mrs. W. was so much alarmed as not to be able to get out; when the driver finding that the carriage would be thrown over into the water, attempted to prevent it – but, it was too late – the whole of the remaining company were precipitated into the creek, which was at that time, some 10 or 15 feet deep. The driver succeeded in saving himself and one mule. The son of Mr. W. swam out. The rest were all drowned.

Thus, in one brief moment, this lovely companion, wife, sister, friend and mother, was called into eternity.

September 7, 1843 ———————— (GM)

UNFORTUNATE CASUALTY. – On Monday evening last, while the train of Passenger Cars on the Central Rail Road, were about two miles above Station No. 16, they ran over a man by the name of Robert Thomas, who was almost instantly killed. It was dusk at the time, and he was lying on the track, probably intoxicated. The train passed over his shoulder and thigh, which were so badly crushed, as to occasion his death immediately. He was discovered after the train had passed him, and taken up and carried to the next station, where the body was left, and an inquest called, but their report we have not learned. No blame could be attached to the Engineer or others superintending the train, as the duskiness of the evening prevented them from seeing him. One thing is certain, that a Rail Road is a most dangerous lodging place, both for man and beast – and particularly for men when beastly drunk.

February 14, 1844

HEARTRENDING ACCIDENT. A friend of ours of Heard county, furnishes us with the following particulars of the death of a young man of that county:

Franklin, Ga., Feb. 6, 1844.

Mr. Editor: a most dreadful circumstance happened in this county on the morning of the 3d inst. It appears that a young man by the name of Pinckney Hill, had gone some two or three hours before day on a hunting excursion, and not having returned by the next evening, his friends became alarmed and collected a considerable force to make a search for him. After a most diligent search, they found his body under the following circumstances: A large poplar tree, some two feet in diameter, which had been felled, under which was found one of the legs of the unfortunate young man. It appeared as though the tree, in falling, had come in contact with another tree which sloped or bent in an angle from the one that was cut, which caused the one that was felled to rebound in the opposite direction, and by this means caught the young man, found it. The leg, when found, had the appearance of having the bones entirely mashed asunder, and to have had the flesh cut by some sharp instrument. The party continued their search for the body; and about eighty yards from the place above named, found it. A large knife was found in one of his pockets, upon which was a quantity of blood – leaving no doubt in the minds of those who saw him, but what he had himself taken the knife from his pocket, cut the skin and flesh that held his leg together, and had placed the knife back in his pocket – leaving a portion of his leg under the tree. He then, no doubt pulled himself by the bushes and underwood to the place where he was found;

although a marsh intervened between the two places, no trace of his passage through it could be traced.

It is painful to contemplate the sufferings of this unfortunate youth. Alone, some two miles from any human habitation, to have received so dreadful a wound, yet not to be deprived of reason (as he evidently must not have been, from the fact of his having used his knife in the manner above stated,) to have been reduced to the necessity of cutting off his own leg, and then starting in the direction of home, but soon bleeding to death, the anguish he must have endured, is most heart rending indeed.

Mr. Hill was a young man of about 18 years of age, of good moral character, industrious and steady habits. He left home at the time before stated, in good health and bouyant (*sic*) spirits; but, alas, how soon was he called from hence to another world, and under what painful circumstances did he leave his friends . . .

March 27, 1845 — (GM)

FATAL ACCIDENT. A man by the name of John Tozier, a citizen of Columbus, left this city for that place in the Stage on Tuesday night of last week. About eight miles from this city, he attempted to get out of the Stage window, when he fell, and both wheels of the Stage passed over him, by which he was severely injured. He was brought back to this City, where he lingered until Monday, when he expired from the injuries he had received by the Stage.

April 2, 1845 ——————————————— (TR)

SUICIDE. The *Savannah Republican* of Saturday last, says:
   Our city has been thrown into a most painful stage of agitation and distress, by the melancholy termination of the life of a young and promising clergyman of the Episcopal Church of this place – the Rev. James Jackson, late of the Diocese of Massachusetts. He had just returned but a few days from the South, where he had been travelling two months for the restoration of his health, which had been impaired by a laborious performance of his clerical duties. He was apparently very much restored by his absence, and his friends hoped that he would be enabled to resume his very acceptable services in St. John's Church. But their hopes and his were doomed to a wretched disappointment, for after exhibiting on the few previous days strong evidences of wildness, he suddenly left the city on Wednesday morning, without giving any notice of his intended departure, and although suspicion was immediately excited and search made during that day and night, he was not found until the next morning, having drowned himself in the river opposite Bonaventure. His body was recovered and the Coroner's inquest had not hesitation upon the very strong testimony submitted to them, to bring an instant verdict of "insanity" . . .

June 10, 1845 ——————————————— (SR)

FATAL ACCIDENT ON THE CENTRAL RAILROAD. On Monday, 2d inst., as the passenger train was passing down, about one mile below Gordon, it ran over Mr. Jesse Collier, killing him instantly. They discovered something on the track some distance ahead, but as they were under such tremendous headway, being down grade, they found it impossible to check the speed in time. . . . His age was 68.

June 25, 1845 ——————————————— (AP)

DEATH BY LIGHTNING. On Tuesday of last week, Mr. Isaac Brinson, of this county (Baker), while gathering cattle about three miles from Newton, was passing through an open pond, when a stroke of lightning killed him and the horse on which he rode. The cloud was a small one, which afforded no rain, and the only severe thunder clap which issued from it, was that which called a mortal to eternity.

March 1, 1848 ——————————————— (GJM)

FATAL RAILROAD ACCIDENT. We regret to learn that Joseph H. Stokes, Esq., an Attorney at Law, of Dalton, was instantly killed at Kingston, on the Western & Atlantic Railroad, on Saturday evening last, the 19 inst., by attempting to enter the passenger train while it was in motion. After jumping on the train his foot slipped and he was caught between the cars and platform, and was crushed to death in an instant.

–Augusta Sentinel.

September 5, 1848 ——————————————— (GT)

DEATH OF FREDERICK SIMS ESQ. We are pained to announce the sudden death of Frederick Sims, Esq., of this city. He was killed on Monday last a few miles above this city, on the Macon & Western Rail Road. The particulars of this death as near as we can learn appear to be these. Mr. Sims was acting as conductor of one of the passenger trains in the absence of the regular officer, and while standing on the steps of the Cars was struck from his position and killed by a projecting post or fence running quite up to the track. He survived the accident but a few moments.

Mr. Sims was one of the oldest and most respectable citizens of Macon. He has left a wife and several children . . .

September 19, 1848 ——————— (CE)

DIED – On Sunday the 3d inst., William M. Evans, aged 37 years. The deceased was a native of Norfolk County, Virginia, but a resident of Havanna (*sic*) for the last 16 years. He had been on a visit to his brother, George W. Evans, of Talbot County, Georgia, and on his return, met his untimely fate in the Steamboat Olive, which was destroyed on the Alabama River on the 2d inst., 60 miles below Montgomery at King's Landing, through the negligence of the Engineer not having any water in the boilers. The deceased was standing between the chimnies (*sic*), when the boilers burst and the explosion took place. The first floor gave away and he was precipitated on the boilers, which not having any water in them were red hot. The first attempt he make (*sic*) to get out was unsuccessful, but still persevering he succeeded in extracating (*sic*) himself by taking hold of the red hot irons, and raising himself up. He was literally burt (*sic*) to death, mortification took place and survived about 24 hours after the sad occurrence. He retained his right mind until a few minutes before he died. Thus a most estimable and good man met a most horrid and torturing death, through the carelessness or neglect of an incompetent and untrustworthy Engineer.

June 26, 1849 ——————————— (CE)

MOURNFUL DEATH. Master P.T. Schley, eldest child of Dr. W.K. and Mary F. Schley, of Columbus, was suddenly killed on Sunday night, June 17th, by the explosion of a tin can containing Camphene, from which the lamp was being supplied. This disastrous event may be safely urged as a proof, that these lamps, whatever may be said of their cheapness as an instrument of light, or of the brilliance and beauty of the light, must be looked upon as a dangerous convenience in a family. . . .

This mournful occurrence took place in the house of his uncle, G.F. Pierce, in Oxford, whither he had been sent to recruit his health, which had been much impaired by Scarlet fever, and also to commence a thorough course of education under his uncle, J.L. Pierce . . . his mother was expecting in a few days to visit him, and to press him again to her fervid bosom. But while her maternal love was reveling in this anticipated delight, came these words in his uncle's sorrowful letter: "Phillip, who four hours ago was buoyant with boyish life, is now a corpse." . . .

July 17, 1849 ——————————— (CE)

DIED. At his residence in Muscogee County on the morning of the 3d inst. and supposed to be a short time before day light, Mr. Joseph Biggers, in the 70th year of his age. The sad messenger, death, visited this aged gentleman in a fit of insanity, and though painful to relate, he terminated his existence by attaching a balerope to a girder of his ginhouse, and suspending himself to it until life departed . . .

About 15 years ago, while engaged in extinguishing a fire which was about to consume a couple of corn cribs, he overheated himself and his physician said that inflammation of the brain was produced – at that time he attempted to destroy his life, but was prevented. His physician said that he might be relieved from that delirium, and it might be thought that he would entirely regain his former intellect, but stated to the family that occasional fits of insanity would follow all along through life, and so it has proved to be. . . .

October 23, 1849 ——————————— (CE)

A HORRID AFFAIR. On Friday evening last, as the regular passenger train on the Macon & Western Railroad was coming from above, when some five miles from this place, the engineer discovered upon the track, a negro girl with her head lying upon the railing. It was down grade, and the car was going very rapidly which rendered it utterly impossible to stop it before it reached her. . . . The whole train passed over her, almost entirely severing her head from her body and frightfully mutilating her otherwise. She was the property of Col. D.W. Collier, aged about 16 years, and was an active and intelligent girl. It is supposed that in a fit of mental aberration, she placed herself in that position for the purpose of selfdestruction. No cause is given for the horrid deed. Col. Collier is a man proverbially kind to his negroes, and has never struck this girl a lick, which makes it so much the more strange. No blame can possibly attach to the engineer, for we are assured that he used every means to prevent it.

—Forsyth Bee.

December 7, 1852 ——————— (CG)

HORRIBLE TRAGEDY! HUSBAND MURDERED BY HIS WIFE!!

On Wednesday, the 10th inst., the good citizens of Gilmer county were startled by the discovery of a crime of most horrible character; the particulars of which, as related to us by a brother-in-law of the murdered man, are as follows:

On the morning mentioned, a woman named Presley, living within a few miles of Ellijay, informed her neighbors that a strange man had stopped at the house the day before, and tarried through that (Tuesday) night; during which he had killed her husband. On repairing to the house, her husband was found in bed, insensible, with an axe still sticking in his cleft skull, and his brains oozing out. He breathed on until Wednesday evening, when death came to his relief. A daughter of the victim disabused the public mind, by denying that any strange man had been on the premises as stated by her mother; upon whom, of course, suspicion then fell, and she was arrested. She thereupon confessed having herself committed the unnatural crime, at the same time expressing regret that she had not done it twenty years ago.

It appears, from the narration to us, that she did in fact, about that time, make the attempt, by tying his arms across his breast, while in a state of beastly intoxication, sitting astride of his person, and essaying to cut his throat with his own shoemaker's knife. She was only prevented consummating the awful deed, by a negro opportunely dragging her from the prostrate body of her husband.

The deceased had formerly been notoriously intemperate; but for some time past, had led a sober life. The immediate occasion of his horrible murder, was a conjugal quarrel. Strange to say, this she-monster was released from her temporary imprisonment in the jail at Ellijay, and is, we understand, now at large.

–Dalton Times.

May 24, 1853 — (CG)

FATAL OCCURRENCE. We regret to learn that Washington Sowell of Scriven (*sic*) County was accidentally killed on the 17th inst., by a blow from the carriage tongue of a timber waggon. The circumstances as we have them from a gentleman of that county, are these: Mr. Sowell and Mr. Jacob Freeman of the same county had gone into the woods on that morning for the purpose of hauling timber, they had succeeded in hoisting a piece on the carriage, and started off when the chain which confined the tongue of the carriage came loose. It flew over and struck Mr. S., on the head and killed him instantly. Mr. Freeman who was near him at the time came near sharing the same fate.

June 14, 1853 — (GJM)

RAIL ROAD ACCIDENT – CONDITION OF MR. STEPHENS.

The cars on the M. & W. Railroad, on their downward trip on Tuesday night, the 7th inst., when within two miles of this city, ran over two cows which were lying on the track. The cowcatcher held one of them, but the other by some means, got under the wheels of the passenger car and threw it off the track. It rushed down the embankment, which was about fifteen feet high, turned twice completely over, and before its progress was arrested, was a mass of ruins. The breakman (*sic*) and mailguard was (*sic*) taken from under its fragments, dead; and all the passengers except one or two, were more or less injured. Among those severely injured were the Hon. Alexander H. Stephens, and a Mr. Lowe and Mrs. Dawson, of this city. All of them are slowly recovering from their injuries.

Mr. Stephens suffered a slight concussion of the brain, from a cut upon the head, by which he was rendered delirious for a few hours, had his left arm broken above the elbow, and was badly bruised. He was taken to the Lanier House, and is now so far recovered as to be able to walk across his room, and will be strong enough to leave it in a few days. . . . He will be at the Gubernatorial Convention, which meets next week.

There is no blame attached to any officer or agent of the Railroad Company. The accident was caused as the majority of railroad accidents in this State are caused, by the runing (sic) over of stock, which are allowed to go at large upon our railroad tracks; and for which if accidentally killed our laws, oblige the Railroad Companies to pay. The Macon & Western Railroad Company will be compelled to pay the value of the cows. . . . Some legislation upon this subject is absolutely necessary.

July 25, 1854 ——————————— (GT)

FOUND DEAD. Coroner Eden was called to hold an inquest, on Sunday last, over the body of William H. Hargroves, on the Louisville Road, some ten miles from the city. The body was discovered at an early hour in the morning of that day, lying near the railroad track, with the right leg, just above the ancle (*sic*), nearly cut off, and having various other wounds. It appeared in evidence before the jury that on Saturday night the deceased was seen sitting on the track awaiting the down train. Before it approached he doubtless fell asleep, and was finally run over and killed.

–Sav. Georgian.

September 26, 1854 ──────── (CE)

DIED at the residence of Mr. H.F. Colly, near Ft Gaines, on the 18th instant, James Hopkins, aged about 21 years. The manner in which this young man came to his death was as singularly strange as unexpected and heartrending to his friends. He, with some two or three of his companions, were standing round looking at a well which had been dug to the depth of some 50 feet without coming to water, when it was proposed, for their amusement, that they should descend to the bottom. Young Hopkins begged that the others should let him go down, and accordingly got into the bucket, and was let down; but upon arriving at the bottom, and finding himself unable to breathe, called out to be drawn up, and upon arriving within about ten feet of the top, the poisonous gas, or air damp as it is called by some, had taken such an effect on him that he let go his hold and fell to the bottom a lifeless corpse. His companions managed to get his body out in about thirty minutes, but found that the brittle thread of life was broken, and their companion who but a few moments before was the pride of the whole circle, was now a lifeless lump of clay! Young Hopkins was respected by all who knew him. He was a model of industry and steady habits, a kind friend, an affectionate brother and dutiful son, and was the hope and stay of a widowed mother.

October 11, 1854 ———————————— (GJM)

FATAL ACCIDENT. We are pained to announce the sudden death of Mr. John Felix McKinne, Discount Clerk in the Bank of Augusta, by one of those casualties which no foresight on his part could avoid. He was coming in from the Sand Hills, in a buggy, between 9 and 10 o'clock yesterday morning and just as he neared Simpson's stable, in Ellis Street, a horse which was running away with a portion of a vehicle turned from McIntosh into Ellis street, passing by and near Mr. McK. His horse took freight (sic) and becoming unmanageable dashed off at a furious rate, running the buggy against a tree just opposite the Ellis-street House, against which Mr. McK. was thrown with such violence that he expired in a few minutes.

—Augusta Chron. & Sent. 6th inst.

October 28, 1854 ———————————— (AWI)

TERRIBLE CALAMITY. We have been permitted to make the following extract from a private letter of a gentleman to a friend in this city:

Marion, Ala. Oct. 16th 1854 – I am sorry to inform you in this connection, of a very sad occurrence which took place here on last (Sunday) night, about 12 o'clock – that is, the burning down of "Howard College." There were sleeping at the time, in the third and fourth stories of the building, about 26 or 28 young men and two negro men; all of whom were required to jump from the windows, a distance of from 30 to 40 feet to the ground below. And, horrible to tell, 22 of the number were mangled in a frightful manner, some more and some less . . . Some of the boys are burned very badly, in addition to other injuries . . . I learned, a few moments since, that one of the black men was dead; he rushed down through the flames to the door. Two or three of the boys are expected to die – the rest will probably recover. . . . The College building, with everything in it, is in ruins. Nothing was saved, as I understand. It is supposed now that the building was set on fire, though at present I cannot believe it . . . The truth will be known in a few days, I suppose.

A postscript says another had died.

–Chronicle & Sentinel.

January 3, 1855 — (GJM)

FATAL AFFRAY. A difficulty occurred in Henry County on Thursday night of last week, between James Hilsman and Wm. Wyatt, which resulted in the death of the former. It appears that Wyatt had eloped with and married Hilsman's daughter, on the day previous, and that the latter had followed them with the expressed determination to kill them both. Wyatt and his wife had retired to a friend's house, and hearing of the threats of Hilsman, barred the door against his approach. Hilsman, however, burst the door open, and discharged one barrel of his gun at Wyatt, who in return snatched up a gun and shot Hilsman, who fell mortally wounded, and died in a few moments. Wyatt has given himself up and demanded an investigation.

–Griffin Union.

January 23, 1855 ———————— (CE)

ACCIDENTS AND DEATHS. – On Wednesday evening last, Mr. John King, who was employed on the Muscogee Railroad, attempted to jump aboard one of the locomotives, while it was going. His foot slipped, and he fell under the wheels, which cut off one of his legs, above the knee, and fracturing it so badly that amputation above the wound was deemed necessary. At the instance of our townsman, Mr. R.R. Goetchius, the wounded man was taken to the residence of the latter, where he was kindly cared for by Mr. G. and his lady, and where the operation was performed by Dr. Stanford of this city. But the sufferer was unable to survive both the wound and operation, and he died on Saturday morning – leaving, as we learn, a widow and one or two children, to mourn their irreparable loss.

On Sunday morning a special train conveyed the corpse to Station No. 3, (near which the deceased formerly resided.) where Masonic burial services were duly performed by the brethren of the Order from this city.

January 23, 1855 ———————— (CE)

Some two weeks ago a gentleman from Harris County, by the name of Cone, was on his way home from this city (Columbus), and when about two miles out, he attempted to pass a buggy, but a wheel of his own buggy ran into a ditch, threw him out with considerable violence, and injured him so seriously that he died on Saturday last. Immediately after the accident, he was conveyed to the residence of W.H. Young, Esq., (not far off,) where he was well attended to, up to the time of his decease.

August 8, 1855

HORRIBLE DEATH OF DAVID WRIGHT. On Saturday night last David Wright, under the sentence of death, for the murder of Deputy Sheriff Robinson, met with a horrid death in the county Prison.

About 12 o'clock at night, he raised the cry of fire in his cell. No attention, however, was paid to it by the jailor as such noises in the night were not at all uncommon. Some hour afterwards coals fell through the floor of Wright's cell, into the room below, occupied by a servant of the jailor, who immediately aroused the inmates and gave the alarm of "fire." Upon entering Wright's room, it was discovered that the flames had not only burnt a hole through the floor, but had caught the ceiling, and that the air of the room was intensely hot. Wright was stone dead; his skin slipped from the flesh; he had been strangled by the smoke and then baked to a crisp by a fire of his own kindling. It was a most awful and appalling death.

It is believed, having sawed his irons nearly off, he set fire to his room in the hope that the jailor would rush heedlessly to his rescue, when he could master him and make his escape, or sell his life in a hand to had (*sic*) engagement. He was dreadfully mistaken in his calculations, and has paid the penalty of his crimes.

January 2, 1856

RAILROAD ACCIDENTS. On Tuesday morning last, about 3 o'clock, the passenger train on the SouthWestern Railroad, while passing over an embankment of some twenty feet in height, in the Tobeesaufky swamp, was thrown from the track by coming in contact with a cow. The locomotive, tender, and passenger car were precipitated down the bank —the locomotive falling on Mr. H.H. Cole, the engineer, who was instantly killed. James Hancock, the fireman, was so badly scalded, that he died a few hours afterwards. Although the car was thrown entirely from the track, none of the passengers were seriously injured.

On Saturday morning last, two passenger trains came in collision near Reynolds, by which the locomotives were considerably damaged. Both trains were out of time, owing to the bad state of the weather, and delay during the night from motives of prudence. One of the train hands was killed, and a passenger by the name of Paulk, formerly of Jones county, but lately of Alabama, in jumping out of one of the trains which was backing at the time of the collision, was very seriously, and it is thought, fatally injured.

Since writing the above, information has reached us that Mr. Paulk died of his wounds on Sunday last.

January 2, 1856 ——————— (GJM)

SHOCKING AFFAIR. A son of Col. A.W. Hammond, of this city, came to his death in a most shocking manner, on Thursday morning last. It seems that he had by some means gotten on the track of the Macon & Western Rail Road, near a mile from the Depot, when the engine attached to the passenger train, which left the Depot at a quarter past five, picked him up on the cowcatcher, and it was not discovered until the train reached East Point, some six miles from this city. His body was dreadfully mangled, and fragments of his person were scattered along the Road for several miles. His remains were brought back by the train Tuesday morning, and a Coroner's Inquest held. At the time of writing the jury had not made up their verdict.

–Atlanta Intelligencer, December 27.

After a lengthy deliberation, the coroner's inquest came to the conclusion that Hammond was murdered by some unknown hands, and his body placed upon the track of the road.

April 23, 1856 ———————————— (GJM)

DEATHS IN DALTON. The *Dalton Expositor* of the 17th inst. says: . . . We also learn that on one of the uptrains yesterday, a gentleman by the name of Austin, while standing on the top of one of the cars, not noticing their approach to a bridge, was precipitated from his position by a stroke to the head, which broke his neck, instantly causing death. The train following found the mangled remains of the unfortunate man.

January 1, 1857 ———————————— (CG)

FROZEN TO DEATH. In Baldwin County, on the night of the 22nd of December, Henry Wood was frozen to death. The night was severely cold and he in a state of intoxication. Drunkards, take warning!

January 14, 1857 ———————————— (GJM)

MELANCHOLY ACCIDENT. A few days since Mrs. Bankston, the estimable wife of Wm. R. Bankston, Clerk of the Superior and Inferior Courts, of Butts County, residing in Jackson, came to her death in a most distressing manner. It appears from information which we have received, that she had lain down before the fire on a pallet with her little child, and fell asleep. While in this condition, her clothes caught on fire, and before assistance could be rendered, she was so severely burned, that she died in a very short time.

–Griffin Empire State.

May 6, 1857 ———————————— (GJM)

Mrs. John H. Neel, of Hancock County, was accidentally burned to death on Friday, 24th ult. Her clothes caught on fire while engaged in cooking, at an open fire place.

July 2, 1857 ———————————— (CG)

HORIBLE (*sic*) **CASUALTY.** On Wednesday night, the 10th inst., Mrs. Wm. J. McKinley, and her daughter were both burned up in their dwelling house in Danville, in this county. The citizens of the place were aroused about one o'clock at night, but when they reached the house it was too late to render any assistance. It seems that the room in which Mrs. McKinley and her daughter slept had no windows and communicated with the other room by a door. It is supposed the house caught fire from carelessness in disposing of clothes with which she had been smoking musquitos (*sic*); and the fire had reached the door leading into her sleeping room before she awoke.

–Americus News.

August 4, 1857 ————————————— (CE)

SAD ACCIDENT. On Sunday morning last, as the 4 o'clock morning train from this place to Macon, reached the crossing of a small stream about 7 miles below the depot, the track gave way, precipitating the locomotive, tender and baggage car into the water and mud below, killing the fireman, Mr. Jackson Bryant, of this place, and so severely injuring Mr. Patrick Sullivan, temporary baggage master, that he died during his transportation to town. Mr. George Smith, the engineer of the train also had one leg and arm broken; and it is something remarkable how he escaped thus lightly, as he was found on the body of Bryant, who was not only killed out right, but so scalded by the hot water, that he had the appearance of having been par boiled. The passenger car was not thrown from the track, and therefore no one else was injured . . .

November 12, 1857 ————————————— (CG)

MAN FOUND DEAD IN A CHURCH – PROBABLE SUICIDE.

(Sparta, Ga.) On Saturday morning last, when the doors of the Baptist church in this place were opened for public worship, was found lying in the pulpit, the dead body of a man. It proved to be Hugh Kelly, who had worked in the carriage shop of Gardner & Martin during the summer. A month ago or more he went into a drinking spree, which continued until his sudden and mysterious disappearance about two weeks since. A two ounce viol containing a small quantity of laudanum was found near him which probably he had drank and that in connection with intemperance was no doubt the immediate cause of his death. This was the substance of the verdict of the Jury of Inquest. A day or two previous to his being found a letter was received from a gentleman in Augusta making enquiry for him, stating that his aged grandmother having heard that he was in a spree in Sparta was nearly crazy about him for fear some evil would befall. Such is the fate of the poor inebriate. Heaven spare the youth of the country from such a ruin and such a death.

December 22, 1857 ——————— (CE)

SINGULAR AND AWFUL OCCURRENCE. We learn from the Fayetteville, North Carolina, papers, that Wm. F. Wightman, late Editor of the *North Carolinian*, and Moses S. Elliot were found dead in the same bed, in a room at the Shemwell House, Fayetteville, on the 10th inst. They left a letter stating their determination to commit suicide by taking poison, and two empty glasses were found on the table by their side.

We believe both the unfortunate gentlemen were native Georgians. Is there another case, on record, of two men committing suicide at the same moment? If there is, it has escaped our observation or memory.

March 16, 1858 (SR)

BURNT TO DEATH. A subscriber in Scriven (*sic*) County writes us under date of 7th inst., that a Mr. Obadiah Dumas was so badly burned on the night of the 5th inst., at Station No. 6 on the Central Railroad, as to cause his death the next morning. He was a school teacher, had been in that county about two years and had a father in or near Forsyth, Monroe County, Georgia.

March 17, 1858 (GJM)

HORRIBLE DEATH. We learn, says the *Rome Courier*, that on Wednesday or Thursday of last week, Mr. Jacob Smyer, the owner of a mill some three or four miles below Coosaville, in this county, was caught in his machinery by his clothes, drawn in between two cog wheels and most horribly mutilated, causing his immediate death.

May 19, 1858 (WGR)

MELANCHOLY ACCIDENT. On Saturday evening last, a son of Mrs. A.E. Hunter, of Greensboro, fell from a wagon loaded with sand; both wheels ran over his chest, crushing him so severely that he died in fifteen or twenty minutes afterwards. He was about fourteen years of age.

−Temperance Crusader.

May 19, 1858 ———————— (WGR)

SUICIDE. In Augusta on the 6th inst., a young man named D.W. Davidson, lately a clerk in the store of Mr. Searling, shot himself with a gun by placing the muzzle in his mouth. – His brains were scattered over the entire room, and presented a most horrible spectacle.

September 22, 1858 ———————— (GJM)

DISASTROUS ACCIDENT ON THE AUGUSTA AND SAVANNAH RAILROAD.

From the *Augusta Chronicle & Sentinel*, 17th.

At an early hour yesterday morning, a dispatch was received at the telegraph office in this city, announcing a serious and fatal accident to the down train on the Augusta and Savannah Railroad, which left this city at one o'clock Wednesday night. The accident which occurred about ten miles this side of Millen, near Station No. 1, was caused by a wash in the roadbed – the result of heavy and continued rains. The engine, tender and three freight cars were thrown from the track, precipitated some ten or fifteen feet down a steep embankment, and are a total wreck. L.M. Northey, Engineer, and two firemen, Patrick Fleury and James Coggins, were killed, and Jesse Farrar, machinist and workman, had his left arm broken above the elbow, and his right leg torn and bruised. The passengers escaped without injury, owing, probably, to there being a larger number of freight cars between the passenger car and the engine . . .

A special train was dispatched to the scene of the disaster at half past eight o'clock yesterday morning, which returned to this city about three o'clock P.M., bringing Jesse Farrar, the wounded man, and the body of James Coggins. The bodies of the engineer and the other fireman were so buried under the shattered engine as to require several hours labor to extricate them. They were brought up to this city about seven o'clock last night.

Mr. Farrar has since died.

November 30, 1858 ──────── (WGT)

CASUALTY. We are informed by Col. Newnan McBain that a man by the name of Green Brown was killed on the 4th inst. near the Plains of Dura, by having a loaded waggon run over him. He was riding in the waggon, and accidentally fell before the wheels and before the team could be stopped the wheel ran over his neck. He survived but a short time. His relatives are said to reside near the city of Macon.

—Americus News.

[Ed. Note: Plains of Dura is now called simply Plains, the home of President Jimmy Carter.]

December 8, 1858 ──────── (GJM)

DEATH OF AN OLD PRINTER. We regret to state that Mr. B.T. Theus died suddenly at his breakfast table yesterday, in the midst of his family. . . . In early life Mr. T. resided in Charleston, where we believe he commenced his career as a practical printer; he subsequently removed to Savannah and continued in the same vocation. . . . It is a somewhat singular coincidence that his wife a year since, also died at the breakfast table without any previous warning.

–Sav. Rep.

December 8, 1858 ——————— (GJM)

SUICIDE BY A PRINTER. Mr. Jas. W. Bennett, a printer by occupation, and for ten or twelve years past foreman of the *Southern Recorder* office at Milledgeville, disappeared Tuesday night last, says the *Savannah Republican* of Monday last, and after diligent search no trace of him could be discovered. Late Saturday afternoon, his body was discovered in a well, in the street, nearly opposite the office. Mr. B. had been for some time, much addicted to intemperance, and it is supposed threw himself into the well while laboring under mania from that cause. He was about forty-two years of age, and left no family.

December 8, 1858 ——————— (GJM)

DEATH OF REV. JOSEPH POLHILL. The numerous friends of this most excellent Divine, says the *Augusta Sentinel*, will learn with sorrow and regret that he expired Thursday, 2d inst., at his residence in Burke County. The occasion of his death is melancholy in the extreme, being a fall from the second story of his gin house four days before.

December 22, 1858 ———————

DEATH OF THE HON. JNO. A. TUCKER

Dawson, Geo., December 16th, 1858.

Mr. Editor: Our little town was thrown into quite an unusual state of excitement yesterday evening, by the announcement of the death of Col. J.A. Tucker, (the Democratic nominee for the Judgeship of the South Western Circuit, and also Senator to the last Legislature of Georgia, from Stewart.) He had been spending a few days in our town and vicinity in a canvassing tour, and on yesterday kept his room all day, (at the Hotel) saying he felt indisposed. On sending to his room for him to dinner, he stated that he was too unwell, and declined any assistance whatever during the whole of the afternoon. On going to his room to see him, about supper time, he was found dead! In his room were two bottles (1 drachm each) morphine untouched; one empty one, and another empty one thrown out of the window, though the cork was left on his table, and several letters, all sealed, with one exception, which was read at the Coroner's inquest. It stated that he had (or would) commit suicide, and directed what disposition to make for his family. The Jury's verdict was that he came to his death by morphine administered by his own hands. Very respectfully, S.C.

February 2, 1859 ———————

THREE MEN KILLED IN STEWART COUNTY.

The steam mill of Mr. Wiley B. Horton, about ten miles north of Florence, was completely destroyed by the explosion of its boiler on the 18th inst., and three men were killed.

A correspondent of the Lumpkin Palladium gives the following account:

"I had rode (sic) over to the mill for the purpose of laying in a bill for some lumber, and had just stepped into the mill and was conversing with Messrs. Dorse and Redick Smith, had not been exceeding five minutes, when the most awful explosion took place that I ever heard. We were standing not far from the saw at the time. Dorse & Smith were precipitated out into the yard unharmed, while I was knocked out of the millhouse and felled to the ground, either by the force of the explosion or by some of the flying missiles from the boiler, being severely bruised in a number of places, the whole house fell over and around me with an awful crash; but fortunately one end of the timbers rested on the floor above and the other end on the ground beyond me, thus leaving sufficient space for my escape. When I crawled out from beneath the fallen house I saw Messrs. Dorse and Smith standing out in the yard in mute astonishment. My appearance seemed to recall their presence of mind and they inquired if I was hurt, and remarked that several persons must be killed. We then went around to the furnace, and the scene which there presented itself to our vision beggars all description. The charred, blackened and mangled forms of John Smith, James Blackburn and John Johnson lay weltering in their gore with scarcely any forms of life. We dragged them out from among the rubbish and carried them to a house near by, and sent for assistance and also for Dr. Wimberly, who lived in the vicinity; but all creature helps were vain, as Mr. Smith died in thirty or forty minutes after the disaster, and Mr. Blackburn did not survive until this morning, and all three were literally scalded to death, if they had received no other injuries. Mr. Johnson still survives, but without a solitary hope of his final recovery.

There were some fifteen persons in all about the mill at

the time, and several others were injured, but not seriously. The boiler was blown, through an embankment of earth, a house and trees, to a distance of fully one hundred yards up the hill. It weighed between seven and eight thousand pound, and the force of the explosion must therefore have been terrific. The correspondent thinks that "a defective boiler and carelessness" was the cause of the explosion.

March 22, 1859 ———————————— (MT)

HOMICIDE IN WARE COUNTY.

We learn that during the past week, Mr. Lamb, the Sheriff of Ware County, killed a man by the name of Cyrus Smith, the son of a Hotel keeper.

It appears that Smith, who is a young and unmarried man, had written and sent a note to a young Lady, a sister-in-law of Lamb, containing proposals of the most insulting character, and which the young Lady exhibited to her brother-in-law, who immediately took a double barreled gun and went in quest of Smith.

Smith was at his father's house, and Lamb upon seeing him taxed him with writing the note and sharp words ensued between the parties. Smith, with a Colt's Repeater in his hand, left the House, advanced to the gate, and as soon as he got out of the enclosure was fired upon by Lamb and killed.

May 18, 1859 ———————————— (GJM)

SAD CASUALTY. On yesterday afternoon, the four o'clock passenger train from Macon ran over and killed a man named Henry Spellers, near East Point. The cars passed over his head severing a portion of it from the body, which fell over the rail and remained in his hat.

On rounding a curve, emerging from a cut, the Engineer observed something on the track with several dogs near it. His first impression was that it was a hog, overrun by a preceding train, which had attracted the dogs, but the second thought or closer approach, which was instantaneous, suggested that it might be a man, and he immediately reversed the Engine, but too late. The unfortunate man was seen some hours previously, on his way to East Point, so much under the influence of liquor as to be almost unable to walk. The dogs proved to be his, and would allow no approach to the body, until they were driven away by throwing stones at them.

The body was brought to this city and an inquest held, after which it was decently interred. Mr. Spellers was an old resident of this county, and leaves a son – an only relative – to deplore his sad fate.

–National American, Atlanta.

July 26, 1859 ———————————— (CE)

NEGROES KILLED BY LIGHTNING. We heard that during a thunderstorm on Saturday afternoon last, about a dozen negroes belonging to Mr. F.M. Biggers, living seven or eight miles north of this city, took refuge in a house in his field, and that the house was struck by lightning, killing two of the negroes instantly and severely injuring two others. There was a very heavy fall of rain in that neighborhood.

July 26, 1859 — (CE)

SUDDEN DEATH. A man named William Manus arrived in this city by the afternoon train on Saturday, from Macon. He spent a portion of the afternoon at the Pleasant Hour bar room, in playing billiards and drinking, at which place, late in the evening, he died quite suddenly. A short time before he died he became helpless, so much so that he could neither stand or sit. In this condition he was laid upon a table, and breathed his last in a few moments. The coroner held an inquest over his body yesterday morning, and found that he died from the effects of liquor. He has on his right hand a star, and on his left hand a heart, made in the skin with India ink.

–Sun.

August 2, 1859 — (WGT)

MELANCHOLY ACCIDENT. Gen. Robert Taylor, an old and well known citizen of Athens, was fatally injured on the Georgia Rail Road near Madison, last Friday. While in the act of leaving the cars, he fell upon the tracks, and the train passed over both feet. Amputation of one of them became necessary, and by last accounts he was rapidly sinking and recovery seemed hopeless.

August 3, 1859 — (GJM)

DIED. In Oglethorpe, July 1, 1859, Dr. Terry Quinn, in the 48th year of his age. He was born in Edgefield District, S.C., December 31, 1811. When he was quite young, his parents removed to Monroe County, Ga. About his twentieth year he engaged in Merchandise in the city of Macon, which business he pursued five years. In 1833 he married Miss Clarinda Nobles, of his native District, within a year thereafter, having taken a course of Lectures, he removed to Chambers County, Ala., where he practiced medicine ten years, and came back to Georgia in 1844. He located at Evansville, Macon County, where he obtained a large practice, and in 1853 he removed to Dooly County. In 1854 he joined the Methodist Episcopal Church. Having purchased a farm in the vicinity of Oglethorpe, he settled there in 1858, and gave his time mainly to agricultural pursuits. His death was occasioned by chloroform, to relive pain caused by the extraction of a tooth, he too incautiously used this subtle agent, and in twelve hours he was a corpse. . . .

He left a widow and seven children well provided. The Rev. Mr. Jackson, presiding elder, preached the funeral discourse, and the Masonic Fraternity buried their brother at Travellers Rest, with the ceremonies usual on such occasions.

August 9, 1859 ———————————— (WS)

Mr. John Bruster, living seven or eight miles from Cowyers (Conyers), Ga., visited the village last Saturday, and became intoxicated. In the evening he mounted his horse and started home; he had gone but a short distance when he fell from his horse and broke his neck, resulting in immediate death.

August 9, 1859 ———————————— (WS)

TERRIBLE EXPLOSION. The steamer Barnett, being engaged in towing a raft on yesterday morning, at about 11 o'clock, when within about four miles of this place, her boiler exploded, instantly killing a Negro named Dave, the property of Capt. Gomez, Michael Kirkland, deck hand, survived only about two hours, having been burned inwardly. Capt. Shaw is badly burnt, and received a severe wound on the left jaw, extending from the lower part of the temple to the chin; Capt. James Jarmon is severely scalded and received injuries on the head; John Towell, 1st engineer, very badly scalded, supposed to be injured inwardly, and no hopes entertained of his recovery; John Irvin, 2nd engineer, severely scalded; Joe, the property of Mrs. Wm. P. DeWees, scalded badly on the right side; Isham, cook, belonging to Capt. Shaw, slightly scalded.

Captains Shaw and Jarmon were sitting by the pilot house at the time of the explosion. Capt. Jarmon landed on the forward deck, but Capt. Shaw was blown overboard, and had it not been for the timely assistance of Isham, his Negro, would have drowned. Joe was also blown overboard, but swam to the wheel.

P.S. Since the above was put in type, Mr. John Towell, 1st engineer, died of injuries received.

–Jacksonville Standard, 4th inst.

September 13, 1859 ———— (CWS)

MYSTERIOUS DEATH. The *Tuskegee Republican* states that on Wednesday morning of last week, the body of Anderson Kilcrease, of Macon county, was found lying in his house lot, quite lifeless and perfectly nude. His clothing, of which he had entirely divested himself, was lying in a heap near his person. His body bore no trace of violence, and the manner of his death remains a mystery. Mr. Kilcrease was a bachelor, and as he lived entirely alone, it is not known how long he had been dead when his body was discovered.

November 8, 1859 ———————— (WGT)

SAD ACCIDENT – A WARNING TO BOYS. Mr. Editor: On Saturday morning, September 29th, J.N. Taylor, Jr., a lad aged 16, left his father's residence near Marshallville, Geo., to shoot ducks in the pond near by. He was in the bateau with a companion; when being in the proper distance for shooting, he seized his gun by the muzzle and drew it suddenly, when unfortunately the hammer struck the cross piece of the boat, discharging the contents of the gun into the left side of the chest, between the fifth and sixth ribs, tearing the heart and its appendages asunder. The blood gushed in the boat – he only had time to say, "Oh me," when his spirit fled to God.

He was buried next day with military honors by the Governor's Guard, of which company he had lately become a member. May the sad end of this hightoned and very intelligent youth, be a warning to boys who are learning to shoot.

November 29, 1859 ———————— (WS)

FATAL ACCIDENT. The *Elberton State of the South*, of Thursday, says:

Captain Wm. H. Harper had employed a young man named Willis Elders to blast in a well that he was having dug on his lot. Young Elders, with a negro man belonging to Capt. Harper, had previously made several blasts in the well, but unfortunately, on that morning the safety fuse which they were using, by some means became ignited, and the explosion was instantaneous, shockingly mangling the body of young Elders in such a manner as to cause his death; he lived until Tuesday night and expired, having been insensible for some time previously.

January 4, 1860 ——————— (GJM)

SERIOUS ACCIDENT. LOSS OF LIFE. With sincere regret, we chronicle a serious accident, occurring to the up freight train, on the Western & Atlantic Railroad at Vining Station, ten miles from this city, between seven and eight o'clock this morning. The freight engine, "Oconee", while at this Station, exploded, instantly killing Thomas Croft, Conductor, and James Rhinehart, Woodpasser, and wounded James Sullivan, Fireman, and Wm. Floyd, Engineer, so severely that their recovery is despaired of. The bodies of Messrs. Croft and Rhinehart were brought to the Western & Atlantic Depot, where, at the time of the writing of this paragraph, they were laid out. The cause of the explosion has not been ascertained. The engine is almost an entire wreck.

–Atlanta American 29th.

January 4, 1860 ——————— (GJM)

MELANCHOLY ACCIDENT. On Friday last, while two boys by the name of Jaugstetter, were hunting, a short distance below the city, one of them, the son of Mr. John Jaugstetter was killed by the accidental discharge of his gun. It appears that while loading, his ramrod was caught in the barrel, and finding it very difficult to get out, the breech of the gun was held by the younger boy. In attempting to draw it out, the gun was discharged, passing it entirely through the body of the other and killing him instantly. His age was about 13 years. Another warning to boys to be more cautious with firearms.

January 31, 1860 ———————————— (WS)

HOMICIDE. We learn that a man named Hampton Dossett, was shot Thursday night last, at a house of ill fame, in the lower part of the city. The shooting occurred during a brawl, and from the attendant circumstances, it is supposed he was shot through mistake. The ball went in between the first and second rib in the right breast, and passed down, wounding the right lung, and probably other vital parts. The wound was a very fatal one, and he survived it about forty-eight hours.

March 7, 1860 ———————————— (CG)

(Sparta, Hancock County) . . . **AN INQUEST** was being held over the body of John Saunders, who was killed in an affray by Ab. Attaway the night previous. His skull was badly fractured by a heavy decanter. He died about twenty hours afterwards. He was the same unfortunate man who killed Horace B. Gardner several years since. Attaway is still at large, and many hope that he will never return, as he is a gambler of the baser sort.

Saturday evening another killing took place at the factory. A drunken man by the name of Calvin Cheek was interfering with Mr. Twilly, one of the watchmen, who drew his pistol and fired at him, as is supposed. It took effect in the chest of a Miss Dickens, who stood near. She died instantly. Both homicides are attributable to the use of ardent spirits, which we are sorry to say has received a premium in the decision of the Supreme Court, to "arm madmen and turn them loose on society", in the emphatic language of Judge Holt. If a man wishes to reck (*sic*) vengeance on an enemy, and have his offence palliated, let him get drunk and do the deed; the court cannot hold him responsible for the act as if he had been sober. A few more such decisions will place the court where it ought to be – numbered with the tombs of the Capulets.

March 21, 1860 ———————————— (GJM)

TERRIBLE DISASTER. EXPLOSION OF STEAMER S.M. Manning. Thirteen Lives Lost – Five Whites and Eight Negroes. Capt. Taylor and two others badly wounded. The boat a wreck.

Gen. Manning's Place, Coffee County, Ga., March 13, 1860. *Editor Republican*: I have just returned from the wreck of the Manning (steamboat;) her boilers exploded last night about 8 o'clock, killing Jefferson Taylor, son of Capt. Taylor, Joseph B. Williams, John Harrell, Jacob Parker, (the three last, citizens of Telfair County) and eight or nine negro hands. Among the negroes lost are Charles, the cook, Jack and Edmond, belonging to William Willcox, Hal and _____, belonging to James Y. Wilcox, and Bill belonging to John F. McRae. A young man got on at Darien, supposed to be young Spencer, who was expected in Jacksonville. Capt. Taylor is badly wounded, so are Messrs. Williams and Bowen.

The boat is now in the middle of the river, two miles above Gen. Manning's – a complete wreck. Some of the heavy freight will be saved; all the light goods will be lost or injured. None of the bodies have as yet been recovered; a portion of clothing has been found in the trees. It is awful to contemplate – so many human beings forced, without a moment's warning, into eternity. Messrs. Williams, Harrell and Parker, are of the best families of Telfair County.

The wounded are at Gen. Manning's, who is doing all he can to alleviate their sufferings. There were no ladies or children aboard.

In great haste, W.W.P.

The Manning was two years old, and was valued at $15,000 upon which there was no insurance. She was owned by Brigham, Baldwin & Co. of this city, Captain Taylor and some parties in Hawkinsville, whose names we have not learned.

–Savannah Republican.

April 10, 1860 ———————— (WS)

SINGULAR DEATH OF A THIEF. In London, lately, a police officer had a desperate struggle with a thief near the docks, during which the thief slipped overboard and sunk (*sic*) immediately. His body was not recovered for some time, when thirteen sheets of stolen copper were found wrapped around it, which was, undoubtedly, the cause of death.

April 10, 1860 ———————— (WS)

CHILD BURNED TO DEATH. A correspondent of the *Atlanta Locomotive*, states that a little daughter, five years old, of Mr. Frederick McWhorter, Greene county, was burned to death on the 10th inst. She and a little brother were playing near some heaps of brush that had been burning early in the day, when a flame kindled and caught her dress, and burned her so severely, that she died the next morning.

April 10, 1860 ——————————— (WS)

FIRE IN MARION – LADY BURNT. We find the following shocking incident in the *Marion Star*, of March 27th:

We learn that, on Wednesday last, the house of Mr. D. W. Larrimore, in the lower part of this district, was destroyed by fire, and that his wife perished in the flames. Mr. Larrimore was absent at the time, and his children were at school. It is thought that Mrs. L., who was subject to fits, was taken with one and fell into the fire, her clothing communicating the flames to the furniture. Her bones only were found in the embers.

April 18, 1860 ——————————— (CG)

Mrs. Jane Gamble, a widow lady of Eatonton, Ga., under the influence of religious monomania, starved herself to death. She died on the 8th instant, having lived twenty days without a particle of food.

June 27, 1860 ——————————— (GJM)

SUDDEN AND PAINFUL. Wade H. Lester, Esq. for a few months a resident of this city, says the *Atlanta American*, died a few days since at the Georgia Lunatic Asylum, whither he had been taken in consequence of a very sudden bereavement of reason, caused by unusual exposure to the intense heat of the sun while seining. The corpse passed through the city yesterday, in charge of his brother, Rev. R.B. Lester, on the way to Marietta, for interment. Mr. Lester leaves an interesting family to mourn his loss. . . .

July 31, 1860 ——————————— (WS)

HORRIBLE DEATH. We learn that a short time since, a negro woman belonging to Ebenezer Kitchens, of Jones county, was killed by a mule in a horrible manner. The negro had been driving the mule in a plow, and had unhitched him, and as is customary with negroes, mounted him to ride home. The mule became refractory and in attempting to subdue him was thrown, and her foot becoming entangled in the traces, the mule started off at the top of its speed dragging her after him for a mile, or perhaps further. When found she presented a horrible and ghastly spectacle. The bones of her head and several of her limbs were dislocated and the skin and flesh worn off to the bone, wherever it had come in contact with the earth.

—Macon Telegraph, 24th.

August 21, 1860 ——————————— (WS)

SAD ACCIDENT IN HOUSTON COUNTY. We learn, says the *Macon Telegraph*, that on Monday the 5th inst., Mark Opry, eldest son of Amos Opry, Esquire, came to his death under very melancholy circumstances. While out "'coon hunting" in company with three other lads, Mark had climbed a tall tree to scare the 'coon down, and was in the act of hasty descent to see the sport below, when his hold broke and he fell to the ground, a distance of forty feet. One of his companions, hearing the fall, ran to him and found his breathless. Procuring assistance they removed him to the nearest house, where he died after an illness of four days.

September 11, 1860 — (WS)

SHOCKING OCCURRENCE. *The Tuscaloosa*, Ala., *Observer*, of the 29th, says that on the Friday previous a negro man, the property of Mr. John Strong, of North Port, while attending the Steam Saw mill of Whitfield & Blackburn, near that city, unfortunately stumbled against the saw while in rapid motion, cutting his body into two pieces, causing his death instantly. This should serve as a warning to others attending saw mills.

September 25, 1860 — (WS)

AWFUL ACCIDENT. On the 17th instant, says the *Rome Courier* of the 20th, while Mr. Henry Hicks was at work in a well on Mr. W.R. Vann's premises, at Coosaville, in this county, the blast exploded prematurely, most horribly and fatally mangling Mr. Hicks. The frontal skull was fractured leaving his brain exposed; the flesh was entirely torn from his right cheek; both jawbones broken, and a piece of rock as large as a goose egg, penetrated the breast and lodged within a half-inch of his heart. He lingered in agony until Tuesday morning when he was relieved by death from his sufferings.

October 2, 1860 —————————————— (WS)

DEATH OF A BRILLIANT YOUNG MAN. We have just learned with deep regret, says the *Atlanta Locomotive*, that William Arnold Sparks, Esq., of Valley Plains, Harris county, committed suicide a few days since by jumping from a window. Mr. Sparks was a high minded, intelligent gentleman, who enjoyed the confidence of all who knew him. He was considered one of the most talented young men that Harris county has ever produced . . . May the beautiful oaks of Valley Plains wave a tuneful requiem over the grave of this brilliant neophyte of the muses.

October 2, 1860 —————————————— (WS)

DIED IN A WELL. The *Greensboro Planters' Weekly*, of the 12th inst., says that Mr. Sylvanus West, died in a well in Oglethorpe county, on Monday last, from the effects of carbonic acid gas. His body had not been removed on the morning of the 11th instant.

October 2, 1860 —————————————— (WS)

DISTRESSING CASUALTY. A large number of both our city and country readers will read with sorrow the following paragraph, taken from the *Atlanta American*, of the 25th inst.:"As the inward train on the Atlanta & West Point Rail Road was leaving Grantville this morning, Mr. George W. Lively attempted to get on while the cars were in motion. Falling between two cars he was crushed so badly that he never spoke afterwards, and expired in about fifteen minutes.

He was about fifty years of age, and leaves a large family. He was extensively engaged, at Grantville, in the Tanning and Shoe-Making business."

Perhaps no man was more widely or better known in this country than George W. Lively; . . . Mr. Lively, it will be remembered, was for many years a citizen of Columbus, and one of our most thorough-going and energetic merchants . . .

October 23, 1860 ——————————— (WS)

CORONER'S INQUEST. On Sunday morning last, 7th inst., says the Bainbridge Argus, a Coroner's inquest was held on the body of one James T. Neal, who, it seems, had been wandering about our streets for some days, in a state of intoxication. On the night previous he had gone into the second story of the Court House to sleep, as has been his habit for a number of years, and from some cause unknown, fell out of one of the windows. Deceased was a soldier in the war of 1812, and one of the earliest settlers of this country (*sic*). Verdict of the jury in accordance with the above facts.

May 8, 1861 ——————————— (GJM)

TERRIBLE ACCIDENT ON A STEAMER. Lieut. Nelson mortally wounded – Col. Miller Grieve seriously injured.

We are pained to record a most melancholy occurrence that took place on our river, late yesterday afternoon, by which a gallant young lieutenant of the Georgia Army was fatally, a prominent and much loved citizen horribly wounded, and another citizen of the up country severely lacerated.

As the steamer *Habersham* was coming up from Fort Pulaski, with a considerable party of officers and visitors on board, as she neared Fort Jackson a small iron swivel was brought out and loaded for a salute – unfortunately over-charged. The fuse being applied, the weapon burst into atoms, the fragments flying in every direction. Though sad as is the result, it was fortunate that it was no worse. One of the pieces of metal struck Lieutenant Wm. Nelson, of the Georgia Army, and son of the late Gen. Chas. H. Nelson, inflicting a fatal injury from which it is impossible for him to recover. The wound is on the right side of the head, just above the eye, and ranging upward and backward. The flesh is much lacerated and the skull broken in for some considerable space. He has not spoken since the accident and his case is considered hopeless, though he is still alive as we write, 7 P.M.

Our old friend, Col. Miller Grieve, of Milledgeville, is the next sufferer. He was standing some twenty feet from the gun when it exploded and was struck on the left cheek, just below the eye, and passing backward suffering a terrible gash and probably breaking in the cheek bone, if not destroying the sight of one eye. The flesh is literally torn up from the bone and thrown back, presenting a frightful spectacle, while his whole person seemed soaked in blood. He had not been thoroughly examined when we saw him. It is hoped that this is the only injury, and that his valuable life is not endangered. He is entirely sensible. He has a son in the service at Fort Pulaski, and had just been down to see him.

Mr. Marshall Perkins, a citizen of Burke County, who had been down on a visit to friends in the service, received a severe gash, to the depth of some 2 inches and three or more in length, on the back part of his left thigh. It is purely a flesh wound, and he will doubtless soon recover.

Should further developments be made in the course of

the surgical examination, and before our paper goes to press, they will be given in a postscript.

We may add, for the satisfaction of friends at a distance, that all the parties were taken to the Pulaski House on the arrival of the boat, where they are receiving every comfort and attention, medical and otherwise.

P.S. – 10 P.M. Lieut. Nelson has been trephined and is somewhat revived, but very little hope is entertained. We regret to hear that upon examination Col. Grieve is ascertained to be far more seriously injured that was first apprehended. The bones of his face are crushed up to the base of the brain, he has had several spasms, and his condition is considered hopeless.

–Savannah Republican of Tuesday.

May 15, 1861 ——————————— (GJM)

THE ACCIDENT. On board the *Habersham*, by which Lt. Nelson was so seriously injured that he subsequently died of his wounds, and our old friend, Col. Miller Grieve, of Milledgeville, sadly mutilated – we noticed in our last. Of the latter gentleman the *Savannah Republican* of yesterday says:

Col. Grieve. – The numerous friends of this gentleman will be gratified to learn that, notwithstanding the serious nature of the injuries received in the late explosion, he is considered much improved, and strong hopes are entertained by his physicians of his eventual recovery – a result which at first was regarded as utterly hopeless.

From the *Daily Sun* of Thursday.

TERRIBLE RAIL ROAD DISASTER! The train that left this city yesterday afternoon, for Macon, when sixteen miles on its way, was precipitated into a broken culvert about one-half or three-fourths of a mile beyond Randell's Creek. The engine, baggage car and tender are a total wreck. The passenger, next to the baggage car, was badly injured, and literally running over the baggage car and the wreck.

Mr. Douglas C. Moore of the Columbus Volunteers, and lately engaged as a clerk at the book store of J.W. Pease, and a Negro boy named Joe, the property of Edward Croft of this city, were instantly killed. Another boy, the servant of Private Thweatt, of the Volunteers, was so badly injured that his recovery is despaired of. Charles J. Williams, of the Harris Guards, had an arm slightly sprained, but not enough to render his return necessary. . . . The engineer, Jacob Burrus, and a fireman and woodhandler, perceiving the danger in time, jumped from the train and escaped injury.

Mr. Landon, of this city, and several citizens of the neighborhood, having discovered and apprehended the danger to the train, repaired to a point some distance this side of the break, and by shaking of handkerchiefs and other demonstrations endeavored to give warning to the engineer; but he mistaking them for signals of encouragement to the military companies on board the train, moved on making a curve in the road and the break was not perceived until within a few car lengths of it.

Mr. Moore and the negro who were killed and the negro badly injured were in the forward baggage car which contained the baggage, provisions and arms of the Volunteers.

Had they been in the car provided for them, they probably would have escaped . . .

The body of Mr. Moore was brought to the city last night, and the funeral services will take place this afternoon at 3 o'clock, from the residence of his brother-in-law, Mr. Wm. Douglas.

August 20, 1861 ——————————— (WS)

The *Macon Citizen* says that on Sunday morning, a man named Rowell Bates was knocked down and nearly decapitated by the South Western train backing into its position at the depot. He was instantly killed.

About the same hour, a lad named Ferrell, son of Mrs. Ferrell of Macon, was run over and dreadfully mangled by the Central train going out. He lived but a little while.

January 21, 1862 ——————————— (WS)

ANOTHER FATAL ACCIDENT FROM MACHINERY.
A very likely negro man belonging to Gov. G.W. Crawford was killed yesterday by being caught in the machinery of the Governor's mill, near Belair. The negro was oiling the machinery when he got entangled in it, and was most dreadfully mangled. He lived but a short time after the accident.

—Augusta Chronicle.

January 21, 1862 ——————— (WS)

SHOCKING ACCIDENT. A distressing casualty happened at the manufactory of C.A. Platt & Co. this morning. The mulatto boy John, belonging to the proprietors, was oiling the machinery while the engine was in motion, when his clothing was caught by the shaft, and he was violently whirled around the shaft, his body striking the column and other woodwork in its rapid revolutions. He was shockingly mangled and bruised, his bones being broken in many places, and his clothes literally torn from him. He died in a short time after the accident.

—Augusta Chronicle, 18th.

January 18, 1865 ——————— (GJM)

DIED. On the 25th inst., Mr. James H. Gillin, probably about 40 years of age. He has long been known as an engineer on railroads, and was at this time employed on the Macon and Brunswick road. The cause of his death is somewhat a mystery, but is supposed to be from inhaling coal gas. He was employed in lighting the furnace in the basement of the Baptist Church, on Saturday night when he laid down. A lad a nephew of his who was with him, was much overcome by its effects, and barely escaped with his life. When he awoke, he was unable to walk, but crawled to where his uncle was lying and finding him insensible succeeded in alarming the police in the vicinity, but too late to save Mr. Gillin. He was buried on Monday in Rose Hill Cemetary (*sic*) by Franklin Lodge of Odd Fellows.

July 27, 1866

HORRIBLE DEATH. Charles H. Tibbs, of this city, a young man of good intellect and fine promise, but for the unfortunate habit of intemperance, was on Monday night, while setting (*sic*) on the railroad in the lower part of the city, run over by a train of cars and instantly killed. He was seen in a state of intoxication some thirty minutes before the fatal accident, but whether he was asleep or not when the train struck him is not known. The engineer discovered him too late to reverse his engine and stop the train. Thus another victim has been sacrificed upon the altar of the relentless monster, Intemperance.

–Dalton Georgian

April 26, 1867

SAD FATALITY – A MAN MISTAKEN AND SHOT FOR GAME. Some two weeks ago, two brothers by the name of Webb, were engaged in turkey hunting, on Spring Creek, in Early County, when the unfortunate man, Allen Gay, Jr., together with a Mr. Evans, entered the same hammock from another direction – also engaged with their fowling pieces in the turkey hunt. Both Gay and Webb being experienced in the search for this valuable game, they were enabled to imitate the peculiar noise of the turkey to perfection. The thickness of the growth prevented their discovering each other – and each, mistaking the other for game, cautiously approached the decoying noise, little thinking of the imminent peril of their respective situations. A portion of Mr. Gay's clothing was at length seen through an opening in the brush wood, and the other, excited with the prospect of a fine haul, instantly fired at the supposed game and ran toward the object in order to get a surer shot when it flew up. But on reaching the spot, he found his friend and neighbor shot directly through the throat.

From the nature of the wound, Mr. G. was unable to talk, but with pencil and paper, told where his horse was, and that he thought he could reach home, which he did, with the aid of his friend. Medical aid was called in, but little hope was given for his recovery. Near night on the third day after the accident, he had gone into an adjoining room, and seeing the great grief of his family, took his pencil and, writing, urged them not to grieve that he was prepared to die willing to go. In a very short time after this he returned to his bed, in the other room, laid down, and in a few moments expired. . . . He leaves a grief-stricken wife and five or six children.

May 10, 1867 (DJ)

SAD ACCIDENT. On Friday of last week, Mr. John Wiseman, son of J.W. Wiseman, Esq. of this county, accidentally inflicted upon himself a gunshot wound, which, we understand, is feared to be mortal.

It seems that when he visited a fish trap in Wolf Creek, on the afternoon of that day, he discovered a large aligator (*sic*) and returned home for a gun with which to shoot it. On returning he found the alligator had escaped and with gun in hand, descended to the trap. After examining the trap and re-ascending the bank, the gun was dragged against a log which struck the hammer, causing it to fire – the ball taking effect in the neck of Mr. Wiseman – entering on the left side of the throat, and being extracted from the back part of the neck.

Up to this writing, Mr. W. is still living, but with little hope of recovery. We are informed that he is a consistent member of the Babtist (*sic*) Church, and bears his affliction with becoming Christian fortitude.

May 22, 1867 (GJM)

DEATH OF IRA H. TAYLOR. The sad intelligence of the death of our old friend and former active citizen, Mr. Ira H. Taylor, reached us on Monday, and produced feelings of deep sorrow and surprise upon all who knew him.

Mr. Taylor was a native of New York State. He removed to Macon when about twenty years of age, and was employed as chief accountant in several of our most flourishing institutions, until, in 1859, he was made Secretary and Treasurer of the Macon and Western Rail Road Company, which important office he filled with great usefulness to the Company and satisfaction to the public for twelve years. He then removed to his plantation in Jefferson County at No. 10 on the Central Rail Road, and devoted himself to agricultural pursuits with his accustomed energy and frugality, and was prospering in his progress until his plantation was plundered by the U.S. forces under General Sherman during his destructive march from Atlanta to the seaboard. Mr. Taylor's place was sacked by the troops, and he lost his year's crop and over two hundred and fifty bales of cotton. When Gov. Jenkins was permitted by the federal government to take charge of the Western and Atlantic Rail Road belonging to the state of Georgia, he prudently sought the best talent and energy he could find to revive this important property from its crippled condition and to restore system out of chaos. He employed Mr. Campbell Wallace as General Superintendent, and Mr. Taylor as Auditor of accounts . . .

On last Sunday morning, after penning a few lines to his

family in a state of partial mental derangement, at twelve o'clock he terminated his earthly existence by shooting himself through the head. He had been very much depressed since the passage of the late military bill and other oppressive acts of Congress, and was crushed to despair at the present prospects of his once happy country . . . His age was about forty-eight years. He leaves a wife and two lovely daughters, and numerous devoted friends, to mourn his loss. His family passed through Macon yesterday to the place of his remains.

May 31, 1867 —————————————— (DJ)

KILLED BY A BEAR. We deeply regret to learn that Mr. John B. Manly, who moved from this vicinity about the first of the present year to Levy county (Florida), was killed a few days since by a bear. He had shot and wounded the animal, and approached to finish him with a revolver, when the bear sprang upon him, caught his head in his mouth and crushed his skull. When found, Mr. Manly and the bear lay side by side.

–Madison (Fla.) *Messenger.*

June 21, 1867 —————————————— (WGT)

KILLED BY A RATTLESNAKE. The *Madison News* is informed of the melancholy death, from the bite of a rattlesnake, of a young man named John Rivers, which occurred the first of last week in Putnam County. Young Rivers was gathering strawberries in his father's patch, on his hands and knees, when the venomous reptile sprung and struck him on the neck. A physician was sent for at once, but before he arrived the young man was dead.

July 16, 1867 ——————————————— (SE)

OBITUARY. – JAMES C. ROSS, ESQ. A few days since we were pained with the intelligence of the sudden death of him whose name heads this brief notice. What a melancholy reflection! that in the vigor of life, one who was endowed with such goodness of heart, should, by an apparent accident, lose his life, breathing his last breath amid the watery waves which a few moments before excited in him no dread of danger.

In his efforts to rescue a boat which he had lost from the shore, at Sunbury, in Liberty County, he was unfortunately precipitated into the bay and was drowned . . .

April 28, 1868 ——————————————— (GJM)

HORRIBLE AND FATAL ACCIDENT. FALLING OF A FLOOR. DEATH OF DOL. (*sic*) **TROUTMAN.** At 5 o'clock yesterday afternoon one of the most horrible accidents ever recorded in the annals of this city occurred.

At that hour Mr. H.A. Troutman, of the firm of Farrar & Troutman, hardware merchants, Third street, in company with a young Mr. Nappier, walked into the branch store of Seymour, Johnson & Co., on Second street. He had been pricing two hogsheads of bacon at an earlier hour during the day, and had come back for the purpose of telling the clerk, Mr. T.D. Tinsley, that he would take them.

Mr. Tinsley immediately lighted a candle, and all three started from near the front door for the cellar, for the purpose of getting the weights of the bacon. When near the head of a stairway which leads below from the front part of the house, Mr. Troutman remarked that he would go back and get a drink of water. After telling him that he would find water near the back door, Mr. Tinsley and Mr. Nappier proceeded down the steps to the cellar where the bacon was kept. When Mr. Tinsley was just in the act of taking down the weight of the first hogshead, thirty feet of the floor above, running from side to side, gave way and fell with a terrible crash. The noise was heard all the block, which instantly brought a great crowd of people to the scene of the calamity. There was a large pile of corn, lard, syrup, flour and salt stored upon that portion of the floor.

When the horrible pit was approached by the crowd they could distinctly hear the cries and groans of Mr. Troutman from the sacks and barrels below. Several sprang into the hole and commenced rolling back the weight that was crushing him. Fainter and fainter came the voice of distress, and in twenty minutes it ceased. Mr. Troutman was dead! The people stood in horror above, except a few who manfully worked removing the debris. At last they came to his body and found a whole barrel of pork lying immediately across his chest, besides an immense pile of corn and barrels of flour were all around and upon it. The body was lifeless when they reached it, although for some time before he conversed with those trying to rescue him, and sent a farewell message to his family.

When the body was taken out it was conveyed across the street to Mr. Flint's store, and examined by Dr. Castellin, who says that no bones were broken. He is supposed to have been suffocated.

He was the son of Mr. Hiram B. Troutman, an old and universally known citizen, who lives in Vineville, and was about thirty-five years old. He leaves a wife and three children, who were unconscious of his terrible death until his body was taken to his home in Vineville.

The immediate cause of the accident was the saturation

of the earth with water by the late heavy rains, which caused the supports to the floor to give way. The floor at the time did not contain near as much weight as had often been upon it, nor half the quantity that is often upon those of other whole-sale houses.

The building belongs to Mr. Jackson Deloach, was almost new, and considered by him and others strong and substantial. No water had got into the cellar, but we all know that the whole earth is now full of it, and consequently very soft.

THE LATE ACCIDENT. An examination of the cellar into which the floor fell the other day, shows that the iron pillars upon which it rested were driven into the ground their entire length. It seems that they tripped from the stone rock upon which they rested, and then went straight down like as stake driven with a maul.

Mr. Troutman was buried yesterday afternoon, from his late home in Vineville, a large number of friends attending his funeral.

June 16, 1868 ——————————— (GJM)

POISONED. Mr. Nathan Lipscombe, of Troup County, was poisoned one day last week by chewing what he supposed was angelica root. He died in half an hour.

September 8, 1868 ——————————— (GJM)

From the *Fort Gaines Mirror*, Extra, Sept. 5th.

FATAL ACCIDENT – MANY KILLED AND WOUNDED. This morning, about 8 o'clock, the new bridge being built across the Chattahoochee river, in consequence of the rising waters, which drifted rafts of timbers against the temporary structures, washed them away, and the whole came down with a tremendous crash and fatal results, taking nearly the entire 2d span, which reached the brick pier, a distance from the wooden one of about 300 feet. The cries and groans of the sufferers, like a panic shock, was soon communicated to the inhabitants, and our city was in general commotion, rushing to the river to save the perishing ones. Skiffs and flatboats were procured, and the dead and wounded were landed along on the banks of the river from the ruins of the fallen bridge, as they drifted down the stream.

About thirty hands were employed on the bridge – many were working underneath – and a large number of spectators were also on the bridge, at the time it fell. All went down together, from an altitude of about 80 feet.

Among the killed and wounded we could only learn the names of the following: Killed: John C. Hill, Sheriff of Clay County, Hooker Steven, missing and supposed to be killed James Middleton, col., and Jerry Sutton. Wounded mortally: William A. Jackson, R.L. Peters and Robert Brown. Wounded slightly: Wm. Walden, W.H. Jernigan, W.G. Jernigan, William Mount and Andrew Newson, colored, mortally. We did not learn the names of all the colored wounded; some that went down with the bridge, have not, up to this time, been heard of.

September 22, 1868 ——————— (SR)

WE REGRET TO ANNOUNCE THE DEATH of Mr. John E. Hayes, editor of the *Savannah Republican*, who died on Wednesday last, it is thought from an over dose of laudanum he took, being unwell at the time. Mr. Hayes came South with Sherman's army, and after it entered Savannah he took charge of the *Republican*, in time, buying out the former proprietors. At first he was of the red hot radical stripe, but in time began to view the Southern people and their cause in a different light, and at the time of his unfortunate death, was doing good service for the South.

As a Northern man, he was mastering his prejudices and had the honesty and candor so to say. Had he lived, and made the South his permanent home, he would in time have been a thorough Southern man in feeling. We therefore regret his untimely death, aged 28 years.

January 19, 1869 ——————————— (WS)

NANCY JOHNSON MURDERED – KEEPER OF THE SAVANNAH HOUSE – THE INQUEST – EVIDENCE – AN ARREST. There are few places better known in this city than the Savannah House, a "Cyprian Hotel for the public" – somewhat removed from the common bawdy house. On Saturday night a murder was committed there which thrills all with horror. The keeper of the house was shot Saturday night and died yesterday.

THE PLACE

The Savannah House is a handsome two story wooden building, painted white with green blinds. On the north side is a long one-story wing. The site is at the corner of Jackson and Early streets, in what is commonly known as "down town". The house was designed and finished in 1863 as a hotel for the frail women who have surrendered their honor to the public.

ITS KEEPER

The mistress and owner of the house was a Miss Nancy Johnson. She came from Gwinett (*sic*) county, North Georgia, and was in her forty-eighth year. She came to Columbus in 1850, when she kept what was known as the Macon House, on Oglethorpe street. Her maiden name was Leverett. For many years she has lived at the place where she died. She has accumulated some $5,000. On Saturday night she bequeathed her property when debts, which are small, are paid to her daughter – once known as a married woman, Mrs. Hulsey – now as Ophelia Jones, the mistress of a house of Cyprians in Atlanta. Nancy has never been married.

THE MURDER

On Saturday night, about 9 o'clock, some four or six persons came to the Savannah House and knocked for admission, which they obtained. They went in. Some muss ensued. Nancy ordered them to leave, as there were no women to see. She had been drinking; so had they. Nancy enforced her order to leave with a drawn pistol. As they went out she slammed the door in their faces. On the second a pistol was fired through the door, the ball entering her left breast inflicting a fatal wound. The ball must have been shot by a tall man, as its course was downward. Nancy was fastening the door bolt when shot. The party hurried away. Immediately there was an uproar in the house. Women in night dresses hurried around. Drs. Stanford and Colzey were sent for. They could do no good. She lingered through Sunday and died yesterday, 2:25 p.m. Policemen could gather nothing on Saturday night.

THE JURY

Last afternoon at 4 o'clock Coroner McCahey summoned the following jury at the Savannah House: A.C. Morton, Foreman, Robert A. Wood, J.P. Murray, John Bush, Frank Gammel, John Philips, Charles Barrow.

THE CORPSE

Was covered with a sheet, on a bed, in a room to the right

of entrance. A placid expression rested on the hard features. When uncovered to the jury two dark spots were visible on the left breast, below the shoulder. One was doubtless caused by a fragment of the fatal ball.

THE EVIDENCE

Mollie Doles Sworn – Knew deceased. Was in her room Saturday night at 9 o'clock. Party of men knocked at front door. I went to my room. Deceased went to door. Heard her ask, "how many more?" Reply was "only two or three." I didn't see them. As they were coming in deceased said, if that was the way they were going to do they must leave her house. They remained about five minutes. As they went out deceased said, "they mustn't do anything like that in her house." She then slammed the door to. Directly after I heard a pistol shot. Deceased laughed and remarked to those outside, "you think you're mighty smart." Directly after she called to me that she was shot through the heart. She died today at 2:25 p.m. I don't know how many, or who the men were – didn't leave my room – the gentleman in there didn't know either. Some time before I could get deceased to lie down. She said the party were strangers to her.

Mrs. Tabitha S. Johnson Sworn – Have no acquaintance with deceased. Know nothing about killing.

After physicians came in from the examination of the body, Drs. Stanford and Colzey testified they knew the deceased, that she had received a gun shot wound, and was then lying dead in that house from its effect.

Dr. Kirkscey, County Physician, submitted the following official report: Columbus, Jan. 11, 1869. To the Coroner and Jury of Muscogee county, Ga.:

GENTLEMEN – I have examined the body of Nancy Jane Leverett, known as Nancy Johnson, who died this evening at 2:25 p.m. from gun shot wound. The examination was made in the presence of Drs. Stanford, Colzey, Moses and Fogarty. The ball entered four inches from middle of sternum, on a line with and two inches below the clavicle, passing inward, backward and downward; entering the cavity of the chest between the third and fourth ribs; traversing the cavity about two inches, penetrating and fracturing sixth rib, passing backward and outward, lodging in the inferior angle of internal surface of scapula, where the ball was found. There was about half gallon of effused blood occupying the left thoracic cavity. It is my opinion death ensued as a consequence of that wound, causing effusion of blood from internal hemorrhage, filling the left thoracic cavity, thereby encroaching and compressing upon left lung and heart sufficiently to obstruct the action. I hereby present to you for your consideration the ball found by me as mentioned.

Very respectfully, E.J. Kirkscey, M.D.

The ball appeared to be an ordinary pistol ball.

THE VERDICT

The jury returned a verdict deceased came to her death by means of a pistol ball, fired by a party unknown.

ARRESTED

We learned late that a man named Gillespie, from over the river, has been arrested.

January 19, 1869 ———————— (WS)

HORRIBLE ACCIDENT – ONE MAN KILLED AND TWO WOUNDED! We have some particulars of a most horrible accident that occurred on Thursday last, about thirty miles below Hawkinsville, in Telfair conty (*sic*) on the line of the Macon and Brunswick Railroad. It seems that a party of white laborers recently hired in the up country to work on that road, were proceeding on foot to the scene of their future operations, and while marching along the dirt road in pretty close order, a musket carried by a negro, and loaded with slugs, went off, accidentally killing a white man walking near the muzzle, and wounding two others. The wounded men were brought to this city on Saturday, to receive medical attention. One of them it is thought, must certainly die, as his brains are protruding from a ghastly hole in the skull. The other was shot in the mouth, and will probably recover.

—Macon Messenger.

September 17, 1869 ———————— (LR)

A SHOCKING DEATH. On Saturday evening last, Mr. J.J. Gilley, a laborer at Jones' saw mill, in this county, while bearing off a puncheon, attempted to raise one end of it over the saw, and failing, bore it against the saw, which caused him to fall across it, under a full head of steam. He was cut through his right shoulder, ranging across towards his right hip to the navel, when the saw turned its course so as to saw into his left thigh. The unfortunate man died instantly.

Mr. Gilley was a stranger in the community, being employed only the day previous, but from a memorandum book found in his possession it was ascertained that he came originally from Sevier county, Tennessee, but of late had been engaged in selling a patent medicine for Dr. Beasley, of Troup county. If any of Mr. Gilly's kindred should see this notice of his death, it will afford them pleasure to know that, although Mr. G. had no money or valuables whatever, he was given a decent burial.

—Newnan Herald, 10th.

January 20, 1870 —————————————— (CI)

A SAD AFFAIR. A young man, aged about sixteen years, named Thomas Wilcox, died at his father's residence, a few miles from this place, on Sunday evening last, from an injury received during Christmas week. Young Wilcox, with some of his companions, were at a neighbor's house. One of them wishing to have some sport at his expense, filled a pipe nearly full of powder, putting some tobacco on top of the powder, and gave it to young Wilcox to smoke. The powder soon exploded, burning his face and mouth dreadfully; and the flame went down his throat, and burned him internally, so severely as to cause his death. Let those who seek amusement at the expense of others take warning from the fate of young Wilcox. –W.M.R. Woodstock, Cherokee Co., Ga., Jan. 13th, 1870.

March 31, 1870 —————————————— (CA)

AWFUL CALAMITY. On Wednesday morning the 29th inst., about 7 o'clock, during the prevalence of a severe thunderstorm the residence of Dr. George B. Smith near Benevolence was struck by lightning and the entire family prostrated and stunned by the shock.

To those who first recovered, an appalling spectacle presented itself. There lay the noble head of the house with his neck broken, a lifeless corpse, while the mother and two of the little ones were grievously injured and blackened by the fluid. To add to the horrors of the scene, in an instant the entire dwelling was wrapped in flames and almost before the dead and suffering could be removed to a place of safety, the whole pile was consumed and a smoking ruin all that remained of the pleasant home of that happy family. Books, papers, clothing, all save two feather beds, fell prey to the devouring element . . .

May 24, 1870 ——————————— (GWT)

The *Marietta Journal* says William Dobbs, of that county, fell off an ox cart Tuesday, while drunk, and broke his neck.

May 24, 1870 ——————————— (GWT)

The Savannah News says: We have received the following particulars of a dreadful accident, resulting in the loss of life of Mr. James H. Butler, near Eden, in Effingham County. Mr. Butler, on last Wednesday morning, while adjusting a belt near the circular saw, was thrown or fell from his position upon the saw, which was in full motion at the time. His right arm and right leg were cut off, and being remote from immediate surgical aid he bled to death in about six hours after the accident, and was buried yesterday at Goshen Hill Cemetery, about twelve miles above Savannah. He was forty years of age and leaves a family consisting of a wife and four children.

May 24, 1870 ——————————— (GJM)

SAD ACCIDENT. Mr. Willie Donaldson, son of Judge Donaldson, of Canton, Ga., while assisting his father in building a bridge near Cartersville, fell into the river on some timbers, on Tuesday last, and was so badly bruised that he died on Wednesday. He was a brother of Mrs. J.W. Davis, of our town.

June 6, 1870 (SMN)

A SAVANNAH MERCHANT FATALLY INJURED BY FALLING FROM A WINDOW.

About half past four o'clock yesterday morning Nelson Knight, colored, a servant in the employ of the Marshall House, found a gentleman, afterwards recognized as Mr. Robert I. Caughey, one of the guests of the Marshall House, and a well known cotton merchant of Savannah, lying in the yard groaning. Dr. Arnold was immediately sent for, who found him sitting up on the pavement in the yard where he was discovered, with a large cut over his forehead and his left thigh broken. Dr. Reed was sent for by Dr. Arnold, and they dressed his wound and had him conveyed to his room, where he died at half-past five o'clock. The base of the skull was found fractured, which was the immediate cause of his death.

The Coroner having been notified, summoned a jury of inquest, when the following facts were testified to, indicating that the deceased had accidentally fallen out of his window into the yard below, while laboring under temporary aberration of mind, superinduced by extreme nervous excitement:

Mr. William Wade, a friend of deceased, testified that he met the deceased on Saturday evening on Bull street; that he appeared to be excited, saying that he wished to go to Dr. Knorr's to get some medicine to quiet his nerves, and speaking of many things which he (Mr. W.) knew had never happened. Dr. Knorr gave him some medicine and he went to his room. He frequently asked Mr. W. if music was not playing, and saying that he heard the church organs playing. Mr. Wade left him, telling him if he got worse to send for him, which he promised to do, but saying that he hoped to be well by morning . . .

The deceased was in his bed by twelve o'clock Saturday night and was not under the influence of liquor . . . the jury found that the deceased had come to his death by falling, accidentally, out of his room window, in the Marshall House, while laboring under temporary aberration of mind, caused by extreme nervous excitement.

The deceased, Robert I. Caughey, was aged about forty-seven years, and a native of Belfast, Ireland, but for the last twenty years has been a resident of this city and engaged in business as a cotton buyer . . . His funeral took place yesterday afternoon.

June 7, 1870 ———————————— (MT)

DIED. A man named Joe Reeves was killed Wednesday, near Cartersville, by a rock falling on him, while being raised by a derrick.

Reuben Statan, white, aged seventeen, was run over by a passenger train on the East Tennessee and Georgia Railroad near Dalton, Tuesday and almost instantly killed. His left leg was cut off near the body and his right foot shockingly crushed.

Mr. Anton Schmitt, a Prussian by birth, who fell from a second story window in Savannah on Tuesday morning, died Thursday morning.

July 5, 1870 ————————— (MT)

DIED. A negro woman named Fanny Frozier, was fatally burned in Savannah, Sunday morning, by the explosion of a can of kerosene oil which she was using to kindle a fire with.

December 17, 1870 ————————— (HHJ)

A SINGULAR MEDICINE AND FATAL RESULT. A singular death occurred in Tishomingo county, Miss. a few days ago. Mr. Pennington, a stout, healthy farmer, had a slight chill last Sunday. The day before he was in excellent health. Monday morning he felt the approach of another chill, and lay down on the bed. After lying awhile he remarked that he had heard that spider webs "were good for the chills". He rose from the bed, and gathering from the walls or ceiling of the room a web, in which were three "spider balls" as they are called, swallowing them. Immediately there was heard within his chest a faint sound as if the ball had burst, and in ten minutes he was dead. Very soon his throat, lips and the whole of his face were greatly swollen by the action of the poison. Who has not seen hundreds of young spiders, not as large as a pinhead swarm from one of these balls when broken open? And who but this ill-fated Mississippian would have ever thought of swallowing them as a remedy for chills or for anything else?

January 24, 1871 ————————— (MT)

A little son of N.S. McCalley, of Troup County, was crushed to death in a gin, one day last week.

February 16, 1871 ——————— (DWJ)

Mr. Thomas Harvill, of Atlanta, seventeen years old, unintentionally shot and killed Mr. Bud Cardonal, on Friday. The two young men were about starting on a hunting expedition, and Mr. Harvill, not knowing his gun was loaded, playfully drew it on Mr. Cardonal. Here is another warning to those who carelessly play with pistols and guns.

February 21, 1871 ——————— (GWT)

SERIOUS ACCIDENT. On Wednesday of last week, while the workmen were engaged at work on a storehouse for Messrs. Gardner & Smith, at Buford, sixteen miles below here, on the AirLine Railroad, the frame gave way and fell with a crash, killing a Mr. White and injuring more or less, three or four others.

February 21, 1871 ——————— (GWT)

SAD ACCIDENT. On Saturday last, Mr. Russel Hall, who was acting as fireman at Colonel Chandler's sawmill, near this place, was accidentally caught between the bandwheel and boiler, and horribly crushed, resulting in instant death.

February 23, 1871 ——————— (DWJ)

A CORPSE DRIVING A HORSE THROUGH NASHVILLE.
    Dr. William Burdett, who resided at No. 336 South Cherry Street, died at six o'clock last evening under the most peculiar circumstances.
    About half an hour previous to his demise he had driven to

the residence of Conductor Edward Wells, near the Decatur Depot, who lay very ill of inflammatory rheumatism. After leaving some instruction with his patient, he got into his buggy and started his horse homeward.

Sudden death, like a stroke of lightning, overtook him probably before he had driven more than a few hundred yards, and the late living, speaking human being, who a few moments before had talked quietly and calmly, after his usual manner, to a patient, and that patients family, and had even joked with a little boy whom he met by the streetside as he entered the buggy, still sat stark and stiff upright upon his seat, the reins clutched in his hands, staring eyes looking out upon the street, driving homeward – a corpse . . . Dr. Burdett's body was taken into the house, where Coroner Brin held an inquest over his remains. The jury returned a verdict that he came to his death from disease of the heart.

February 23, 1871 ———————— (DWJ)

A MAN DROWNED WHILE BEING BAPTIZED. A few weeks since Dr. A.P. Pownall, of Sand Hill, Ky., after a brief courtship, was married to Miss Mary J. Wilson. Shortly after his marriage Dr. Pownall united with the Christian Church, and Sunday last was appointed as the day of his baptism, he having requested his paster (*sic*), the Rev. J.B. Hough, to perform the rite. At the appointed hour a large number of persons had assembled on the banks of Crooked Creek, the place chosen for the immersion. After singing and a prayer the Rev. Mr. Hough entered the creek, leading the Doctor.

They were obliged to proceed some distance from the shore in order to reach a sufficient depth, but suddenly both were seen to go down. They soon arose to the surface, and the minister regained the bank, but the Doctor, being unable to swim, was swept by the current under a flood gate, only a short distance below. Every exertion was made to save him but in vain.

The body was soon after found and brought to shore amid the most heart rending screams from his wife and friends. Everything possible was done to resuscitate the Doctor, but alas the vital spark had flown.

February 23, 1871 ——————————— (DWJ)

SAD. A child of Mr. S.F. Bennett, living not far from our town, was very slightly burned the other day, but different applications being made to the wounds, ease was restored to the little sufferer. Subsequently it was suggested that Kerosene Oil was an excellent antidote, and it was not long after the application of that article was made before the little sufferer was a corpse.

March 7, 1871 ——————————— (GWT)

We clip the following from the *Atlanta Constitution*, of Sunday:

A Mr. Robert Foster left this city for Chattanooga, on the 10 1/2 o'clock train on Friday night. Just after passing the Rolling Mill in making an attempt to pass from one car to another, he fell, and both his legs, from the knees down, were horribly smashed by the cars running over them. He also received one or two flesh wounds on the head. After laying in this condition for sometime, he was brought to the city and carried to the Stubblefield House.

At the time of this writing he is supposed to be dying. We

have heard that he was under the influence of liquor at the time of the accident.

March 7, 1871 ——————————— (GWT)

The wife of Mr. James McCampbell, who lives about one mile above Marietta, was killed on yesterday. Mrs. McCampbell, hearing the Dalton freight train coming, and seeing her hogs on the track, went to drive them off. While doing so, her dress caught on the track, throwing her down, the train passing over and killing her.

March 7, 1871 ——————————— (GWT)

Benjamin Thompson fell into a ditch at Savannah on Friday, and was drowned. Drunk.

March 28, 1871 ——————————— (GWT)

There were two alarms of fire Thursday night, at Atlanta, and while responding to the second, Mr. Dan Lynch, Foreman of Company No. 3, fell under the engine, which ran over his abdomen, causing his death in a few minutes.

April 4, 1871 ——————————— (GWT)

Mr. Joseph White, who lived near Centreville, Fla., fell off a train just starting from Thomasville for Savannah last Monday night, and several cars passed over his head, killing him instantly. He was drunk.

April 20, 1871 ————————————— (DWJ)

SAD DEATH. A very worthy young man by the name of "Bony" Edwards, an operative in the Car factory, came to his death the other day by jumping or running against a plank. It appears that he and some of his friends were amusing themselves by slapping each other with boards. – Young Edwards, having struck one of his friends, turned to run, when he came in contact with the end of a plank, and the internal injuries received were such as to cause his death in less than fortyeight hours.

June 20, 1871 ————————————— (GWT)

A little boy aged three years, son of Mr. Ben. Callier, of Talbotton, was poisoned last Thursday by eating cobalt, and died in a few hours.

June 20, 1871 ————————————— (GWT)

Captain C.B. Cluskey, late of Washington City, died at Brunswick, Wednesday, from the effects of exposure to the sun on St. Simon's Island, where he was engaged in con-structing a lighthouse.

August 8, 1871 ————————————— (GWT)

Mrs. John Charles was killed in the old Eagle and Phoenix building in Augusta, by a portion of the plastering falling on her head and breast as she lay sick in bed.

August 8, 1871 ———————————— (GWT)

The Columbus Enquirer says that at the steam mill of Mr. McCormick, on the Eufaula and Montgomery Railroad, Saturday, there occurred a sad accident – such as are often recorded about machines run by steam. A laborer (colored) in the employ of Mr. McCormick, while moving some plank from the mill, allowed the plank to touch the saw, and was thrown down, and before he could rise was caught by the saw, and was immediately killed; the saw cutting diagonally through his body from his shoulder to the waist, cutting through the lungs and heart. Mr. McCormick was standing near, and made a desperate effort to save the unfortunate man, but was too late. It was but the work of a second – so sudden and terrible that the lungs and heart were observed still in action after the body had been torn asunder.

October 31, 1871 ———————————— (SR)

Mrs. Mary Woodall, wife of William Woodall, of Gwinnett County, in attempting to grease a cogwheel while running, was caught in the wheel and crushed to death. She leaves five children. She was a member of the Methodist Church . . . *Gwinnett Atlas.*

November 28, 1871 ———————————— (SR)

KILLED. A negro man named Henry Lawson was run over and killed by the train on the M. & A. R., on Friday night last, about four miles west of Sparta. Cause – drunkenness and asleep on the track.

January 16, 1872 ——————— (GWT)

Mr. George Wilson, while working in Talmadge's Saw-mill, at Monticello, last week, was caught in the machinery and so terribly mutilated as to cause his death that night.

Emma Bland, a white woman, living at Augusta, who was accidentally burned last Wednesday by falling into the fire, died on Friday

A man named Shepherd was found frozen stiff and dead, one night last week, in the road near Damascus, Early county. Benzine.

January 16, 1872 ——————— (GWT)

SCALDED TO DEATH. A little negro child, about two years old, met with a fearful accident in this city on Thursday. She was playing alone in the kitchen and fell backwards into a pot of boiling water, in which situation she was not discovered until a part of her body was parboiled. The little unfortunate lingered in great agony until Friday, when death released her from her sufferings.

January 25, 1872 ——————— (DWJ)

WE REGRET to chronicle the horrid death of Miss Emma Hall, daughter of Mr. Ira J. Hall of this county which occurred on Tuesday last, the circumstances of which are as follows: Miss Hall was at a spring near her father's residence washing, the day being windy, she ventured too near the fire that was burning briskly under a pot, when her clothes caught on fire and in an instant she was enveloped in flames.

Under the excitement she made no effort to extinguish the flames, but ran as fast as she could towards the house, thereby adding fury to the flames. Besides being dreadfully seared and scorched outwardly, she was also burned inwardly to an extent that would have caused her death.

February 6, 1872 ───────────── (GWT)

We quote as follows from the *West Point News* of Wednesday:
TERRIBLE FREAK OF A FLASH OF LIGHTNING – ONE LIFE LOST – TWO PERSONS SEVERELY INJURED.

Mr. Gresham is a tenant of Mr. H.G. Slaughter, who lives some eight miles from this place, between Long Cane and the river. Last Saturday afternoon, as Mr. G. and his family were sitting around the fire the chimney was struck by lightning. The electric current passed through the gable end of the house down to the mantlepiece, totally destroying a clock which was thereon. From thence it passed along the end and side of the house to the other end, knocking the gable out. Two little children were in a bed near which the lightning passed, but escaped any injury. Mr. G. and his wife were both knocked senseless. The former had one of his feet seriously injured. The skin was lacerated and his foot presented the appearance of having been badly bruised. He was also severely burnt. The hair on his body looked like it had been singed over a fire, and his skin was intensely red. The clothing of Mrs. G. was set on fire, and she was burned from her feet to half way up her body. A son of Mr. Gresham, some twelve or fourteen years of age, was instantly killed. Another son, who was afflicted, together with Mr. Reading, a nephew of Mr. G., were both in the group, and escaped unharmed. A large chest containing clothing, was torn into atoms and the contents set on fire. The roof of the house was almost blown off. A singular fact in connection with this accident is that neither the shoes of Mr. G. nor a single piece of the clock are to be found.

March 5, 1872 —————————————— (GWT)

We quote these items from the *Dalton Citizen*, of Friday:

TERRIBLE ACCIDENT – FOUR PERSONS KILLED. As we go to press we learn that the engine at Broker's saw mill, five miles above this place, exploded its boiler yesterday evening, killing Stewart Wilson, John Brinkley, Clem Quillian and a boy named Chastain. The engineer and several others were badly scalded, the former it is thought dangerously. The explosion is said to have been terrific, tearing the engine into fragments. The scene around the mill after the accident is represented to have been terrible in the extreme, those that were killed being awfully mangled, one of whom was thrown at least a hundred yards and split wide open, and another against a large stump, fifty yards off, bruising and mangling him in a horrible manner. We did not learn the cause of the explosion.

March 19, 1872 —————————————— (GWT)

We find the following in the *Republican*, of Sunday:

MELANCHOLY ACCIDENT. Mr. Joshua Friar, an old and respected citizen of Coffee County, Georgia, sixty-two years of age, met his death about ten days since in a most remarkable manner. He was smoothing a stick with a drawing knife, when the catch of the blade slipped from the stick and its keen edge was pulled with such force by his own hands against his person, that his abdomen was cut open across the middle, severing his bowels and causing death in thirty-six hours.

April 2, 1872 (GWT)

We quote as follows from the *Savannah* News, of Tuesday:

KILLED BY A FALLING TREE. On Saturday last, in the afternoon, Mr. W.H. Edwards, Sr., of Tattnall County, started in his buggy to visit his grandson, residing in an adjoining county, Bryan, who was confined by illness to his bed. Mr. E. appeared in his usual health when he left his home, and there was no cause to suppose he was in danger. A gentleman from Bryan County informs us that late in the afternoon an empty buggy was seen standing near the bridge over the Canoochiee (*sic*) river, which divides the two counties. On closer approach of the party, Mr. Edwards was discovered on the ground leaning against the buggy, perfectly dead. The horse had broken loose and was standing a short distance off. A large branch of a tree was lying across the front of the buggy, almost concealing Mr. Edwards from view. The supposition is that he was killed by the tree limb. The buggy was badly broken, but the horse was uninjured. Mr. Edwards was an old and respected citizen of Tattnall County, and had lived to the good old age of seventy-two years, in the enjoyment of the good will and opinion of all his neighbors.

May 28, 1872 (GWT)

THE RECENT AFFRAY AT ST. MARY'S. We have the following particulars through private sources of the recent homicide at St. Mary's. It appears that Warren Scott and John Grovenstein, school boys, became engaged in a dispute during a game of base ball. Both parties used their bats freely, and an unfortunate blow from Scott upon the back of Grovenstein's head fractured the skull and produced death in about thirty-six hours.

Three Justices have pronounced it a case of involuntary manslaughter. Young Scott was bound over to appear at the next term of the Superior Court in St. Mary's. The distressing affair is deeply lamented by the people of that vicinity.

June 4, 1872 ——————————— (GWT)

The Senoia Journal, of Thursday, says:

HORRIBLE. As an extra train passed up the Savannah, Griffin and North Alabama Railroad Tuesday night, the engineer discovered something on the track a few hundred yards above Turin, but was unable to stop the engine before reaching the object and some of the wheels of the locomotive passing over it. Upon examination, the body of Mr. Frank Jones, of Sharpsburg, was found in a very mangled condition. His thighs were both crushed, his shoulder dislocated, and other terrible wounds upon his head and other portions of the body. We learn that the wounds of his body bled but little when found, and that it was cold or nearly so. It is supposed by some that he was killed by unknown parties, and his body placed on the track by his murderers. The deceased was a son of Miles Jones, Esq. and highly respected where he was known. He had no enemies so far as we know.

June 18, 1872

Mr. William Gaskins, of Coffee County, suicided one day last week. He had a wife and family, but fell desperately in love with a young lady in his neighborhood, and his brains, or heart, or something else, couldn't stand the pressure. If he had lived in Utah, Mr. G. might be alive and numerously happy now.

June 18, 1872

The *Journal* says a little child of Mr. T. Stephens, of Cobb county, met with a horrible death last Thursday. It wandered to the well near the house, and "pushing its little head through some lattice work around the well, it caught hold of the iron windlass and began pulling and tugging at it, until the bucket was lifted to the opening and began to descend. The first revolution of the windlass struck it on the head, which was fastened to the lattice work, knocking it insensible, and each successive revolution increasing in momentum and force, struck it on the head, also, fearfully battering the skull until its brains were almost visible."

August 20, 1872

We find these items in the last *Dalton Citizen*:

FATAL ACCIDENT. Last Wednesday evening the Selma, Rome and Dalton Railroad train, going southward, knocked an old decrepid (*sic*) gentleman by the name of Tate, from the track, near the line of Gordon and Whitfield, killing him instantly. The man was very old and deaf, and quite feeble. The crossing was very near a curve in the road, and the witnesses, who have made affidavits to the facts of the sad disaster, exonerate the engineer from any fault, and think that it could not have been prevented under the circumstances.

August 20, 1872 ————————— (GWT)

DEATH FROM A THORN. We learn that a Mr. Bailey, of Murray county, stuck a thorn in his foot on Saturday the 3d inst., while in his field at work, which he at once extracted. The wound from the thorn, which was very slight, gave him but little pain at the time; but the next morning his foot was swelled to twice its natural size, and by Monday evening it was found that mortification had commenced, and he soon after died.

August 20, 1872 ————————— (GWT)

MAN KILLED ON THE STATE ROAD. We understand that a brakeman on the above Road (new hand) had his head knocked off at one of the Chickamauga bridges, between this place and Chattanooga, one day last week. Did not learn the unfortunate man's name.

September 24, 1872 ————————— (GWT)

The *Chronicle and Sentinel* says the body of a white man named Lewis Morris was found dead on the Georgia Railroad, three miles from Augusta, on Tuesday morning. Morris was drunk the previous afternoon, and is supposed to have gone to sleep on the track. The up night passenger train for Atlanta run (*sic*) over his head and cut off half the skull.

November 21, 1872 ——————— (DWJ)

DISTRESSING CALAMITY. From the *Griffin News* we learn of the occurrence of one of the most distressing casualties which it has been our province to chronicle in a great while. The heart-rending misfortune occurred last Saturday night, on the line of Spalding and Monroe Counties. The particulars, as we have them, are as follows: On the night above mentioned, Messrs. Harper and Ogletree were packing cotton, and had a lantern in the gin house. By some means the lantern fell, and setting fire to the lint burned to death one child of Mr. Green Harper, two of his sister's – Mrs. Gardner – two negro children, and burning Mr. Harper severely; also burning another child of Mr. Harper's so that he cannot live. This is by far the most distressing occurrence ever known in our section of the country, and the bereaved families will have the sympathy of every one. The gin house and six bales of cotton were also consumed.

November 26, 1872 ——————— (GWT)

The *Covington Enterprise* prints the following:

A REMARKABLE PREMONITION. On Sunday night, the 12th inst., Mr. Henry Maddox dreamed that his father, Mr. John Maddox, was dead. The old gentleman lived some three miles from him, between the Yellow and South rivers, in the southern part of Newton County, and had been suffering from paralysis for several months. The dream rendered Henry so uneasy that he went to see his father on

Monday, whom he found to be about as he usually had been for some weeks. After spending some time with the old man, the son started to leave, but his mother called to him that his father was worse, and he returned only in time to find him breathing his last.

November 26, 1872 ———————— (GWT)

We find these items in the *Columbus Sun*, of Wednesday:

THREE YOUNG LADIES DROWNED – TWO MEN NARROWLY ESCAPE – BATTEAU OVERTURNED. Mr. William Kildree reports one of the saddest incidents that we have yet had occasion to record. It happened Sunday afternoon on the Chattahoochee River, twenty miles above Columbus, near Mechanicsville, Lee county, Ala. A party of two men and three young ladies were crossing the river in a batteau. One of the survivors states that one of the ladies arose in the boat to scare some ducks, when the vessel capsized and the entire party were precipitated into the water. The day was very cold, must have been intensely so on the river. The three young ladies were drowned. Their names are Misses Susan and Elizabeth Teel, and Josie Pike. The latter was formerly a resident of this city. Her body was recovered late Sunday night. The other two bodies had not been recovered when our informant left the locality Monday morning. It was with the utmost difficulty the two men were saved. One would have been drowned also had it not been for the assistance rendered by a person on shore who happened to be near the scene of the terrible accident. The names of the men are Charlton Carver and Cicero Godwin.

February 11, 1873 ———————— (GWT)

A MAN KILLED BY A FALLING WELL BUCKET.
The *Lawrenceville Herald* says on last Monday, Wellington
Jones of that county, was down in a well cleaning it out, his
son drawing up the bucket. By some means the bucket while
filled with dirt, broke loose from the rope and fell on Mr. J's
head, fracturing his skull and causing his death in a short
time.

February 14, 1873 ———————— (QB)

A TERRIBLE ACCIDENT. Mr. M.E. Parramore, an aged
citizen of Quitman, was seriously injured on last Friday, by
being thrown from a wagon – the horses having taken fright
and run away. From the character of the injuries received, it
is presumed that Mr. Parramore was dragged some distance
– his head particularly being terribly mangled. He lies in a
critical condition at his residence, near the Academy.

Since the foregoing was placed in type, death relieved the
sufferer. Mr. Parramore died at about one o'clock Wednesday
Morning.

February 14, 1873 ———————— (QB)

DEATH IN THE SWAMP. It is reported and generally
believed that an unfortunate white girl, generally known in
Quitman by the name of Clifford Pucket, was found dead on
the edge of a swamp, near Boston, Thomas County, the latter
part of last week. The indications are that she had been dead
several days, as birds of prey had feasted on her carcass. The

cause of her death is not stated, but the inference is that she was murdered. She was about 18 or 20 years of age, an ignorant, dissipated girl of very easy virtue, and formerly resided on the suberbs (*sic*) of Quitman. She led a wretched, depraved career in life, and died a horrible death in the swamp.

March 28, 1873 — (HWV)

Mr. Joshua Riggins, of Upson County, was attacked with a toothache, on the 11th. After the tooth ceased to ache, his tongue swelled up and filled his mouth. The tongue assuaged, the throat began to swell, and projected as far out as his chin, producing death. Three physicians were in attendance, but could not designate the disease. So reports the *Thomaston Herald*.

April 10, 1873 — (DWJ)

Albany News and *Central City*:

Mr. Samuel Gaff, a young man of this city, aged eighteen years, died at his home on Sunday night last, of suffocation from an abscess of the larynx. When first visited by Dr. Hilsman he was in no apparent danger, but late in the evening of Sunday he became rapidly worse. The Doctor was sent for too late, for before he arrived, the young man was a corpse.

April 10, 1873 — (DWJ)

SUDDEN DEATH. Mr. Henry Miller, who lived near Chickasawhatchie, in this county, met death suddenly and rather mysteriously on Thursday night last. After eating supper he went to a neighbor's house, not far distant, to sit until bedtime, and was apparently in good health. Returning about the usual bedtime, he retired. During the night his wife was aroused by a noise in the room and inquired what it meant. She was answered by Mr. Miller that he believed he would choke to death. Mrs. Miller gave the alarm – medical aid was hastily procured, but no relief could be had, and he died in a few hours.

April 24, 1873 — (QB)

The body of W.E. Reese, of Warren County, was recently discovered in a dense canebrake. The head was torn from the body by dogs, and the remains horribly mutillated (*sic*). The deceased was of unsound mind, and it is supposed committed suicide.

April 29, 1873 — (GWT)

Mr. S.M. Goodwin was thrown from a mule last Friday, on the plantation of Mr. Redwine, near Powell's Station, and killed instantly. After he stopped plowing he hitched the end of the trace chains on the top of the harness and led his mule about 75 yards. He then attempted to mount the mule, and was thrown and became entangled in the harness. He was dragged about 893 yards, and when found his skull was broken and his body horribly mangled.

April 29, 1873 ————————————

HORRIBLE DEATH. We quote the following from the *Fort Valley Mirror*: Monday morning a young man named Wm. Lowe, living with Mr. Seab. Mims, about three miles in the country, hitched two mules to the front wheel of the wagon and went down to the mill to get a log cart. The lines by some means became disconnected, and the mules began to run at a fearful speed. The young man fell over in front of the wheel, and his feet being fastened between the boards he was unable to extricate himself. The mules ran against a telegraph pole and then he came loose from the wagon. It is supposed from the bruises on his chest that the wagon wheel was on him all the time. The body was badly bruised from the back of the neck all the way down the spinal column. He did not live but a few minutes after the accident happened. Mr. Lowe was raised in Twiggs County, and this will be sad news to his friends and relatives in that county.

May 15, 1873 ————————————

TERRIBLE ACCIDENT. One of the most terrible and heart-rending accidents that has ever been our misfortune to chronicle, occurred yesterday about half past one o'clock at Mercer University.

While some workmen were engaged in putting up a cornice or mitre on one of the corners of the building, the scaffolding on which they were standing gave way and precipitated them to the ground – a fall of sixty feet. Mr. John Rowe alighted on his feet, but the rebound threw him under the brick, and he lived only fifteen minutes. Mr. James Globler fell on his head and died in about half an hour. William B. Procter fell on his side and is also dead. Ed Holt and Ben White, both colored, were horribly mashed and bruised, and their legs and arms broken. Messrs. Rowe and Globler were from Philadelphia, and were skilled workmen. Mr. Proctor was well known in the city as a tinner.

—Macon Enterprise.

May 23, 1873 — (LR)

HORRIBLE ACCIDENT. We are pained to record a horrible accident, resulting in death, from the imprudent use of kerosene oil. Miss Susan Grady, a young lady about eighteen years old, living in West Point with her sister, Mrs. James Scott, was attempting to kindle a fire in a stove, last Thursday evening, and in order to facilitate it, she poured on kerosene oil. The fire was communicated to the oil in the can which exploded, scattering the oil in every direction, and saturating her clothing with it, which took fire. In a moment she was frantic with excitement and ran screaming through the house into the yard. Here she fell to the ground, enveloped in flames, and Mrs. Scott, who had pursued her, wrapped blankets about her. The flames were extinguished, but the unfortunate young lady was burned frightfully. Her lower limbs, right side and arm, were perfectly charred, while the remainder of her person was covered with blisters, crisps of skin and flesh. She lived nearly twenty-four hours, after the occurrence, in great suffering.

June 5, 1873 ————————————— (DWJ)

SKELETON IN A TREE. A Most Remarkable Suicide. The readers of the *Telegraph & Messenger* will probably remember some notices that were made in the early part of April of the disappearance from Macon of a German confectioner named Charles Baswildebald. At the same time a notice was published by some of the friends of the missing man offering a reward for his recovery.

The man had been drinking and was known to have been laboring under a mental aberration caused by the use of strong drink, and it was apprehended that he was wandering in the woods somewhere around Macon, or had perhaps lost himself in the swamps down the river. Several parties went out to search for him, but without finding any trace of him. Once, however, they thought they found indications that he had wandered into the swamp and had sunk forever in the water and mud, finding therein a grave, the precise location of which would never be ascertained.

When these signs were discovered further search was deemed useless, and his friends gave up all hope of ever finding his remains. They were fully satisfied that he had lost his life in the swamp, and though they desired to give him christian burial, they felt compelled to forego the performance of that melancholy duty.

The man wandered away on the 28th day of March, and for three or four weeks the search for him was kept up pretty steadily.

The mystery of this disappearance was not fully explained until yesterday, when some boys, who were in the woods, about two and a half miles from the city, near the Houston road, discovered the body of a man hanging in a pine tree, near the top, and some fifty or sixty feet from the ground.

The unfortunate man seems to have climbed the tree, made a noose of his suspenders and hanged himself to the limb, where for two months his remains have been hanging, beaten upon by the rain, withered by the sun, swung and swayed by the winds, while his requiem was sung in the branches of the pines in grander diapasons than were ever breathed from the organ.

There is no doubt that this skeleton which is dangling there in the top of that tall pine, is all that is left of the mortal part of Charles Baswildebald. Though it has not yet been cut down, his friends are all entirely satisfied that the lost is found. Coroner Dewberry will go at nine o'clock this morning, when the remains will be cut down and an inquest held. It is almost certain that he will be identified by the clothing, as well as by the contents of his pockets. He had some fifty or sixty dollars in his possession when he left his room. The remains are hanging in full view of the residence of Mr. J.R. Rice, and can be distinctly seen therefrom.

The deceased was a native of the Kingdom of Bavaria, and came of a good German family. He was liberally educated and was a confectioner by trade. He came to Macon in 1868, and obtained employment with S. Helfrich, with whom he remained up to the time of his disappearance. For two years after he came here he was strictly sober, but he got to drinking and finally began to take sprees which lasted several days at a time. Mr. Helfrich frequently remonstrated with him, but his reply always was that he would as soon die as live. He kept drinking more and more until his mind became unsettled, and in this derangement he wandered off and put an end to his existence.

There is some romance connected with this man, the facts

of which are not known, but which may have had much to do with bringing about the facts. He was evidently in an unhappy state of mind, and took to drink to drown some trouble that was preying upon him. At the head of his bed hung a picture of a beautiful German girl. To this picture he often expressed the greatest attachment, but he would not tell whose the picture was, nor any connection he may have had with the original of it. It remains a secret, probably forever, and the reader can only conjecture the real nature of the romantic particulars.

–Telegraph & Messenger.

From the same paper of Tuesday we copy the following additional particulars:

The deceased appears to have been very deliberate in his work. His suspenders were made of osnaburg. These he tied together and then fastened one end around his neck, the other end to the limb of a tree, let go his hold, and was launched into eternity. There was nothing to show that his death struggle was a severe one. One arm hung by his side, and the other rested on an adjacent limb as if it had been placed there in a position of ease. His feet hung down perfectly straight.

The body was not disturbed until the arrival of Coroner Dewberry, when a man ascended the tree, made a rope fast to the body, loosened the suspenders from the limb and lowered the skeleton to the ground. There was little more than a skeleton left, and this was ready to fall to pieces. Both feet dropped off, as it was being lowered. The clothing remained intact, preserving the body of the deceased from the birds of prey, but all the flesh had been removed from his face and neck, his eyes plucked out, and his hair was all gone. The beard, however, still adhered to his fleshless cheeks.

The body was identified by the clothing, and also by a receipt found in one of the pockets for dues paid by the deceased to the Germania Lodge of Odd Fellows, of which he was a member.

August 1, 1873 ——————— (HWV)

HORRIBLE DEATH. The *Washington Gazette* says: A young man named Turner, living near Danburg, in this county, died on Saturday after a few days illness, and it is supposed from the following singular cause: Some days previous to his attack he assisted in the disinterment of a corpse, for the purpose of removal to another place of burial. The body had been buried some months, and was exceedingly offensive when the grave was opened. Young Turner began to complain of headache and other symptoms soon after the removal, and in a few days became seriously ill, and died on Saturday. He complained during his entire illness of smelling and even tasting the horrible effluvia arising from the corpse. It is supposed that this effluvia or exhalation penetrated and saturated his entire system, thus poisoning his blood and causing death. We hear that a brother of his is also very ill from the same cause, though we do not know that the report is authentic.

August 21, 1873 ——————— (DWJ)

Mr. James Morgan, a well known lumber merchant in Albany, hearing a loud noise in his barn a few nights ago, dressed himself, and taking a kerosene lamp in his hand, went out to learn the cause. – He remained so long that his wife became alarmed and going out herself to see what detained him, found the horses trampling him under their feet, and the horses and stables in flames. It is presumed that when he reached the barn one of the horses must have knocked the lamp out of his hand and set the place on fire. After the fire had been extinguished, the body of Mr. Morgan, burned to a crisp, was recovered.

–Savannah News, 14th.

August 26, 1873 ——————— (GWT)

On Thursday morning Mr. G.H. Crabbe, of Hogansville, took an overdose of morphine and died in a few hours.

August 27, 1873 ——————— (ET)

KILLED. On Tuesday morning last, young Charles Buntin, son of Rev. Wm. Buntin, of Worth, and Albert Faircloth, were on their way to a protracted Methodist meeting at Puckett's Chapel, on the Troupville road. In a pretty piece of road they concluded to try the speed of their horses. At the top of their speed, Buntin's horse flew the track, and throwing the rider high up above the saddle against a tree, killing him instantly.

September 9, 1873. ——————— (GWT)

We find the following in the *Atlanta Herald* of yesterday:

A DOUBLE HOMICIDE. A TEACHER AND PUPIL IN BANKS COUNTY STAB EACH OTHER TO DEATH. A horrible tragedy was enacted in Banks county, near Homer, the county site, on Friday last, the 28th of August. The teacher of the school was Mr. Alfred Alexander, aged forty years, and the student, Mr. John H. Moss, a young man aged about twenty-one years. It appears that once again a woman was at the bottom of the affair. Mrs. Alexander, wife of the principal, was, we learn, present of her own volition, but not in the discharge of any regular duly as teacher or in any other capacity. Her custom, however, had been to observe the conduct and deportment of the pupils, and when she considered them guilty of any breach of decorum, to report them to her husband for reproof or other punishment. On this occasion the subject of her reportorial capacity was the young man referred to, Mr. Moss. When his attention was called to the matter in question he denied the charge made by Mrs. Alexander, which led to an animated and angry dispute. Alexander became enraged at the young man for the part taken in the controversy by him, and advancing towards Mr. Moss, drew his knife and stabbed him in the breast. Moss in return advanced with a dagger and plunged it into Alexander's heart. This was a fatal wound, and the man fell. Just then Moss turned to leave, but Mrs. Alexander, who was at the side of her husband, wrung the knife from his hand and administered one or two severe cuts to Moss in the back, near the region of the spine. The result was that both lay mortally wounded on the scene of the conflict, and both expired in a short time, the one within three minutes of the other.

September 12, 1873 ———————— (GWT)

William Abernathy, of Cherokee County, was ran (*sic*) over and killed near that place, last Saturday night, by a train on the State road. In one of his pockets was found a loaded pistol, and in the other a bottle of whisky.

September 12, 1873 ——————— (GWT)

Mr. Daniel Molene, a Swede living at Palmetto, was killed at Whitesburg, on the Savannah, Griffin and North Alabama Railroad, on Monday, while attempting to get on a train which was in motion.

September 12, 1873 ——————— (GWT)

KILLED BY LIGHTNING – SINGULAR FREAK. On Monday last during the thunderstorm, John Long, a colored man employed on Colonel McLarin's Oakey Woods Place, was lighting his pipe at the fire place, and while in the act was instantly killed by a current of lightning that came down the chimney. We learn from Col. McLarin, who was called to the negro a few minutes after he was stricken down, that there was no explosion; that the man was thrown back upon the floor, and that the clothing was literally stripped from onehalf his body from head to foot, and his right shoe torn off.

September 23, 1873 ——————— (GWT)

Mr. W.H. Thomas, of Floyd County, went down into his well last Saturday, and was so overcome by the foul air as to fall to the bottom, and receive injuries that caused his death.

September 23, 1873 ——————— (GWT)

W. N. Norris, a train hand on the State road, was crushed to death last Tuesday by being caught between a bridge near Graysville and the top of a car.

September 30, 1873 ———— (GWT)

Mr. Welcome Spears, of Harris County, died last Sunday from an overdose of morphine taken for relief of cramp colic.

October 16, 1873 ———— (DWJ)

FATAL ACCIDENT. We regret to learn that a little son of Mr. Augustus Bivins of Schley County, was instantly killed on Thursday last by coming in contact with a cog wheel of a cotton gin which was in motion while the hands were ginning cotton. His father was feeding the gin at the time, and the little fellow, unconscious of danger, got on the cog wheel and instantly his arm became entangled between the trundle head and cogs, crushing his head to pieces. The little fellow was only 7 years old and was the idol of his parents. The accident occurred at the gin house of Mr. A.G. Goodson of Schley County.

—Sumter Republican.

November 6, 1873 ———— (QB)

DEATH OF ANGUS MORRISON. We are pained to have to record the death of this good citizen under circumstances that are peculiarly distressing. It seems that Judge Morrison left Valdosta on Tuesday evening of last week, on horseback, for his home in Brooks, being somewhat under the influence of liquor. As nothing was heard of him during Wednesday and Thursday, his friends became uneasy and commenced a search for him. They learned that he had crossed Little River at Tucker's bridge Tuesday evening or night, but could hear nothing more of him. By tracking his horse it appears that he had been thrown off not long after leaving the bridge, and when he remounted he doubtless missed his direction (it being dark.) At least the horse's track, instead of keeping the road towards home, turned off into the swamp and went towards the river until the stream was reached at a high and steep bank, where he either jumped or fell over. The horse was found on Saturday on a nob in the river near that place, in a starving condition, as the banks on either side were too steep for him to get out. Of course it was concluded that Judge Morrison had been drowned, and after a little further search his body was discovered under the water, not far off. Upon being taken out no marks of violence were found upon his person. He was decently buried last Sunday . . . He left a wife and eight children, most of whom are girls, and with them we deeply sympathize in this their great affliction.

November 13, 1873 ——————— (HD)

SAD OCCURRENCE. A few days since a Mrs. Hughes, of Bulloch County, through mistake gave two of her sons, who were unwell, a dose of arsenic for cream tartar. Both died in a few hours. One of the young men had a wife and three children, the other was single and aged about 21 years. The feeling of the frantic mother cannot be described when she discovered her fatal mistake.

November 18, 1873 ——————— (GWT)

The *Sandersville Central Georgian* has the following: . . .

We regret to learn that Mr. John Pittman, residing near the line of Washington and Johnson County, was killed on

Monday last, by being crushed in a cane mill while grinding his cane for syrup. So severe was the crushing that Mr. Pittman died instantly from the effects of his bruises.

November 20, 1873 ———————— (HD)

Dr. Henry Shirrer, of Wilkes County, met with a horrible accident, on the thirtieth of October, which resulted in his death, last Saturday. The *Washington Gazette* says he was on his way to visit a patient, and while riding at considerable speed, a cow attempted to cross the road in front of his horse. He was unable to check the horse in time, and the consequence was that the rider, horse and cow were all thrown together in a heap.

November 20, 1873 ———————— (HD)

POSSIBLE DEATH BY LIGHTNING. Mr. Joseph Wilcox the Victim. We learn from Dr. Fleetwood, who has just reached here from Jacksonville, Telfair county, that he left Mr. Joseph Wilcox in a dying state on Monday evening from the effects of a stroke of lightning received on Sunday night while in bed asleep. His wife and sister, Miss Rebecca Wilcox, were sleeping in an adjoining room and were awakened by the terrific storm and loud peal of thunder. His sister arose and called him, but he made no response, whereupon she called his brother-in-law, a little son of Mr. John Hamilton, to arouse her brother. He was shaken violently, but gave no signs of life.

This was about eleven o'clock. Becoming alarmed, Miss Wilcox procured a light and entered his room to ascertain the matter. She was horror-stricken to behold her brother apparently in the agonies of death. This was about eleven o'clock. His wife immediately sent a freedman to convey the news to Mr. Wilcox's father, and summon Dr. Fleetwood. The distance being almost ten miles, they did not receive the news until after daylight on Monday morning. They hastened to Jacksonville and found the stricken man still showing signs of life. All had been done for him that could possibly be done – pouring water over him, etc.

The lightning passed down the chimney and shivered the fire board, and passed to the bed nearby. The hair on the forehead was singed, and the electric current passed to the left shoulder, then under it, thence across the left lung down the abdomen to the right leg, from which it burned the hair in a streak to the foot. The body was considerably bruised. The left lung became filled with phlegm as if affected by pneumonia. Mr. Wilcox was alive at a late hour on Monday evening, but there seemed no possible hope for recovery. He was speechless and unconscious, and had not moved a muscle save an occasional drawing up of the right foot.

December 4, 1873 ———————— (DWJ)

MILTON MALONE. This unfortunate man, who was to have been hung in Atlanta on Friday last, committed suicide in the prison cell the night previous to the time fixed for his execution, by swallowing morphine. He had saved the poison at different times from the physic given him by physician, to be taken in case every effort for his relief should fail. He had sewed it up in the binding of his undershirt. He swallowed the fatal dose sometime during Thursday night, and died about 11 o'clock Friday.

January 10, 1874 ———————————— (QI)

Mrs. Angeline Bond, of Banks County, hung herself with a hank of cotton. A love affair is supposed to have been the cause.

January 10, 1874 ———————————— (QI)

Mr. Joseph Allford was killed at a ball in Bartow County recently by a man named Thomas Dawson. The difficulty grew out of the fact that Allford slapped the face of Dawson's nephew, who persisted in throwing fireworks into the ballroom among the ladies.

January 10, 1874 ———————————— (QI)

A HORRIBLE ACCIDENT occurred in Murray county recently. A Mr. Johnson, in preparing to kill hogs, had sunk a large box in the ground, filled it with boiling water and placed a blanket over it. His little son, three or four years old, walked on to the blanket and into the scalding water. He lived twentyfour hours.

January 29, 1874 ———————————— (DWJ)

Samuel Williford, living on Dr. N.B. Hail's farm, near Floyd Springs, in Floyd County, was cutting down a tree on Thursday, and as it was falling, he discovered his little son, about five years old, coming in the direction the tree was falling, but too late to save him. The tree fell on the little fellow's head and crushed him so that he died instantly.

A SAD AFFAIR. Rutledge, Ga., February 14, 1874.

Messrs. Editors: On Saturday morning, 14th inst., a colored boy mounted on horse, came down from the premises of John W. Wood, a mile distant from Rutledge, telling the neighbors along the road as he passed that Mr. Wood had killed himself.

As Mr. Wood has been on a drunken spree for some time past, but little attention was paid to the alarm, and scarcely any disposition on the part of his neighbors to visit the house. Hastening to the premises at sunrise, accompanied by two other gentlemen, we found the doors firmly secured and barricaded, and all as still as death. On entering a window, the body of J.W. Wood, stained with gore, was first to meet our gaze – feet to the hearth and back to the floor, and pistol, with one barrel discharged, within eighteen inches of his head; in this room, we noticed his little boy, George, ten years old, apparently asleep in bed; on approaching to awaken him, we found him cold in death. On entering an adjoining room, the mind cannot conceive of our horror, on finding his oldest boy, Thomas, 14 years old, a corpse, and his little daughter, four years old, lying on her brother, Tommy's arm, her life fast ebbing away. We did all in our power to resuscitate her, but alas! life was too nearly extinct.

Wood overdosed his children with Morphine and shot himself through the body, between the eighth and ninth ribs, one inch to the right of the median line, the ball cutting the descending aorta in its transit, and lodging in the supraficial facia of the back at an opposite point of its entry.

This was all premeditated, as he addressed a communication to his mother on the 9th inst., which was found over the mantlepiece of his chamber, telling her that he was going to administer morphine to his children, and also end his own existence. He leaves an amiable and brokenhearted widow.

Such are the bitter fruits of strong drink.

March 5, 1874 ———————————— (DWJ)

DIED. Mrs. Malissa Bearman, of Sumpter (sic) County, was burned to death on Thursday morning last. She was accustomed to having fits, and it is supposed she fell in the fire after being attacked with one, as her waist and head were burned to a crisp when she was discovered.

April 16, 1874 ———————————— (DWJ)

FOUND DEAD. A correspondent of the *Atlanta Herald* states that the mutilated remains of a white man was found near Hampton, Henry County, Ga., last week. In his coat pocket was found a small memorandum book together with several letters addressed to Mr. Ed. Clark, which is supposed to be the name of the unfortunate man. Those letters were written by a lady, signing her name C.M. Turner, written from Quitman County, Georgia. Judging from the affectionate tone of these letters I am sure that fair correspondent will be overwhelmed with sorrow, should it fall to her lot to read this account of her dear friend's sad fate.

The body was completely torn up, his heart, liver, lungs, bowels, ribs and one arm had all been devoured by dogs, buzzards, and hogs, his hair had slipped off his head, his pocket knife was lying open by his coat. He had a memorandum book with several pictures in it, two ladies and three men. C.H. Turner, near Eufaula, Ala., wrote him two letters, and in one requesting him to come back and plow for his father, as some one of the family had the rheumatism, and wanted to see him badly, and requested him when he wrote to send his picture, and when they went to Eufaula they would send theirs.

We came to the conclusion that he cut his throat, as his knife was lying open by him. We put him in a box, or the fragments, and buried him at Mr. Griffin's, this evening. This is a statement of facts as I saw them. P.B.

April 21, 1874 —————————————— (GWT)

A Negro man named George Patton, who was sleeping on the track of the AirLine road near Atlanta, Saturday night, was run over by a passing train and instantly killed. He was almost dismembered.

May 19, 1874 —————————————— (GWT)

Mr. J. Davison was run over and killed last Tuesday night about four miles above Union Point on the Athens branch road. He is supposed to have been drunk and asleep on the track.

June 11, 1874 —————————————— (DWJ)

FATAL ACCIDENT AT ATHENS. Marion Oats, of Augusta, a student at the University at Athens, as we learn from the *Constitutionalist*, of Sunday, was fatally shot last Saturday afternoon by a little girl. She was playing with his pistol and he told her there was no load in it, and to snap it at him. She did so, and it fired lodging the ball in his stomach.

June 16, 1874 ——————— (GWT)

M.S. Whitfield, of Troup County, was run over and killed near LaGrange, by the express train from Atlanta to West Point, last Saturday morning. A whisky flask, with a drink or two in it, was found in his pocket.

June 16, 1874 ——————— (GWT)

(*Hawkinsville Dispatch*) **HAS THIS WARNING TO BOYS** who go in bathing while overheated: William Smithhart, aged sixteen years, of Dooly county, raced to the Alapaha river in company with other boys for the purpose of bathing, and as soon as he could get his clothes off plunged in, but had only made two strokes when he went to the bottom and was drowned.

June 16, 1874 ——————— (GWT)

CREMATION IN GILMER COUNTY. The *Marietta Journal* says an old man in Gilmer county who was absent a week on a visit "to his still house hid in the mountains, was found by his friends dead in his still house with two or three large rattlesnakes wrapped around his body. The men being afraid to enter, set fire to the house and burned all in one heap, making a successful cremation of snakes, man, house, and whisky."

HORRIBLE CASUALTY. FATAL BOILER EXPLOSION AT TEBEAUVILLE. THREE MEN BLOWN INTO ETERNITY. The Result of Removing a Steam Gauge. (Special Telegram to the *Morning News*.)

Tebeauville, June 29, An explosion of a locomotive boiler on J. McDonough's Tram Road occurred at about 2 o'clock this evening, about four miles from his mill, at the fiftyseven mile post, Brunswick and Albany Railroad, and three miles from this place. It was caused by too great pressure of steam upon the boiler.

Mr. Joseph W. Bender, the engineer, and his fireman, a colored boy by the name of Shingleton Ahl, were instantly killed. William Douglass, who was riding on the engine to the mill, was also killed.

Mr. Bender took the steam gauge off on Saturday, and did not replace it. When taking the engine out this morning, the safety valve stuck fast, which caused the explosion.

The engineer had made one trip with the engine, and had loaded at Log Way and gone some four hundred yards on the second trip, when the explosion occurred. The engine was blown to atoms. The tram road was also torn up the length of the engine.

Mr. Bender's body was found about two hundred and fifty yards from the engine. The lower portion of the body was badly mangled and the bowels ripped open. The right arm and leg were almost severed from the body.

Shingleton Ahl's body was found in an opposite direction on the other side of the track, about fifty yards off, badly scalded, and injured.

William Douglass's body was found in a sitting position

on the tram road, in rear of the train, fifty yards off, bruised and badly scalded.

A portion of Bender's clothing now hangs to the limbs of trees some forty or fifty feet high.

The coroner's inquest this afternoon exonerates Mr. J. McDonough of all blame in the matter.

July 24, 1874 — (SMN)

A SAD ACCIDENT TO A SAVANNAH LAD. Fatal Result of Playing with Firearms.

On Monday morning last, Angus McAlpin, a promising youth, and the only son of our well known and esteemed citizen, Mr. Angus McAlpin, whilst on a visit to Col. George S. Owens' place, about five miles from Clarksville, accidentally shot himself in the head with a pistol with which he was playing, and died from the effects of the wound received about ten o'clock the same night . . .

Mrs. McAlpin has for some time past been keeping the hotel at Clarksville. On Monday morning young Angus, who had been of great assistance to his mother, in attending to various matters about the hotel, left Clarksville to pay a brief visit to some friends at Col. Owens' place. While there the proposition was made to play a game of cards, and young Angus, with one of his companions, entered a room for the purpose of finding the pack. Whilst looking for the cards, Angus came across a pistol, and for the time was diverted from the object of his search, and amused himself snapping the caps. There was no discharge, and imagining the weapon was not loaded, he said to his companion, who had advised him to put the pistol down, "I WILL PLAY KILLING MYSELF, as it is not loaded", and raising the barrel towards his head, pulled the trigger. Unfortunately the chamber was loaded and the weapon was discharged, the ball penetrating the right temple and coming out from behind the left ear. He fell to the floor, and remained entirely unconscious until a late hour, when the silver cord was broken and the youthful spirit winged its flight to the celestial realms. . . . The deceased was about twelve years of age, and was regarded as a remarkably promising youth . . .

It is a mournful, yet singular occurrence that Tinsley, the oldest son of Mr. McAlpin, met his death by accident when about the same age, or very little older than Angus. About two years ago, whilst at play with some boys, he was run against by one of his companions whose teeth struck him in the forehead knocking him down. He was taken sick, and erysipelas ensuing from the wound, he died shortly afterwards . . .

October 22, 1874 ——————— (HD)

TERRIBLE AFFAIR. DIFFICULTY BETWEEN TWO BROTHERS, AND ONE OF THEM KILLED.

On Tuesday, the 6th of October, a most awful tragedy occurred on Swift Creek, in Worth County. Jack and Charley Judge, two brothers, quarreled about some oats, and the quarrel led to a fatal difficulty.

We are informed by a kinsman of the unfortunate brothers that Jack Judge attempted to strike his brother Charley with a pitchfork. Charley evaded the lick, and the weapon was broken against the wall of the crib near where they were standing. Jack then rushed with open knife upon his brother, who, in self-defense, drew his knife and began cutting. He inflicted upon Jack one gash, about eleven inches in length, clear across the lower abdomen, letting out the entrails upon the ground. In the meantime Jack had stabbed Charley in several places about the hip.

Charley, though wounded seriously, got upon his horse and went at once to a neighbor's house. He related the circumstance, and asked his neighbor to go back with him, as he had killed Jack. The neighbor examined Charley's wounds before leaving and found in one of them the knife blade, which had been broken off.

The men returned to the dreadful scene, and found the unfortunate brother still living. Dr. Joseph Forbes, of Dooly, was immediately summoned, and he rendered surgical aid by washing the entrails, replacing them, and sewing up the wound.

In this horrible condition, the wounded man lived until 2 o'clock Saturday afternoon, when he expired.

It is said that the brothers were not allowed to meet or speak to each other after the difficulty. While Jack lived and was rational, it is said he still censured his brother, but when reason would leave him for a while he lamented the affair and believed himself to blame for it. Jack left a wife and two children. Charley is a single man, and it is reported deeply regretted the necessity that forced himself to defend himself at the life of his brother. At last accounts he was recovering from his wounds.

November 3, 1874 ———————— (GWT)

The *Thomasville Times* reports the death of Mr. Jacob Ricks, of that county, last Friday, under shocking circumstances. He was dragged through the woods by a runaway mule and literally beaten to death, his foot having caught in the stirrup.

November 5, 1874 ———————————— (DWJ)

SAD DEATH OF A CHILD. On Tuesday last a little daughter of Mr. Wm. Holt found a cup in which was some potash. The little girl drank the water and ate a lump of potash. Immediately thereafter she commenced screaming as if in great agony, which greatly alarmed the family. Medical aid was called in but the little sufferer continued agonizing until a late hour at night when death relieved and God took her.

November 5, 1874 ———————————— (DWJ)

CRUSHED AND MANGLED. – A Young Lady Killed by an Engine. (Atlanta)

. . . When at noon yesterday the news thrilled along our streets and sidewalks, that a young lady had been run over and killed at Whitehall crossing, it created the most intense excitement. In a few minutes hundreds gathered at the spot. Just in front of Thompson's restaurant on the side of the railroad track was the lifeless form of a young lady presenting

A SICKENING SPECTACLE.

The iron wheels of the engine had taken off scalp and skin and flesh from one side of her head, while brains and blood had collected in great pools underneath her and were all oozing out. Pools of blood and brains were also on the track. No one knew her at first, so changed by the mangling had she become. But the scene was one never to be forgotten. The writer saw many cheeks blanch at the sight . . . Never have we before witnessed

SUCH INTENSE EXCITEMENT

as powerful here. Some were clamorous for administering

speedy justice to the engineer of the train; others were for tearing up the railroad tracks; others for stopping the passage of cars across Whitehall crossing, except passenger trains . . .

THE VICTIM

It was discovered after a while that the victim of this tragic affair was Miss Elizabeth McDowell, daughter of a worthy horticulturist, living at Rosdale Garden, near this city. Miss McDowell was about 18 or 19 years of age, and noted for loveliness of character and amiability of disposition. She had been for two years connected with the military establishment of Miss Mary McDowell. She was a member of the Central Presbyterian Church and Sabbath school.

THE TRAGEDY

From what we can gather the particulars, are about those of the sad tragedy: Miss McDowell last Saturday morning received a letter from a friend in LaGrange, requesting her to purchase a pair of shoes for her, and send them to her by the first train. With that obliging disposition for which she was noted, she started out between eleven and twelve o'clock, to go to a shoe house on Peachtree street and get the shoes and was hurrying back when the horrible affair occurred. While coming across Whitehall crossing, a switch train of the Georgia railroad was backing down a track that passes between the Union passenger depot and Garrett & Bro's store, with one attached. The tender of the engine was in front, the engine backing. Miss McDowell passed down a little from the crossing – As soon as she reached the middle of the track, the engine of the switch train gave a whistle which confused Miss McDowell, causing her to look in the contrary direction. The

TENDER STRUCK HER

which she grasped in a vain endeavor to protect herself. But the momentum being too great, knocked her down, and she was

DRAGGED TWENTY FEET

or more along the track, being rolled over and over, until her head was forced under the wheels and crushed, in the manner related in the beginning of this article. A gentleman on Wall street saw the whole scene. He states that the engine was going at

DOUBLE ITS USUAL SPEED

when the accident happened. This gentleman rushed to the spot, and with the assistance of one or two others, pulled out the body from under the cars, but

LIFE WAS EXTINCT.

Others concur in the statement that the engine was going faster than usual.

THE ENGINE

is the "South Carolina", one of the oldest on the Georgia railroad, one of the cars technically called "cabbage cutters".

THE ENGINEER,

Mr. Joe Bennett, was immediately arrested by policeman Haynes and lodged in the station house. Mr. Bennett says none can regret it more than he does; that he saw her and endeavored to check it but owing to its being the old style, failed to do so in time. Mr. Bennett's wife, we learn, is quite ill.

THE FUNERAL

services of Miss McDowell will take place at the Central Presbyterian church, at 4 o'clock P.M. today, Rev. J.T. Leftwich, D.D., officiating.

March 4, 1875

FATAL RESULT OF AN AMOUR. The citizens on the west side of the river, were shocked on last Tuesday morning by the killing of S.W. Wilcox by G.W. Forester. The circumstances were as follows, taken from the verdict of the coroners jury: It seems suspected that there were improper relations existing between his wife and Wilcox. On Tuesday morning Forester left home telling his wife that he would be gone all day. Returning during the morning he found his wife and Wilcox secreted in a thicket near the house. He rushed upon Wilcox, and it is said literally carved him into pieces. He was stabbed three times we understand in the region of the heart; his throat cut from ear to ear, and disemboweled. –The verdict of the jury makes the act justifiable. The killing took place a few miles from Cairo.

–Thomasville Times.

March 11, 1875

A YOUTH DROWNED WHILE ATTEMPTING TO CROSS A SLOUGH. Johnnie Buchanan, a youth of some fifteen years, was carrying a lady to Mr. Lovetts, five miles northeast of this city yesterday, and at 12 o'clock, four miles from town, he attempted to cross the slough known as "Dry Creek", which is caused by the backing of water from the river.

He drove the buggy in, little dreaming of its treacherous depth, or of his sudden doom. Finding himself in swimming water, with rare presence of mind he took his knife and immediately went to free the struggling horse, which he did by cutting the hamestring (*sic*).

The animal was plunging furiously, and the person who

witnessed the calamity called to John to swim to shore and save himself, which he attempted to do, but sank to the bottom after having swam but a few yards.

The lady, still clinging to the buggy, was rescued by getting on a log which the bystander managed to shove out to her.

March 18, 1875 —————————— (BWD)

SAD AFFAIR. On Monday last, Conrad Buchannan, was cleaning a musket belonging to the Bainbridge Independents. After finishing he concluded to burst a cap to clear out the tube; laying it across his lap, the muzzle pointed towards Silas Shockley, a lad of fourteen, who was stretched out on the ground a few yards off, he placed a cap on the tube and drew the trigger. To his utter consternation the musket went off, and its contents, three buckshot and a ball, struck young Shockley, killing him almost instantly. A Coroner's jury found a verdict of accidental killing.

March 23, 1875 —————————— (AtC)

SUDDEN DEATH. GENTLEMAN TAKES TOO MUCH OPIUM.

Yesterday morning a death occurred at the residence of Mr. G.W. Cook, on Spring street, under circumstances unusually painful. The deceased was a son of Mr. Cook's half sister, and was named Beall. He reached Atlanta, from Montgomery, Ala., on Monday, and went immediately to the residence of Mr. Cook . . . he was put in the room with Mr. Ira Cook to pass the night, and before entering he told Mr. Cook that if he heard him breathing very loud and heavily to wake him up. About 2 o'clock in the night Mr. Cook did hear Mr. Beall making a choking noise, and tried unsuccessfully to arouse him. Becoming thoroughly alarmed he woke up the family, and Dr. Drake was sent for. As soon as the doctor saw his patient he pronounced him to be suffering from the effects of opium. He set to work to relieve him, and after some time left him under the impression that the worst was over . . . Mr. Beall suffered a relapse, and in spite of every attention died at an early hour yesterday morning . . . Mr. Beall was a corpse before he had been twenty-four hours in the city . . . He was unmarried . . . How he came to give himself too much opium is a fact not yet known . . .

March 25, 1875 ———————————— (DWJ)

THE CYCLONE. Particulars of the Dreadful Storm of Saturday. (March 20) Fearful Loss of Life. A Belt of Ruin Across the State. (Excerpts)

The march of the tornado was west from Harris county, across Talbot, Upson, Monroe, Jones, Baldwin, Hancock, Glascock, McDuffie and Columbia, touching Richmond also, and passing into Carolina.

. . . Mr. Cannon, of Harris county, lost five children, and his wife and two other children were badly hurt. He was not at his house at the time, but knowing that his family were in danger he was struggling to them when he met the bodies of two of his little daughters being carried along by the cyclone.

Mrs. Culpepper found her husband crushed under a heavy sill. With superhuman strength she lifted the immense piece of timber from his body, only to find him crushed to death. —No two men in the county could lift the piece of timber under ordinary circumstances.

BALDWIN COUNTY

The absorbing topic of interest here now is the great tornado of Saturday. A little after one o'clock in the afternoon it swept across the southern limit of our city from west to east, prostrating everything before it. . . . The broad apex of the funnel formed demon of the cloud floated rapidly along, probably at the rate of more than one hundred miles an hour; and the narrow base which touched the earth lifted up and destroyed everything in its path. Within our corporation limits Mrs. Johnson, wife of Mr. Thomas Johnson, was killed, and her husband severely wounded, and Dick Gonder, a colored man of good charity, instantly killed, and his mother badly wounded . . .

To illustrate the force of the wind, we may mention that a shingle is driven, sharp end foremost, several inches into the body of a small oak tree it happened to strike directly. To the west of us, some miles, a lifeless negro woman was found lodged in the branches of a lofty tree not exactly in the hurricane's path; and a child of the same race was blown away and has not been found at all. Dick Gonder, already mentioned, was killed by having the upper half of his head cut off smooth by a plank driven by the wind, and the missing top of his head has not been found.

HANCOCK COUNTY

When he saw the storm coming Mr. Massey made a frantic effort to save his wife and child. . . . He thrust them toward the door and was himself caught in the timbers. When the storm had passed he saw his wife lying near him with her brains crushed out. His child, an only one, about two years old, he found in the garden, with a fearful hole torn in her side. It was dead. Miss

Sallie Berry had been blown into the top of a pine tree, which had fallen near by. Her legs were broken in seven places, and she was otherwise awfully mangled. She lived four hours. A negro man on the place ran to the nearest house for help, and when neighbors arrived they found Mr. Massey, who was badly hurt, sitting beside his dead wife, with his dead child in his arms and the dying girl lying near him. No words can describe the horror of the spectacle.

WARREN COUNTY

At Camak on the Georgia railroad the depot and office, two stores, one large hotel, one large guano house, four dwelling houses, saw mill, gin house and ten or fifteen smaller houses were literally torn to pieces. The night watchman, Mr. Tom Geesling, was crushed under a loaded guano car and killed. In the hotel Mrs. Wright and her five daughters and two sons – all were injured. Mrs. Wright had two ribs broken. They were taken from under the fallen timbers . . . Three negroes were in a little house which was torn to pieces. Two will die, the other may recover . . .

COLUMBIA COUNTY

Mrs. Dorsey, an old widow, was killed at her house, also a young child. Miss Dorsey, her daughter, was badly injured . . . An old negro man near by was killed. . . . About four miles from Appling six or seven negroes were killed. A party of six young men were hunting and passing through an open field saw the storm and fell down on the ground. They were picked up and carried a hundred yards into a pine thicket, but were not seriously injured.

McDUFFIE COUNTY

. . . The house of Mr. John Stovall was blown down, breaking his leg and crushing the ankle of his wife. . . . At Benson's gin one negro was killed. At John E. Smith's place two negroes were killed and two others have died since of their injuries. . . . Elam Church, four miles east of Mayfield, was blown down during services, killing Mrs. Lewis Jones and wounding nearly all present – about thirty persons. Mr. Hubbert's large two story house was blown down; also John Hubert's house near the church, killing one negro woman.

June 8, 1875 ——————————————— (MT)

We learn from the *Columbus Times* that Arad Williams, light house keeper at East Pass, near Apalachicola, Florida, fell off the top on Monday last and was instantly killed. He was leaning on a railing which ran around at the top, when it gave way and he fell to the rocks below landing upon his feet. It is said that when he hit the rocks he bounced three yards in the air.

June 10, 1875 —————————————— (DWJ)

Dr. R.T. Persons committed suicide at Fort Valley on the 1st instant, by taking morphine. He was found insensible upon the counter of his drug store, with symptoms of his having taken a large dose of that fatal drug. Medical skill was at once summoned and stomach pumps brought into requisition, but to no avail, and the man died about 2 o'clock on Tuesday night. Deceased was the son of Rev. G.W. Persons, a local Methodist minister of Fort Valley. He was about thirty years old, and leaves a wife and two children. Dissipation was the main cause of the suicide.

August 19, 1875 ———————————— (ET)

FATAL ACCIDENT. On yesterday morning about 6:30 o'clock, the boiler of the steam saw mill of Mr. De Vaughan, about eight miles above this point on our line of road exploded, killing two men, Mr. J.W. Briggs, the sawyer, and Mr. J. Coons, another employee of the mill . . . Mr. Coon, was blown some 20 or 30 steps from the mill, whilst the other party, Mr. Briggs, was completely torn to pieces, his arms and legs being broken, and his head terribly mangled. Mr. Coons expired immediately, but Mr. Briggs was alive up to several hours after the explosion, though without the slightest chance of recovery. Two other parties were somewhat injured, but not dangerously . . .

August 19, 1875 ———————————— (BWD)

A HORRIBLE ACCIDENT. [*Marietta Journal*]

We learn from Mr. J.R. Groover, of Pickens County, that a sad and fatal accident occurred to Mr. Wm. Page, who resided near Heard's Store, in Dawson County, on last Thursday week, the 29th ult. Mr. A.J. Kelley recently erected a new circular saw on Yellow Creek, near the Cherokee line, and Mr. Page having never seen a circular saw in operation, went over to see it. When the stock had been put on and the saw had cut off the first slab, Mr. Page and his neighbor, Mr. Nelems, picked up the slab to carry it off, when the saw caught the slab and jerked Mr. Page against the saw, which inflicted a wound that killed him instantaneously. The saw struck him between the point of his right shoulder and neck, ripping his body open to the lower part of his breast bone, exposing his lungs, while the quivering flesh was covered with his life's blood. He leaves a wife and two or three children to mourn his untimely and sad taking off.

September 7, 1875 ——————— (GWT)

Thos. A. Dutton, Postmaster at Marlow, on the Central Railway, suicided on Monday by taking an overdose of morphine; and Harrison Achard, of No. 12 1/2, on the same road, had his head blown off by the discharge of a gun he was playing with.

October 7, 1875 ——————— (DWJ)

And again this news column has to chronicle another sad death from the careless use of kerosene. On the morning of October 1st, Mrs. John Welsh. of Savannah, poured from a can a quantity of oil on wood shavings that were then ignited, and the result is, that an explosion occurred, the burning oil covering her body, from the effects of which she died.

October 7, 1875 ——————— (DWJ)

SAD DEATH. Leroy, aged eight years, a son of W.M. Gresham, was aiding in the packing of cotton, on the 28th, ult., and by some means was caught in the machinery and so badly crushed that he died in a few hours. We regret this sad accident, not only on account of the loss of a noble boy, but from the fact of his trying to aid his father, and in the effort lost his life.

November 5, 1875 ——————————— (HV)

William White, an operative in the Atlanta paper mill, met a horrible death, a day or two ago. Some part of his clothing got caught by the main shaft, and before the machinery could be stopped, he had been whirled round several times, and his brains beat out.

November 26, 1875 ——————————— (HV)

A TERRIBLE AFFAIR. The *Middleport* (Ohio) *News* tells the following horrible story:

In Jackson county, W. Va., last week, a grand houseraising took place. As is customary on such occasions, chickens had been killed by chopping off their heads. Two little sons of the owner of the house to be raised saw the chickens thus guillotined, and during the day concluded to repeat the operation. It was just at a time when the men were lifting a heavy log into its place. The father, who was holding one end of the log, casting his eyes toward the little fellows, one of whom had the ax raised to sever the neck of his brother, let go of the log to save the boy, and it fell, killing six men, two instantly, the others living only a few hours. The axe fell before the father could reach the scene, cutting off the head of his son.

December 9, 1875 ——————————— (DWJ)

J.H. Braswell of Norcross, was found dead in his bed last week, and the *Lawrenceville Herald* says he told a gentleman of the place recently, that within two years he had swallowed nearly fourteen hundred gallons of whiskey – about two gallons per day.

December 16, 1875 ———————— (HD)

HORRIBLE CATASTROPHE – A Man Burned to Death in a Stump Hole.

A most awful catastrophe occurred on Wednesday night of last week in Dooly County, near the line of Worth. The unfortunate victim was Elder Samuel Wright Story, a Primitive Baptist, very highly esteemed. Mr. Story had been to mill on Swift Creek, and was returning home late in the evening. He stopped to warm himself in front of the house of Mr. Stevens, on the roadside, where an old stump of a tree had been fired, and had burned into a hole. None of Mr. Stevens' family went out where he was or paid any attention to his being there. They only noticed that his cart remained there for an unusual length of time for a person merely to warm. About ten o'clock at night, they observed that his cart was still on the road side and finally concluded to go and see if anything was the matter. On arriving at the stump hole a most horrible sight was before them. The head and shoulders of Mr. Story's body were lying in the hole and had burned to a crisp. It seemed as if he had fallen into the burning hole headforemost. Whether he had struck his foot against some obstacle and fallen, or whether he had been prostrated from a fit, is unknown. In either case, he was unable to rise himself out of the hole, and death, in its most terrible form, put an end to his struggles.

The citizens of the neighborhood were informed of the accident, and assembled to hold an inquest and bury the remains. Our informant, Mr. S.P. Willson, passed the place on

Thursday morning, and a crowd had already collected for the objects stated.

December 16, 1875 ————————— (HD)

EXPLOSION AND INSTANT DEATH OF AN ENGINEER.
On Friday morning last the down passenger train from Macon for Brunswick met with a terrible accident near Buzzard Roost, just about daylight. The train was running at full speed, when the boiler of the engine exploded. George Horning, the engineer, was instantly killed, and the fireman, as if by a miracle, escaped with his life, though considerably bruised. The baggage car was almost a complete wreck, but none of the passengers in the other cars were hurt. The track was torn up several yards. The explosion was terrific.

Major John A. Grant, the Superintendent of the road, was on the train, and only a few minutes before the explosion had decided to take a seat on the engine in order to observe the condition of the road. Finding that it was too dark to see to advantage, he had concluded to wait a little while, and this conclusion, no doubt, saved his life.

January 13, 1876 ————————— (DWJ)

Mr. H.M. Brown, of Macon, died on the 10th instant from an overdose of morphine. He had been suffering from an attack of cholera morbus, and took several doses of the drugs to relieve him, but instead of the hoped for effects, it brought over him an unconsciousness from which he never aroused. Peace to his ashes.

May 18, 1876 ——————————— (BWD)

SAD DEATH. We are pained to announce the death, on Thursday afternoon last, of Samuel C. Borum, son of V.M. Borum, Esq., of this city, in the 16th year of his age. On the Saturday previous, Sammy was kicked in the stomach by a mule, at the plantation of Mr. Brennan across the river. At the time it was supposed he was not seriously injured, but on the next day (Sunday) took to his bed and died on Thursday, suffering very much in the interim . . .

June 8, 1876 ——————————— (DWJ)

DEATH FROM SNAKE BITE. Mr. Henry Paulk, of Coffee County, living about twelve miles from Alapaha, was bitten last Saturday evening by a rattlesnake, from which he died Sunday morning at 3 o'clock.

Mr. Paulk and some of his neighbors were out driving near the Alapaha River swamp, while the dogs were in the swamp after a deer. Hearing the dogs coming somewhat in the direction of where he was, he ran to a stand and had been standing there about three minutes when the deer run up in shooting distance. As he fired the snake struck him on the back part of the leg about five inches above the ankle. He was carried to Mr. Arche Gaskins', his brotherinlaw and his wife and children sent after, which was but a mile distant. When they arrived, the poison had taken such effect that he was insensible of their presence. Liquor was administered to him to counteract the poison, but it took no more effect than water, and he continued to grow worse until death ended his suffering.

—Alapaha News.

June 8, 1876 ———————————————————————— (DWJ)

Mr. Alex Irvin and his little son, aged seven years, were drowned in Savannah one day last week. They had been on a pleasure excursion. – The boat arrived at the wharf in the night and Mr. Irvin, with his child in his arms, stepped overboard, in the darkness, and both were drown. (*sic*)

June 8, 1876 ———————————————————————— (DWJ)

DEATH OF MILLARD SEALS. This community was startled and saddened yesterday by a telegraphic announcement of the sudden death of Millard Seals, only child of Col. Jno. H. Seals, of this city, and proprietor of the *Sunny South*.

The young man left Atlanta on Thursday morning with a party of excursionists for Port Royal. While the train was passing over Salt Creek, seven miles this side of that place, he was standing on a step of one of the cars and was precipitated into the creek and drowned. The bridge over the stream had been recently repaired and in finishing the work certain timbers projecting upward were sawed off to admit the free passage of the regular Port Royal cars, but not sufficient to allow the passage of cars from certain other roads. Millard was on a car belonging to the Savannah road, the steps of which came in contact with the projecting timbers, and were torn from under him by the collision.

The train passed on about four hundred yards before it could be reversed, and when a return to the place of the accident was effected, it proved too late. The body, after an inquest, was properly prepared and, under escort, brought to this city, arriving by the 6 o'clock a.m. train this day, and now lies in the editorial rooms of the *Sunny South*, where it is being visited by many of his friends, who mourn his early and unexpected death. Though only in his eighteenth year, he had won, as a scholar and an orator, fame which would have been considered a proud trophy if achieved by matured intellect and what he had accomplished while so young constituted an index of a splendid future of usefulness to his race and his country. –*Atlanta Commonwealth.*

Young Mr. Seals was well known to many of our citizens, his father having resided a few years ago, in the neighboring town of Cuthbert.

June 8, 1876 ——————————————— (DWJ)

HORRIBLE SCENE ON THE SCAFFOLD. A Man's Head Jerked from the Body by the Hangman's Rope.

Worchester (*sic*), Mass., May 26. – Samuel J. Frost was executed this morning in this city, for the murder of his wife's brother, Franklin P. Towne, July 4, 1875, in the barn on the farm owned by Towne. Frost has stoutly maintained all along that he killed Towne in self-defense, and today, in an interview said, 'I declare to all men that I die innocent of willful murder.' He has been apparently indifferent to his fate, refusing all counsel or advice. . . . Politics has been his principal theme and checkers his amusement. . . . As the hour of his death drew near, he was calm and determined, and walked unassisted to the scaffold.

As the drop fell the first thrill of a shudder had not run through the spectators when the body was seen spinning at the end of the rope almost headless, a fearful tear extending over the front of the throat and the blood gushing out in streams. – The blood, forced upward by the arterial movements, spurted fountainlike upward from one to two feet, the stream falling to the floor in a circle round the hanging body. This circle extended even to the framework of the gallows, which was in many places sprinkled with blood. The blood poured from the wound down the front of the body and trickled from the feet, forming a pool directly beneath the body. For some two minutes the arterial gushings of blood continued, and the slow dripping of the blood from the body continued longer. The knot of the rope had been placed behind Frost's left ear, almost around to the centre of the neck. The drop was enough not only to break his neck, but to sever the spinal column entirely, leaving the body hanging by the fragments of the rear portion only.

August 10, 1876 ——————————— (DWJ)

Leary, Ga., August 9, 1876. Dear *Journal*: On Friday last, about 3 o'clock, Mr. H.O. Stanford, a gentleman in the employ of Mr. S.F. Dasher, while engaged in getting cross ties for the S.W. R.R. Co., near this place, was accidentally caught under a falling tree, bursting his scull (*sic*) and so horribly mutilating his body as to cause instant death. Mr. Stanford was a citizen of Terrell County, . . . The deceased leaves a wife and one child . . .

August 10, 1876 ——————————— (DWJ)

On Sunday morning, the 6th, inst. about sun rise, another of Dasher's hands, a negro named Starling Clark, was accidentally shot with a pistol in the hand of Martin Tinsley, col. while engaged in a tussle. He was struck centerly in the forehead, the ball passing through his brain and lodging against the back portion of his neck. He lingered ten hours and died. Another warning against the careless handling of firearms.

August 17, 1876 ——————————— (BWD)

A DREADFUL CALAMITY. From passengers we learn that on Sunday last, about 1 o'clock a.m., a fire broke out in Quincy, Florida, originating in a stable belonging to and in rear of Mr. Garish's store, near the public square, and in a short time destroyed the store and stock of Mr. Garish, the store of Mr. Desmukes, and one other building, all new frame buildings, with the exception of Mr. Garish's, which was brick.

In order to arrest the spread of the flames, it was deemed necessary to blow up with powder one of the buildings, and the matter was taken in hand by Dr. Jno. H. Gee. The powder was placed in position and the fuse ignited by the Doctor, who retired to a safe distance. The explosion being delayed for some reason he ventured in to the building to relight the fuse. While in there the building blew up and he lost his life in the flames. A prominent and esteemed citizen, he fell doing his duty, bravely not hesitating even at the risk of his life . . . The fire is believed to be from the torch of the incendiary.

August 24, 1876 ——————————— (DWJ)

A young man named Thomas Jordan working in Langley and Robinson's factory, in Atlanta last week, slipped and fell on the revolving knives of a moulding machine, and was cut to pieces. He died soon afterward.

August 31, 1876 ——————— (DWJ)

ACCIDENT ON THE MACON AND BRUNSWICK ROAD.
Engineer Richards Killed. The down passenger train on the
Macon and Brunswick road was thrown from the track night
before last near station No. 13, and the engineer, Ed. Richards,
of this city, was killed instantly. The accident was caused by a
cow which had got caught in a trestle. The engineer ran upon
her and being unable to throw her off, was untracked and turned
entirely over. – One box car was thrown across the track and the
second class passenger car was thrown off, but not damaged.

Young Richards, the engineer, died at his post. He was
found upon his seat, lifeless, and it required half an hour to
extricate him from the wreck. His body was not mangled,
but was considerably bruised, and the flow of blood from his
mouth indicated internal injuries. His remains will reach
Macon at 8 o'clock this morning and will be interred at half
past four this afternoon. The wreck was cleared from the
track in a few hours and trains are now running on regular
schedule time.

–Telegraph & Messenger.

September 28, 1876 ——————— (BWD)

A SHOCKING ACCIDENT. Last Thursday evening, a fatal accident occurred at Mobley Mill ten miles from this city.
Mr. D.B. McKenzie, the engineer, was sawing when the lever
which controls the steam became detached and the throttle
valve was pulled "wide open". The tremendous velocity of
the fly wheel caused it to burst into pieces, and a large piece
struck Mr. McKenzie on the head, nearly severing it from his
body, killing him instantly. His death is generally regretted.

October 19, 1876 ——————————— (DWJ)

A little daughter of W.D. Hudson, of Elberton, was smothered to death in a bank of cotton seed, at his gin house last week. She was one of the triplets born five years ago, and a sprightly, promising child.

October 19, 1876 ——————————— (DWJ)

The *Newnan Herald:* We have to record a very serious and fatal accident at the gin of Mr. Ad. Brooks on the Robinson place east of town. On Monday last Bob Amy and Cooper Dominick both colored, were under the press spreading the bagging, when hearing a noise above them, they arose and looked up, and were immediately struck by the driving block, which by some means had become detached and came falling with terrible effect. The two men were standing on opposite sides, and far enough out for the ends of the falling block to strike them on their foreheads, knocking both of them back from under the press and killing them instantly.

November 23, 1876 ——————————— (DWJ)

Samuel C. Robinson, a flagman on the Western and Atlantic railroad, was killed on the night of the 17th inst., by his head coming in contact with a bridge over the road just beyond Atlanta. His dead body was found on top of one of the cars, after arriving at Marietta.

December 14, 1876 ───────── (DWJ)

Columbus Times: On Thursday afternoon, as a lumber train was coming to the city, when at Baker's creek bridge, in ran over Mr. Lewis C. Coleman, aged 57 years, and his little son, six years of age, killing both instantly. They were seen by Mr. Scovil, the engineer, when some two hundred yards distant, but supposing they would keep clear of the track, he did not take up in time to stop the train. All proper signals are said to have been given, but Mr. Coleman, from intoxication it is supposed, in his confused anxiety to save his little boy, fell on the track and pushed the little fellow with him, and before they could recover from the fall the fatal train crushed their life out.

December 28, 1876 ───────── (DWJ)

The *Thomasville Times* chronicles the death, by accident, of M.E.J. Young, better known to almost all the citizens of that county as 'Uncle Jenks.' He was on his place engaged in clearing up a small piece of ground with two boys to do the cutting. The boys were cutting down a pine sapling about two and a half or three inches in diameter, when they remarked to Mr. Young that he had better move or the tree would hit him. Almost as they spoke the tree fell and a small knot struck Mr. Y. and broke his skull, hilling him almost instantly. – He was in his sixty-fourth year.

January 19, 1877 ───────── (HJ)

HICCOUGHED TO DEATH. Dr. Elton says he called to see a man named Henry Hoskins, a slate miner aged forty-five years. Hoskins said that he had gone to work without breakfast, as he had not felt well. About eight o'clock he had drank (*sic*) some cold water, and hiccough set in violently at first, but subsequently he did not mind it much thinking it would soon disappear. It did not, however, and he then tried several local remedies, such as drinking nine swallows of water, putting a cold piece of slate down his back, and such like cures. He became alarmed, for he felt he was getting weaker every minute. It continued with renewed violence, and Hoskins was advised to go home by the boss. His wife made him hot coffee and he tried to eat his breakfast, but his appetite was entirely gone. He began to shiver, and his hiccough still continued as bad as ever. The doctor was sent for. He at once administered twenty drops of sal volatile and fifteen drops of ether in a wine glass full of camphor and water, but that did not do any good. The doctor tried to divert the man's attention from it; but it was all to no purpose. He then gave the man thirty drops of laudanum, and drove back to his home to procure another medicate. Still the hiccough continued and in fifteen minutes after the doctor left the man was a corpse. Hoskins seemed to be perfectly healthy in every respect. His throat swelled a great deal before he died, and he seemed to strangle before his suffering was over. [Ed. Note: The location of this incident is not given, but it probably took place in a state other than Georgia.]

January 26, 1877 ———————— (ECN)

MILLER COUNTY DEPARTMENT. Dr. E.B. Bush recently returned from Milledgeville. He says Dr. Knowles, of Early County, who is now an inmate of the Asylum, is recovering. C.B. Bean, of this county, who is also in the same institution, is some better, than when he first entered the Asylum. Recently he killed one of the lunatics with his wooden leg.

February 22, 1877 ——————— (DWJ)

A DISTRESSING ACCIDENT. A Young Man Killed By a Ball. On Monday last, about noon, young Milton Chapman, oldest son of our old and esteemed friend, Nathan Chapman, Esq., of Cave Spring, in this county (Floyd), was almost instantly killed by being struck with an India-rubber base ball. It seems that at recess the school boys were in the habit of playing ball, and upon this occasion young Chapman was acting as catcher, and in attempting to catch the ball was hit immediately behind the right ear. Upon being struck he threw his hands up to his head, walked a few steps, and sat down, and fell over dead in an instant. He never spoke after being struck . . . Young Chapman was about seventeen years of age, and was looked upon as a model young man. He was a great favorite of young and old . . .

—Salem Register.

February 23, 1877 ——————— (CA)

On Friday evening last, as the Macon freight was approaching the depot at this place, James Stirkes, a train hand, was knocked from the train and immediately crushed to death. The unfortunate man was upon the cars arranging the bell-rope, preparatory to shifting some cars, and while walking from one car to another, with his back towards the engine, the train passed under the bridge just above the depot, when his head was struck by a stringer of the bridge, with such force as to break his skull. – He then fell between the cars several wheels passed over him mutilating his body horribly. His remains were carried back to Macon next morning, where he has a wife to whom he had been married but a few months.

March 1, 1877 ——————————— (DWJ)

Dr. Swet Cox, of Homer, Ga., says the *Gainesville Eagle*, committed suicide on the 7th by taking morphine and strichnia. He had been absent two days and his wife supposed he was absent on professional business. He was found in his office, with his nose and lips eaten by mice – several of which were lying dead near him. They were doubtless killed by the poison on his lips.

March 1, 1877 ——————————— (DWJ)

The *Dalton Citizen* says that a frightful accident occurred Tuesday between Maddox's mill and Conasauga river bridge. Mr. Pierce Miller, of Murray Co., had brought a load of hay to this place in the morning, and when returning home, it is supposed that his horses ran away and threw him out of the wagon. No one was with him, and he was afterwards found in the road in a dying condition, his skull being badly fractured. He was still breathing but speechless, and died in a short time.

March 22, 1877 ——————————————— (DWJ)

On Monday, 12th instant, a young white man named Henry Kitchen, living on Col. W.D. Mitchell's place, Thomas County, went out turkey hunting. He soon heard a flock of turkeys and concealed himself to await their approach. He had not long been in this position before he saw the bushes shaking about the place where he thought the turkeys were, and catching sight of what he believed to be a turkey, he fired. Hearing a noise like the fluttering of a wounded turkey he ran up to secure his game and found, to his astonishment, a negro man named Ben Goldwire, in the agonies of death. The explanation of Ben's presence at that place is that he too was after the turkeys and was trying to creep on them through the bushes.

March 22, 1877 ——————————————— (DWJ)

Mr. Terrel Hulsey, of Paulding County, while at a neighbor's house last Saturday evening, took a gun and went out to shoot a chicken. He put the gun down on the ground and placed the muzzle in his mouth and blew down its deathly cavern to see if it was loaded. The hammer being on the tube, he could not determine, so he put his foot on the hammer, and the gun fired, the ball lodging in the brain. Some gentlemen caught him before he could fall and laid him down, and he died instantly. Mr. Hulsey was a nice young man and highly respected. The sad accident is deeply regretted by our citizens. So says the *Marietta Journal*.

April 26, 1877 ———————————— (DWJ)

FATAL ACCIDENT. We learn that Robert Williams, son of Mr. R.M. Williams living near Buena Vista, Marion county, met with a fatal accident on his father's premises last Saturday afternoon while throwing off a load of logs from a wagon. It seems he was standing on the ground throwing the logs over his head, and while holding a heavy one in his hands he made a step backwards and fell across a log lying behind him, when the piece of timber he had hold of fell across his head, breaking the skull and causing instant death. Deceased was 17 or 18 years of age, and was considered a very promising young man.

—Sumter Republican.

April 26, 1877 ———————————— (DWJ)

SUDDEN DEATH. On Tuesday of last week Mr. James Jernigan, of Greene county, went into a grove near his house to shoot a squirrel his dogs had treed. As he was nearing the tree, "he complained of great pain in his eyes, and said he believed he should die. He went to the tree, however, shot and killed the squirrel, falling to the ground himself at the report of the gun, and before he could be carried into the house, only a few yards distant, he was a corpse. There was no apparent cause for his death, and he had been for some time past enjoying his usual good health."

April 26, 1877 ———————————————— (DWJ)

MURDER. EIGHT CHAIN GANG CONVICTS MURDER THEIR GUARD AND ESCAPE.

Macon, April 24, 1877.

Editors *Telegraph and Messenger*: This morning, among my various squads of convicts, one of eight men was started out in charge of James McMichael, one of my most experienced guards, and when within a short distance of the field of work – clearing up a new ground – one of the prisoners, Moses Butler, of Richmond, felled him with an axe, which was followed by second blow by George Washington, of Muscogee, either of which would have killed him.

After the fatal blow they pilfered his pockets, first getting the key that locked the prisoners together on a chain. They also got from his person ninety dollars in money – took his double-barrel gun and repeater, and after getting off the squad chain, cut their shackles off with axes and made for Oconee Swamp, about one mile off. There were eight convicts in the squad, all of whom escaped save one who fled for camp to tell the awful story of the killing. We pursued them with one of the finest pack of nine hounds in the country, but after four hours' pursuit they swam the Oconee river, the dogs following them; but the hunters, so fatigued from the race, declined to swim the river, hence the demons are at large. A liberal reward will be paid for them or either one of them. T.J. Smith.

May 17, 1877 ———————————————— (DWJ)

OGLETHORPE ECHO: On the plantation of Mr. Lawson Cason, in this county, lives a Mr. Chalker and family, who are tenants on the place. On last Thursday a daughter of Mr. Chalker met with a horrible death, the circumstances of which are as follows: She is a grown young lady, and assists her father and other members of the family in their work on the farm. On the day in question, she had been plowing a mule, and at night mounted the animal with the gear on to ride to the house. On the way the mule became frightened at something and dashed off unseating the young lady, one of whose feet caught in the gear, and thus suspended she was dragged by the frightened animal a considerable distance over rocks, stumps and undergrowth, and horribly bruised and mangled. She survived the injuries only a few hours . . .

June 14, 1877 (DWJ)

DISTRESSING ACCIDENT. Miss Della Rentz, a young lady about 16 years old, and niece of Mr. Tiner Rentz who resides in Baker County, was assisting her uncle in hauling oats, one morning last week, and while enroute home with a load, the oxen that were drawing the wagon became frightened and ran away, throwing the young lady off under the wagon, the hind wheel passing directly across her breast, producing internal injuries from which she died the following evening.

We also learn that a day or two previous to the above, a little two year old son of Mr. Rentz, happened to the misfortune of swallowing a piece of potash that was lying carelessly about the house the effects of which produced death in less than two hours.

A HORRIBLE CONFLAGRATION. On Wednesday night of last week, a negro cabin, situated in what is known as the "fork field" on Mr. J.M. Taylor's plantation, about 2 miles south east of Leary, was entirely consumed by fire, together with four of its occupants, a negro man named Tim White and three of his children. Being situated in the forks of two large creeks, the mosquitoes are very troublesome, and not being provided with bars, it had been Tim's custom for several years previous to build a slow fire directly under the door in a clay-hole for the purpose of smoking off these insects; and on the night in question the fire was built and the family consisting of Tim, his wife, and four children, retired. About ten or eleven o'clock, Tim awoke to find the house completely enveloped in flames (it having caught from the fire in the clay-hole), and under such headway as to render escape through the door impossible. By his frantic screams, he aroused his wife from her slumbers, who realizing their dangerous situation, took the baby child in her arms and knowing of a loose plank in the floor, raised it up and succeeded in making her escape just as the roof began to fall in, leaving her husband, who in the attempt to save the other three children perished in the flames with them. As soon as it became known to the other inhabitants of the quarter, they repaired to the horrible scene of the conflagration, and, as soon as the fire had burned sufficiently low to allow it, a search was made, and only a portion of the body of the man and two of the children were found and removed from the embers, while the other, supposed to be the youngest child was entirely cremated.

Tim was about thirty years of age, and, although he professed to be a minister of the Gospel, was considered by most every one that knew him as a rather notorious character. The ages of the children were, respectively, four, six and eight years, and that portion of their bodies, as well as their father's, that was saved, was all placed in a large dry goods box and burried (*sic*) on the evening following this terrible calamity.

August 3, 1877 ——————————— (ECN)

On Tuesday of last week, the down passenger train on the Georgia Road met with a terrible accident, about three miles above Union Point, by running into a cow on the track. The engine, in running over the cow, was thrown off the track and completely twisted across it. Upon the engine came the rushing train, and there was a shock which threw the entire contents of the baggage, mail and express cars on the tender in a confused mass, these cars being run into each other and almost telescoped. The two hindmost cars were not thrown from the track, but the shock hurled the passengers from their seats, and many were severely bruised. These two cars were mostly filled with United States soldiers, on their way to Louisville, Ky. All the baggage of the passengers, the U.S. Mail and the entire contents of the express car were burnt to ashes, as were the cars also. And horrible to relate, Mr. Zach Armstead, the engineer, was caught fast in the tender and burned to death in a few minutes. Not a trace of his remains was to be found, save a small white mass which seemed to be charred bone.

August 23, 1877 ——————————— (DWJ)

Old Uncle Simon McKenzie (Col.) who has dug more wells than any other man in the State, and another colored man named Gus Green, met with sudden and unexpected deaths last Saturday. On Mr. Joel Fokes' plantation, near this place, there is a well which needed cleaning out; Mr. F. employed uncle Simon to do the job. As usual, the old man suffered himself lowered to the bottom of the well, when it was soon discovered, by those on the outside, that something had happened to the old man, as he seemed to have lost consciousness. Upon consultation, Gus Green agreed to descend and see what was the matter. He refused to allow himself tied, and went down the rope. When near the bottom, he called to those above to draw him out, which they proceeded to do; but when about half way to the surface, Gus let go the rope and fell to the bottom – dead. An accumulation of noxious gases in the well had done the work.

–Montezuma Weekly.

August 24, 1877 ——————————— (ECN)

A SERIOUS ACCIDENT occurred in Savannah, on the evening of the 16th. A platform in front of Stoddard Range, Bay Street, gave way that evening under the weight of an iron safe which was being moved. Dennis Willis, colored, was instantly killed; John W. Reilly had both legs broken; John Daley and Richard Brode and five negroes were injured.

October 19, 1877 ———————————— (CA)

We learn that a man named Brunson shot and killed himself near Harrison's Mill, in this county, on Thursday night of last week. He was out hunting, in company with several young men, and while cutting down a tree, the ax handle struck and discharged a pistol, which he carried in his pocket – the ball passing through his abdomen. He died almost instantly.

October 25, 1877 ———————————— (DWJ)

The *Rome Courier*: About noon, little Charlie Rounsaville, son of Mr. J.W. Rounsaville, was killed on Broad street by the running away of his pony. He had got on the pony for a short ride. Using a saddle with stirrups too long, he put his feet through the straps and the pony taking fright at something ran down the street. The brave little fellow held on for a while, but eventually was thrown, and, with his foot hanging in the stirrup leather, he was dragged by the terrified horse about seventy yards, when the girth breaking, his little lifeless form was released . . .

December 6, 1877 ———————————— (DWJ)

SHOCKING MURDER of a young girl in Jones County. Miss Addie Hodge, a daughter of Mr. Samuel Hodge, an old and highly respected citizen of the upper part of Jones County, was shot and killed while on a visit to her brother-in-law, Mr. Robert Gordon, by some unknown party, about dark Saturday evening, the 24th inst. While the family of Mr. Gordon were at tea in the kitchen, a house adjacent and directly behind the dwelling from the road, the discharge of a gun was heard in the direction of the road. Miss Hodge at the time happened to be passing from the back part of the dwelling toward the fire place and received the ball, it taking effect on the side of her head, just above the ear and ranging upward. She survived about an hour. – It is supposed the shot was aimed at some one in the kitchen.

Miss Hodge was about fifteen years of age greatly esteemed for her many estimable traits of character, and her untoward death has cast a gloom over the entire community. The funeral service took place yesterday at Cany Creek Church where the remains were intered. (*sic*) The Rev. Mr. Bozemore officiated.

–Macon Telegraph & Messenger.

December 6, 1877 ——————————— (DWJ)

SAD ACCIDENT. The *Berrien County News:* Mr. Peter Troup, of Irwin County, had his little son, ten years of age, crushed to death under the following circumstances: Mr. Troup had been boiling syrup at a neighbor's house, and had filled a barrel, placed it in his cart and carried it home. His little son who was with him in the cart had fallen asleep, and when the father reached home he jumped out, leaving the child still asleep, and unhitched the tongue of the cart. He let it fall with some force, to the ground, which caused the barrel to pass over the child, crushing him to death.

December 20, 1877 ———————— (DWJ)

The *Sandersville Courier* has the following account of a heartrending accident: "On Friday last Mr. C.H. Odum, who resides three miles west of this city, went to the grist mill of the Messrs. Warthen, known as the Carter's Mill, for his grist. While standing near the flouring mill his overcoat was caught by the upright shaft of the elevator and in an instant drew hm so firmly to the shaft it was impossible to extricate himself. He was whirled around at the rate of one hundred and twenty circles to the minute. He was compelled to pass at each revolution, between four upright posts, all in such close proximity that any one of them would have crushed him to death. Before the water could be shut off he was mangled and torn to pieces. We are informed that his bones, flesh and blood were literally showered over the house." Mr. Odum leaves a helpless and dependent family to mourn his untimely death.

December 27, 1877 ———————— (DWJ)

THE EFFECT OF LIQUOR. Thomas T. Dorough, at one time, a prominent citizen of North Georgia, was run over and killed by a train of cars on the Northeastern railroad, in November last. He was buried, but his friends not being satisfied, and suspecting foul play, had his body exhumed, a few days ago, and an inquest held. The following is the verdict of the jury:

"We, the jury, after a post mortem examination of the body of T.T. Dorough, deceased, by Dr. L. G. Hardeman, find that he, the deceased, came to his death on the night of the 3d of November last by being intoxicated and being on the track of the Northeastern Railroad one a half miles above Harmony Grove, in Jackson county, when the down train, about 10 o'clock at night, ran over him and cut his head from his body, with many other bruises, and caused his immediate death. This December 14th, 1877."

January 10, 1878 — (ET)

The *Dublin Gazette* says: "On Wednesday, Mrs. Dominy, wife of Mr. S. Dominy, living about seven miles from town, drank a small quantity of whisky from a bottle from which others had been drinking, by which she was soon thrown into convulsions. Dr. R.H. Hightower, of this place, was sent for in great haste and did all that medical skill could do, but without avail. The remainder of the liquor when shaken was of a white milky appearance. Dr. H. decided that the death was caused by poison, but to make the matter doubly sure he brought the bottle to town and gave a portion of its contents to a cat which died in a few minutes. Dr. Hightower says it was strychnine. The community are much distressed about it."

February 7, 1878 — (DWJ)

The *Dahlonega Signal* has the following fatal accident, the result of imprudence: "On Wednesday, Thomas, little son of Mrs. John Hulsey, a widow lady residing in the neighborhood of Auraria, and aged about eleven years, entered the house gathered up a gun and began an examination of it. Not being aware that it was loaded, he placed the toe of his foot upon the hammer, pressing it back, and at the same time placing his mouth over the muzzle for the purpose of blowing in the barrel, when his foot slipped, a loud report followed and the almost headless corps (*sic*) of the boy lay stretched at the feet of his mother, while the room was bespattered with blood and brains. The gun was heavily charged with slugs and had been loaded for some time."

April 18, 1878 ——————————— (DWJ)

Mr. T.E. Collins, a prominent young merchant of Macon, fell through a trap door in the floor of his storehouse to the ground, 12 feet below. He struck his head and his skull was so fractured that he died in a few hours afterwards.

May 23, 1878 ——————————— (ET)

SAD AND FATAL ACCIDENT. From the *Hawkinsville Dispatch*, 16th inst.

About 5 o'clock on Sunday evening last a sad and shocking casualty occurred in our midst. As Mr. D.P. Searing, a painter employed on a job or work for Dr. W.N. Fleetwood, and Mr. M. O'Brien were taking a stroll on the river a short distance below town, Mr. Searing discovered some magnolia blooms and at once commenced climbing the tree after them. When he had reached a height of about forty feet he missed his footing and fell to the ground, receiving injuries which caused his death in about three hours. Mr. O'Brien placed the injured man in as comfortable position as possible and came to town for help. A party of gentlemen were soon collected and the suffering man was conveyed to the Hudspeth House, where he received every attention that surgical skill could devise of kind and sympathizing friends could bestow.

The unfortunate man in falling came in contact with the branches of the tree, breaking his ribs and receiving the most internal injuries ever witnessed. He spoke only a few words after his fatal fall, and they were in regard to his sufferings.

From papers found on the person of deceased, we learn that he left New York City, where he has a wife and two children, on the 9th day of October last. He arrived in Hawkinsville about the 22d of January, and had been engaged on jobs of painting for different parties up to the time of his sad and untimely end. – He received an affectionate letter from his daughter on Saturday evening, and had an answer to the same in his pocket at the time of his death.

Mr. Searing was a Mason in good standing, and bore a certificate of membership from Chapter No. 288 of New York City. He was a first-class painter, and had, by his gentlemanly deportment, won the esteem and confidence of our people generally.

The remains were decently interred in Orange Hill Cemetery on Monday evening by Mt. Hope Lodge, No. 9, F. & A.M.

The papers, books, and other effects of deceased are now in the hands of Dr. W.N. Fleetwood of this place.

May 30, 1878 ——————————————— (DJ)

Mr. J.B. Scott tells the *Americus Republican* that Mr. Player, once of Houston, seemingly died in Wilcox County and was laid out, in six or more hours he rose up in his graveclothes and conversed several minutes, then fell back dead.

May 30, 1878 ——————————————— (DJ)

KEROSENE. Sad Death of Little Eva Gilmer. Little Eva Gilmer, youngest child of Mr. and Mrs. Joseph Gilmer, is no more. Just before retiring on Thursday night Miss Mattie Badger, a young lady who is staying with the family, went into the dining room to get some Kerosene, which had been requested by Mrs. Gilmer, who was sick. Little Eva had been undressed and prepared to retire, but followed Miss Badger. The latter took the Kerosene can, and holding it near the lamp which sat on the cupboard, commenced pouring the fluid into a saucer. All of a sudden she became aware that the kerosene had ignited. The gas escaping from the can which had just been opened is supposed to have reached the top of the lamp chimney, which conveyed the blaze to the saucer and to the can. Miss Badger, thinking the trouble was with the lamp, threw it out doors, and about this time the can, which she had dropped, discharged its contents and a sheet of fire. Little Eva was standing near by, and was drenched with the burning fluid. She ran out into the yard, and with remarkable presence of mind, jumped into a tub of water and extinguished the flames, not, however, until she had been fearfully burned. She bore her sufferings like a little hero until about 3 o'clock a.m., when death came and relieved her. Little Eva was about five and ahalf years old, and was one of the brightest, sweetest little girls we ever knew.

–Albany Advertiser.

June 6, 1878 —————————————— (DJ)

A HORRIBLE AFFAIR. John Caldwell Kills his Wife, His Wife's Sister, Three Children, and Then Kills Himself. – From Mr. Luke Roberts, deputy Sheriff of this county, who, on Tuesday, returned from near the scene of the action, we learn the following particulars of a horrible tragedy that was enacted near Davidson's Mill, in Sumter County, on last Monday:

John Caldwell killed his wife, his wife's sister, three of his children, ranging in age from 4 to 10 years, and then himself. Their brains were scattered all over the floor and walls of his house. One daughter, whom he tried to kill, escaped and ran to a field where a brother was at work. These two are the only members of the family left. After killing all these persons, Caldwell jumped into the well twice in an attempt to kill himself. He then got on the house and jumped off. This failing to kill him, he climbed to the top of the gin house and jumped off, fracturing his skull and killing him. His son, who had returned from the field, saw him just before he jumped from the gin house, and implored him not to leap.

The six bodies were buried at the Providence Church on Tuesday evening. . . . Mr. Caldwell was a man of about middle age, in easy circumstances and of good character. He had long been a member of the Primitive Baptist Church, and was well liked by his acquaintances.

We have now learned the following particulars: Mr. Caldwell's sister-in-law, whom he killed was named Francis Mitchell. The children killed were Allen, aged 10 years, Robert, aged 6 years and Lyda, aged 2 years. Mr. Caldwell had eight children, three of whom were absent from home at the time of the killing, and one of whom escaped, as above stated. He first killed his wife and children in the house with a smoothing iron, and then went out in the yard and killed his sister-in-law with a hoe.

June 13, 1878 —————————————— (DJ)

On Monday at noon, says the *Albany News,* Mr. Abram Shiver, son of Mr. John Shiver, of Worth, met his death under most peculiar circumstances. He had been complaining for some time – ever since cutting oats. On Saturday night the family heard screams from the young man, and running to him, found him on the front porch suffering intensely and tearing the garments from his person and uttering yells of agony. He was put to bed at once, and after thirty seven hours of horrible agony, breathed his last. The physicians pronounced the case overheat and dropsy. Deceased was about twenty years of age.

June 13, 1878 —————————————— (DJ)

The *Marietta Field and Fireside* says that Atlas Daniell, living near Smyrna, and Bailiff of that district, while turning his horse and plow at the end of a furrow last Friday afternoon, struck himself in the abdomen with the handle of the plow, and although medical aid was brought to him, his hour had arrived and on Sunday he died . . .

August 15, 1878 —————————————— (ET)

Columbus had a very severe storm last week. A heavy door was blown against Mr. Wm. Egles, foreman of the Southwestern railroad shops, fracturing his skull and causing his death.

August 22, 1878 —————————— (ET)

The *Franklin News* says that a little son of Mr. James Deloach, of Texas district, on Monday the 5th inst., went out a short distance from the house to hunt a hen's nest. Finding a nest the child put his hand in to get the eggs, when the fangs of a rattlesnake were plunged into his wrist. The entrails of a chicken were applied immediately, and Drs. Morgan and Gaffney summoned as quickly as possible. The most efficient antidotes were administered but without arresting the deadly poison, and the unfortunate little boy died on Wednesday following. The snake measured four feet nine inches in length and had thirteen rattles.

October 31, 1878 —————————— (DJ)

Albany News: Last night B. & A. Mail brought us information of the finding of the remains of some unknown man, ten miles south of Ty Ty, by Mr. W.E. Williams. . . . Our correspondent stated that "he had been dead so long that his bones were scattered over a quarter of an acre of ground, and were bleached and whitened by the rains and sun." Scattered about over a considerable space were found were a valise, violin, some clockmakers' implements, and various papers. His identity could not be traced on any of them. The papers were old and dim, and the lettering obliterated by exposure to the weather.

November 7, 1878 ——————— (DJ)

TERRIBLE ACCIDENT. *Washington Gazette:* "Little George Gunter, son of a widow who lives on Mr. Zeb Colley's place, three miles from town, had his head terribly mangled in the running gear of a gin last Tuesday morning. The little fellow was standing on the lever riding around when he put his head a little above the larger cog wheel, which crushed it against the piece of machinery in which the journal of the band wheel works. – The cheek bones of one side of his face and the jaw bone were broken in several places and the flesh all torn from that side. He was thought to be conscious though he was unable to speak. Dr. Andrews says he has never seen a more terrible looking wound. The patient died the next morning about daylight. He was only seven years old."

December 5, 1878 ——————— (DJ)

A SINGULAR AND MELANCHOLY ACCIDENT. A few days ago it was reported that Rev. R.E. White, of South Carolina, had been fatally shot while riding in his carriage by some unknown person, and that a negro named Coleman suspected of being the assassin had been arrested. It now turns out that Mr. White was really the victim of a singular accident. A special dispatch to the *Charleston News and Courier* says he was killed by a twelve year old son of Mr. Spencer Davis, who was hunting for hawks in the woods near the road. The rifle used was a Remington, and the heavy ball missing its aim and probably glancing downward from contact with a twig sped through the forest to the road, two hundred yards distant, and struck down Mr. White with instantaneous fatal effect. The little fellow was too much horrified and frightened when the body was taken to his father's house to tell how the killing occurred . . . the negro Coleman, who was arrested, has been released.

–Savannah News.

December 5, 1878 ———————————— (DJ)

A negro woman by the name of Tinnie Gray died at Savannah recently from an overdose of religion taken at a revival.

December 5, 1878 ———————————— (DJ)

DEATH IN THE WOODS. Near Arlington, Ga., November 25th, 1878. We are pained to note the death of Mr. Wm. A. James, whose body was found this day by a colored boy in the Northwest corner of Baker County, on the farm owned by the Ivey estate. After the boy found the body he notified young Mr. Ivey, and he immediately made it known to his brothers and neighbors. As soon as possible they assembled, called in a physician and a proper officer. He impanelled a jury, which found a verdict "that the deceased met his death by being thrown from his horse against a pine tree". His body was carried by his brothers and friends to his parents in Randolph County, near Brooksville, where he was raised. He was about thirty-five years of age, unmarried, a citizen of high standing, and was once a member of the 13th Georgia Regiment, and was a gallant soldier and ever at his post . . . Strange to note that this is the third dead person found within the space of 200 yards of the spot – all killed from the same cause. *–Telegraph and Messenger.*

December 26, 1878 ——————— (DJ)

Cartersville Free Press: On last Monday afternoon Captain William H. Stiles, a popular and prominent citizen of our county, was most frightfully gored by an infuriated bull. He was walking through his yard in the direction of some laborers in a field near by when he encountered the bull in his pathway, and lightly struck him over the head with a stick to drive him out of the way, and passed on. This instantly put the bull in a fearful rage, and he flew at the captain, who, taken by surprise, was, of course, felled to the ground. After running back a few steps the bull made the second plunge, and one of his horns entered Captain Stile's thigh, and he was thrown into the air five or six feet. As soon as the captain struck the ground the bull made the third attack, hitting him in the breast. At that moment the farm hands came to the rescue, and succeeded in driving the brute off. Captain Stile's wounds are very ugly, and he has been suffering intense agonies. . . . The horn entered the inside of the left thigh, and tore a frightful gash some seven or eight inches, laying bare the bone and femoral artery. A piece of flesh from this wound, of considerable size, was found on the ground. He also sustained internal injuries . . . Just as we go to press a messenger has arrived in town for Capt. Stile's coffin, and tolling church bells are announcing his death, he having breathed his last at 11:30 o'clock this a.m. . . .

January 9, 1879 ——————— (ET)

On the 25th of December, Mr. Henry Boyd, a young man about 23 years of age, was found frozen to death two miles west of LaGrange. He was on his way home, and was not very far from it, when it is supposed he was attacked with an epileptic fit.

January 9, 1879 ——————————— (DJ)

Butler Herald: A very sad and fatal accident occurred in our town last Thursday. While Peter McCrary, colored, was out in his back yard quite early in the morning preparing for killing hogs, a large iron kettle had been placed in the ground and filled with boiling water for the purpose of scalding hogs. Over the kettle had been placed a white cloth. A little two-years-old son of Peter McCrary's thinking that the cloth had been placed upon the ground, stepped on the cloth and was immediately plunged into the boiling water up to his armpits, from the effects of which it died at ten o'clock the following night.

January 23, 1879 ——————————— (DJ)

Fort Valley Mirror: On Wednesday Mr. Allen Davis, an old gentleman who was living on Dr. Flournoy's place, went into the lot with the doctor's son, Joe, to catch Reuben, the doctor's mule, both parties being armed with sticks. The mule ran Mr. Davis down and jumped or fell on him, when Joe hit him and drove him off, but as the mule rose he kicked the old gentleman on the temple, breaking his skull, from the effects of which he died that night. The mule is a regular fighter and is well known as dangerous, so much so that no one but Dr. Flournoy and his little son ever attempts to handle him. It is a pity that he does not belong to someone able to blow his brains out.

January 23, 1879 ──────────── (DJ)

Cedartown Express: Last Friday evening Mr. Martin Harris, a citizen of this county, and a very clever man, left this place for his home, about 7 miles distant. It will be remembered that it was a very cold night. He was found on the roadside between Cedartown and D.A. Whitehead's. When come upon he was fighting fire, his clothing from his waist up being nearly all burned off. The theory is that he had put a lighted cigar in his vest pocket and it ignited his clothing. He was removed to the hospitable roof of Mr. D.A. Whitehead, and thence by his family to his home. The services of Dr. Harris were brought into requisition, but the man's body had been burned to a crisp, and of course no human art could save him. After a few short but painful hours he was relieved.

February 28, 1879 ──────────── (ECN)

A TERRIBLE ACCIDENT occurred on the 8th inst., by a train falling through a rotten bridge on Selma, Rome and Dalton Railroad. George Evans, a prominent young man, was killed. Two or three negroes are dead in the wreck, and two white men are fatally wounded. Mr. Stanton, general superintendent, and conductor White are both believed to be fatally hurt. Ten or twelve others are slightly hurt. The train, except the engine, is badly wrecked. The sleeper went down but the rear end hung to the abutment, allowing the inmates to escape.

P.S. Mr. Stanton has since died of his injuries.

March 14, 1879

COL. ROBT. A. ALSTON KILLED. The following particulars of the tragic death of Col. Alston is found in the press dispatched from Atlanta of the 11th:

At 3:20 o'clock p.m. the office of the State Treasurer, at the Capitol, in this city, was the scene of a bloody tragedy, the parties being Col. Robert A. Alston, member of the Legislature, and Capt. E.S. Cox, of DeKalb county. Alston fired three shots and Cox two. Alston was shot in the right temple, the ball passing through his brain. Cox was shot in the mouth and through the left hand. Alston is dying, but Cox is not seriously hurt.

The difficulty arose from Alston having a power of attorney from Senator Gordon to sell the latter's interest in the State convict lease. Cox is sub-lessee under Gordon, and wanted Alston to sell Gordon's interest to Walters, who had promised to buy Cox out. Alston sold to another person. Cox threatened Alston at noon that he would kill him before sundown if the trade was not cancelled and made with his man. He hunted Alston down, Governor Colquitt and others having detained Alston at the capitol, the quarrel was renewed, and both drew their pistols, with the result above stated.

Colonel Alston died at four minutes after six this evening.

The coroner's jury rendered a verdict that the killing of Colonel Robert A. Alston by E.S. Cox was wilful (*sic*) and premeditated murder. Cox is in jail to await trial.

April 1, 1879

HORRIBLE FATE OF JEFF DOWNING – HE IS EATEN BY ALLIGATORS.

The *Quitman Free Press* thus tells of the horrible fate

of one Jeff Downing. It says: "Many citizens of this county, and almost everybody in Lowndes County, knew Downing. He was a fisherman, and for years has supplied the Valdosta market with fish from the Ocean Pond. His plan was to fish for several days, or until he had a load, and then carry them to market. His protracted absence the first part of last week attracted the attention of his friends, who finally went to see what was the matter. Arriving at the landing where he kept his boat, they found his fish box and canoe all right, but the fisherman was missing. Soon after they reached the bank of the pond, however, the parties were astonished to see two huge alligators emerge from the grass near by and come towards the shore, apparently wanting to fight. A gun was procured, and both alligators were finally killed and dragged ashore. Upon opening the animals, their stomachs were found to contain human flesh, bones, particles of clothing and other unmistakable evidences, showing plainly the fate of poor Downing. The supposition is that he was transferring fish from his boat to the box where he kept them, when the alligators made the fatal attack. A more horrible affair has never occurred in our section."

April 4, 1879 ———————————— (ECN)

The *Sandersville Herald* says that last Saturday while Mr. Aylesbury Wiggins, who resided in the western part of Washington County, was riding toward his home from the field, accompanied by one of his laborers, who was also on a horse, they were overtaken by the storm which had just arisen, and when about a mile from the house a large pine tree fell on them, almost instantly killing Mr. Wiggins, and severely injuring the negro man, as well as the two horses they rode. Before Mr. Wiggins could be conveyed to the house he expired, in full view of his agonized family, who had hastened to his assistance . . .

April 4, 1879 ——————————— (ECN)

A special dispatch from Nacoochee to the *Atlanta Constitution,* on the 27th ult., states that Prof. Frank H. Bradley, former Assistant State Geologist, was crushed to death at his gold mines near that point, by the caving in of a bank of earth under which he was at work.

April 10, 1879 ——————————— (DJ)

The *Marietta Journal* tells us of a shocking tragedy. It says: "Mrs. George Scroggins, a widow lady, living near Powder Springs, who has several children, missed her ten-year-old boy Thursday morning, and after a diligent search she found him hanging from a loft in the stable dead. Evidently he had attempted to climb through a small opening into the loft, his foot slipped, his head caught on the inside of the plank, leaving his body dangling in the air by the neck, and being unable to extricate himself from his perilous position, life was soon extinct. He had been dead about two hours when he was found."

May 3, 1879 ——————————— (TT)

REV. ALLISON DEKLE DROWNED. At one o'clock on last Thursday Rev. Allison Dekle was drowned at his mill, known as the Folsom Mill, 14 miles north of Thomasville, on the Big Ocklockonee river. The recent freshet had broken the mill, but the dam had been repaired and water again stopped. At one o'clock Mr. Dekle and perhaps his son-in-law discovered a leak which they feared would endanger the dam, and went down to the gate to let off the water. One of the uprights supporting this gate was held in position by a prop, and this gave way as soon as the pressure of water came against it, pushing Mr. Dekle into the current. His son-in-law caught him and attempted to pull him back, but the force of the water was too strong and sucked him under. He rose some ten or fifteen feet below in the river, but went down again and had not been found up too three o'clock that day . . .

May 8, 1879 (DJ)

KILLED BY LIGHTNING. On Tuesday afternoon about the time the severe gust of wind and a slight shower of rain passed over Albany, Mr. John Cox, the overseer for Mr. R.G. Carleton, on the Frog Pond place, nine miles south of the city, was struck and instantly killed by lightning. He was out in the field sitting on a stump, about a hundred yards from where the hands were at work, when killed. Mr. Cox was forty-five or fifty years of age, and moved to this county from Green (*sic*) County in January last. He leaves a wife and three children . . .

–Albany Advertiser.

June 26, 1879 (DJ)

Marianna Courier: On Wednesday of last week, while Mr. John Aarons was bathing in J. Davis' mill Pond, Mr. Henry

Glover concluded to join him. Aarons had dived into the water and was immediately followed by Glover, who jumped in, striking Aarons with his head between the shoulders. Both parties for a few moments were unconscious. Aarons receiving the blow soon rallied, but his companion died within an hour. He was buried on Thursday last. Aarons is still living, but is reported to be in critical condition.

July 24, 1879 ——————————— (DJ)

The *Northeastern Progress* is informed that Mr. Brantly Strickland, of Banks County, happened to singular accident on Thursday last. Mr. Strickland had dammed up a creek on his premises for the purpose of irrigating some part of his land. After the water had risen to a sufficient depth, he concluded to jump in and take a bath, and in so doing, it is supposed his head stuck in the mud and his body went over with such force as to dislocate his neck. A brother-in-law was with him, and rendered all assistance possible, but the poor man died in eight hours after the occurrence.

July 25, 1879 ——————————— (ECN)

A SHOCKING SUICIDE occurred on the Western and Atlantic Railroad on Friday of last week. Just as the train approached the Fair Grounds near Atlanta, a man threw himself across the track, and before the train could be stopped, he was crushed to death. The unfortunate man was a young German named Max Franklin, who had been in bad health for several months.

October 9, 1879 ———————————— (DJ)

. . . The *Leesburg Advance* says: "The party who attended the coroner's inquest on the body of Mr. Harry Keller, drowned in the Withlacoochee River on the 5th instant, and found on the 7th, with his head off, returned last Sunday. Dr. Stevens' sworn statement clears up all suspicion of a murder having been committed. The body of Mr. Keller was dissected and it was found that he came to his death by drowning. The head of the drowned man had been twisted from the body by an alligator, and the neck eaten away by turtles and fish. When the body was found a large alligator was swimming within twenty feet of it, while the turtles had to be kept off with a stick. Alligators are very numerous in this river . . ."

October 16, 1879 ———————————— (DJ)

A SAD ACCIDENT occurred in Athens last Wednesday morning, Rev. James Smith, while descending the steps of DuPree Hall, made a misstep and was precipitated to the bottom. The fall was so rapid and severe as to break his neck and proved fatal in a few minutes. The *Chronicle* says he was a very old man, had been a presiding elder in the M.E. Church South for fifty years or more and was highly respected.

October 16, 1879 ———————————— (DJ)

SAD. We understand that a one year old child of Mr. Thomas Jay, of Ward's Station, was scalded to death one day last week. The child was playing near a stove in the kitchen and took hold of a kettle of boiling water. The handle of the kettle was so hot that the child could not let it go, screamed and fell upon the floor, the contents of the kettle scalding the child so badly that it died in a few hours.

December 4, 1879 ———————— (DJ)

SUDDEN DEATH – KICKED BY A MULE. On Monday evening last, on the plantation of Dr. John Laidler, of Houston County, a Mr. McWilliams was kicked by a mule and died in a few minutes. The deceased, with another person, we are informed, had hidden themselves under a bridge, and as some freedmen, riding mules, passed over the bridge, McWilliams jumped out and struck one of the mules in the flank with a sack. The frightened animal kicked violently with its hind foot, striking the man, and causing almost instant death. – *Hawkinsville Dispatch.*

December 11, 1879 ———————— (DJ)

The *Independent* gives an account of a terrible death which recently occurred near Lumpkin, as follows: "On yesterday morning the shocking intelligence reached town that Mr. Frank Dunaway, who lived about three miles from town, had been crushed to death in a cane mill. He had carried his cane to the mill of Mr. J.B. Griffis and his little boy and girl were driving the mules while he was feeding the mill. It seems that in feeding some mills it is necessary for a man to stoop to avoid the lever as it passes around. In this instance Mr. Dunaway got his cane too close to the mill, which prevented him from stooping as much as he should have done. We learn that as the lever came around he was struck and his head jammed between the driver and the wedges, and that his head was instantly terrible (*sic*) crushed. One of his children gave the alarm and Mr. Griffis ran to his assistance. He pulled the mule and lever back, when Mr. Dunaway fell to the ground, drew only a breath or two and was dead. . . . He was about thirty-five years of age, and leaves a wife and four small children . . .

December 11, 1879 — (DJ)

The body of Oscar Ricks, of Florida, who mysteriously disappeared while attending the Bainbridge fair, was found in Flint River six miles below that city a few days ago. It was supposed that he had purposely drowned himself, as his gold watch was found on his person. He had been drinking hard for some time before his disappearance.

December 25, 1879 — (DJ)

SAD OCCURRENCE – DROWNING OF TWO MEN. – [*Athens Watchman*]: It becomes our sad duty to announce, this morning, the drowning, on Sunday night, of Rev. Father Doyle, the Catholic priest who has supplied the church at this place for some time past, and Mr. M.H. Moynehan, one of the popular clerks at Gray & Co.

They had been to Lexington, where Father Doyle held services on Sunday, and were endeavoring to return to this city, where Father D. wished to hold service on Monday morning.

It seems that they had gotten off the regular road, and, in crossing Stewart's Creek, about 6 miles below this city, they and the horse they were driving, were all drowned . . .

December 25, 1879 ——————— (DJ)

John Duncan, a train hand on the Southwestern railroad, while walking on top of the cars, last Thursday night, near Butler, fell between them and was run over and killed.

January 15, 1880 ——————— (DJ)

Mr. Frank Goodman, of Irwin County, called on Miss Mary Payne, and while talking to her, began examining a small pistol; the pistol went off, as usual, and shot Miss Mary through the brain, killing her instantly.

February 19, 1880 ——————— (ET)

SERIOUS ACCIDENT. On Monday last, while engaged in taking down Mr. Leitch's mills, preparatory to removal, Mr. Geo. Davis, an employee at the mills, was overhead removing some timbers, and walking too far out on a plank, it gave way and he fell to the floor, a distance of about ten feet, his head striking against the timber carriage, producing a severe concussion of the brain. For a short time he was apparently lifeless and thought to be dead, but such means as were convenient were used for his restoration, a physician dispatched for, and at last accounts, Mr. D., though suffering severely, was thought to be out of danger.

LATER. Since the above was in type we learn that on Tuesday night Mr. Davis grew rapidly worse, and died on Wednesday morning.

He was a young man of good character, and a consistent member of the Methodist church. He has a widowed mother in Florence, S.C., besides other friends and relatives to mourn his premature death. His only relatives with him was a twin brother, Mr. Fuller Davis, engineer at Mr. Leitch's mills, and his wife, who watched him with tender care all through his suffering. He was about 27 years of age.

April 15, 1880 ——————————————— (DJ)

THE FOLLOWING INSTANCE OF A SUDDEN AND HORRIBLE DEATH is related in the *Macon Telegraph*: "At two o'clock yesterday morning as the Macon and Brunswick passenger train was nearing Baxley on the upward trip, Captain Sharp, the conductor, as usually, called the name of the station, in order to allow passengers for that point, of whom there were several, time to make their preparations for leaving the car. A man named Jones was among the number, and lay upon a bench asleep. He arose, passed down the car, out through the door on the platform, apparently to get off. Instead of waiting, however, for the train to stop, or of passing down the steps, he walked upon the little platform which lies above the coupling, turned and stepped off into the darkness between the two cars. The brakeman caught at and succeeded in catching hold of him, but was unable to retain his grasp. Down unto death beneath the thundering train went the unfortunate man, and in a few moments was but a mass of broken bones and mutilated flesh. The wheels did not pass over the body. He was caught by the truck and doubled up along the cross ties until the train stopped. He was alive when picked up, but died in an hour. No blame can attach to the road or its officers for this unfortunate death. About the dead man were found fragments of a whisky flask. It is supposed that, being in a stupor from drink, and dazed by the lights, at the sound of "Baxley" he rose and walked out on the platform, and thinking himself opposite the steps, and the train at a stand-still, took the fatal step."

April 15, 1880 ——————————— (DJ)

Thomaston Times: "On the 2nd Inst., while a Mr. Crawford and his son were out cutting wood for Flint River Factory, the younger Mr. Crawford came to his death under the following circumstances: It seems that they had cut one tree down and it had lodged against another, and fearing that this one would lodge also, they placed a heavy prop against it to force it to fall in another direction. While cutting on this tree the prop fell, striking young Crawford on the back of the head and knocking him senseless. He was carried home, and upon examination it was found that his skull was fractured. He lived about six hours after the accident."

April 22, 1880 ——————————— (DJ)

The *Swainsboro Herald* thus tells of a horrible and fatal accident which recently occurred near that town: "Last Wednesday morning Mr. Solomon Canady went out to hunt wild turkeys that frequent a certain swamp and Mr. John P. Edenfield, his son-in-law, had gone to the same place for the same purpose, neither of the gentlemen knowing the other was there. About sunrise a turkey flew down, as well as we can learn, near the two men, and Mr. Edenfield spied Mr. Canady's hat and mistook it for a turkey and fired at it with a rifle, and on going the spot he was horrified to find that he had shot and instantly killed Mr. Canady. – The ball struck Mr. Canady in the right temple, penetrated the brain and lodged in the back of the head. Mr. Canaday (*sic*) and Mr. Edenfield were devoted to each other as father and son . . .

May 13, 1880 ———————————————— (DJ)

SAD AND FATAL ACCIDENT. The *Middle Georgia Times* publishes the following:

We are pained to chronicle the sad death of Mr. Robert Millen, of Upson County, which occurred last Thursday about dark. The facts, as we get them, are that his wife being absent, he put his little children to bed, and had concluded to go over to his brother-in-law's, Mr. Doc Alford, for a short while, and having lost the front door key, fastened it on the inside, and attempted to get out of a window by means of a short ladder, which slipped, and he fell to the ground, breaking his nose and neck. He died instantly. The children heard the fall, but did not know that their father was lying dead under the window. Mr. Alford, who lives only a short distance from Mr. Millen's, came over in about five minutes after the fall, and it was he who first discovered the corpse.

May 16, 1880 ———————————————— (AtC)

A SHOCKING SCENE THAT APPALS THE WHOLE CITY. A Fire Takes Place on the Stage of DeGive's Opera House, in Which the Young Ladies Become Enveloped – The Wild Excitement of the Moment. [Ed. Note: This is a very long article and has been condensed to give the most significant details.]

Wednesday afternoon, a few minutes past three o'clock, just before the curtain had risen upon the matinee performance of the spectacular of Paradise and the Peri, the audience were startled by the cry of fire . . . the audience, which, happily, was small, passed to the street without accident.

. . . It seems that just before the time for the performance to begin a troup of eight or ten young ladies were collected in one of the upper dressing rooms which is reached from the stage floor by means of a short flight of steps leading up to a narrow balcony from the edge of which rises a low wooden railing. These young ladies were dressed to represent angels. They wore full flowing tarleton robes, with very large sleeves, relieved by long broad wings standing stiffly out behind, and made of common batting. The mind staggers in the effort to imagine a more combustible costume. A gas jet was burning in this room. It had been lighted for the purpose of burning cork, which . . . is used by amateurs and professionals . . . in making up the face for artistic effect upon the stage.

Among the ladies in this dressing room were Miss Maggie Chapman, Mrs. Abbie Hammond, of Baltimore, Miss Madge Ellis, Miss Minnie Bellamy and Miss Katie Mayrant, who is a visitor here from Charleston. One of the above named ladies . . . in turning about, thrust her wing into the blazing jet. In less than one minute she was in flames, and in wheeling around in her fright had communicated them to the other two. . . . Mrs. Bellamy, who was also in the room, violently shoved the girls nearest the door – her daughter and Miss Mayrant among the number – out upon the balcony. The three flaming angels rushed madly from the room, and two of them, in passing down the balcony to the stage, set fire to the wings of Misses Bellamy and Mayrant. The third, Mrs. Hammond, frantic from fright, took a shorter path to the stage, throwing herself over the balcony railing and falling a distance of nearly ten feet to the floor below . . . Miss Chapman ran down the balcony steps . . . Miss Bellamy, as soon as the tip of her wings caught from the passing flames . . . threw herself upon her back on the balcony and rubbed the fire out before it had time to spread over her dress. Miss Ellis did not leave the balcony, but made her way to an adjoining dressing-room, and throwing a piece of carpet around her rolled over and over upon the floor until the flames were extinguished.

Miss Mayrant was doubly unfortunate. In her desperate effort to escape from the balcony she was not only set on fire, but knocked down. She fell at the head of the steps leading to the stage, and Miss Chapman passed over her. . . She shot like a meteor through the stage door, rushed down two flights of steps and reached the pavement screaming and with the flames shooting high above her head. The very minute she struck the sidewalk two brave and stalwart arms . . . had her carefully wrapped up and tenderly placed upon a lounge in his office. And thus another life was saved.

Miss Maggie Chapman was horribly burned about the neck, throat and arms. She inhaled the flames, affecting most seriously thereby the bronchial tubes. She was borne to her home on Houston street, late in the afternoon, upon a bed.

Mrs. Abbie Hammond is dangerously burned about the neck, shoulders and arms. She was first taken to the residence of Dr. Willis Westmoreland . . . Later in the afternoon she was removed upon a lounge to the home of her friends on Luckie street.

Miss Madge Ellis was painfully burned upon both arms, and Miss Mamie Bellamy was severely burned upon each shoulder . . . Dr. Thad Johnson thinks their condition by no means serious.

Miss Katie Mayrant was conveyed in a carriage . . . to the residence of Mrs. Boylston, on Peachtree street. She has three very painful burns – one on either arm and one upon her right shoulder.

LATER.

Miss Chapman died on Thursday afternoon and was

buried on Friday. Mrs. Hammond died on Thursday night and was buried on Saturday morning. Both funerals were large and imposing. Misses Ellis, Mayrant and Bellamy are recovering.

May 27, 1880 —————————————— (DJ)

Some one put out poison to kill a dog belonging to Mr. Jas. Martin, of Dubois. A fifteen months old child of Mr. Martin got hold of some of the poison, ate it, and died.

May 27, 1880 —————————————— (DJ)

The *Berrien County News* reports a most horrible and sickening occurrence in Telfair county as follows: "Mr. R.J. Odum, writing us from Dorminey's Mill, under date of May 16th, gives an account of a white woman named Susan Dossen, who had been on a visit to her brother in Telfair County, and who on her return was taken sick. She stopped at a house and asked to be allowed to stay until she became able to resume her journey, but was refused, and went her way. Three days later the attention of someone was attracted by a swarm of buzzards which flew up from near the roadside, and an examination revealed the mutilated remains of the poor woman, who had breathed her last far from her friends, and with only the sky as her shelter. Her body was almost entirely eaten up by the dogs, hogs and buzzards . . ."

May 28, 1880 ——————————————— (ECN)

The rain in Columbus on Friday and Friday night of last week was the heaviest known in that city for years. In two hours, during Friday night, the river rose from ten to fifteen feet. The low grounds of the city were flooded, and families had to leave their homes and seek higher grounds. One of the wooden piers of the lower foot bridge was swept down the river. The bridge over Girard creek was swept away. A press dispatch from the city, on Saturday says, from Friday at 9 a.m. to Saturday at 5 p.m., 9.92 inches of rain fell. All of the railroads are injured, and no trains have arrived or departed today. The through freight and accommodation train from Macon to Montgomery, last night ran into Schatulga creek on the Southwestern road, nine miles east of this place. Engineer John T. Wade, fireman, Joe Schaefer, wood passers Charles Taylor and Joseph T. Lane, were killed. All are white, and from Macon, Ga. The engine and eleven cars were wrecked. A construction train is repairing the breaks from here to the point where the accident occurred.

June 10, 1880 ——————————————— (DJ)

SUICIDE. Yesterday about one o'clock Mr. Upshaw, who was boarding with Mr. J.C. Harris, his brother-in-law, dressed himself in a suit of conventional black, which he had purchased for the purpose of a wedding suit, and binding a towel around his neck to keep the blood from soiling his clothes, he put a blanket on the bed, and taking a pistol, a single barrel, forty-one calibre derringer, he placed it against his right temple and pulled the trigger, discharging the ball, which passed directly through his head. He lingered until near four o'clock, when he died.

Mr. Upshaw was about forty-five years of age and came here about five years ago. He was born in Elbert County, Georgia and came from South west Georgia to this city.

He left a letter addressed to his sister and Mr. Harris requesting them to bury him quietly and just as they found him, as he had prepared himself for the grave.

—Columbus Times.

June 10, 1880 ——————————— (DJ)

The two story dwelling of Mr. Ed Bradly, near Florence, was burned a few days ago. His cook perished in the flames.

June 24, 1880 ——————————— (DJ)

Quitman Free Press: A colored well digger, named Levi Myers, while digging a well on Mr. Dick Harris' place about three miles from Quitman, on Wednesday last, was suffocated by gas at a depth of thirty-one feet. No one was at the windlass at the time, but it is supposed that he died almost immediately after reaching the bottom of the well. An inquest was held by coroner Ponder and a verdict rendered in accordance with the above facts.

July 1, 1880 —————————————————— (DJ)

Mr. J.M. Gatewood, of Dougherty County, gave his sick son a dose of morphine, mistaking it for quinine. The child died the next day.

July 1, 1880 —————————————————— (DJ)

A young man, named Ed Stephens, of Eufaula, Ala., was so severely hurt by the premature explosion of a cannon, while firing a salute over the democratic nominations, that he died.

August 12, 1880 ————————————————— (DJ)

Frank Harrison, of Pike County, was arrested for bastardy. He mounted a horse and tried to escape, pursued by the bailiff. During the race Harrison's horse fell and so injured him that he died soon afterwards.

August 12, 1880 ————————————————— (DJ)

A FEARFUL SCENE. That Stupefies Webster County. A Stepmother Administers Morphine to Herself and Nine Children, Three of Whom Will Die.

Americus, Ga., August 6. – A terrible crime was committed in Webster County, twenty miles west of this place, on the evening of August 4. Woodson L. Gunnells, a well to do farmer, left home to visit a sick neighbor, and returning at 10 p.m., found his wife and nine of ten small children in a horrible sleep, from the effects of morphine administered in lemonade by Mrs. Gunnells. There is no doubt she prepared the fatal beverage and administered it to the children and drank of it herself with fatal intent. Mr. Gunnells was married to this his second wife seven years ago, and has by her four children. The other six is (*sic*) by his previous wife, and as far as known the stepmother has been dutiful and a kind parent to them. Mrs. Gunnells is from a highly respectable family. A note in the handwriting of Mrs. Gunnells, found under the morphia bottle on the table, in which she stated she had deliberately administered morphia to the children and herself with the intention of destroying them all, and that she was not actuated by any domestic trouble. Owing to the lapse of time before medical aid arrived, Mrs. Gunnell's case was hopeless . . . The case of the children was not so hopeless, and by the unceasing efforts of the physicians some of them showed signs of returning consciousness. All of the stepchildren and some of the younger children are now thought to be out of danger. The youngest child, and infant of a few months, was saved by the fact that the mother could not introduce enough fluid down its little throat to destroy life. Probably three of the children will die. . . . All of the evidence taken negatives the idea of insanity and points directly to a cool, deliberate determination on the part of the hitherto quiet, kind-hearted lady to take away her own life and that of her family, and at the same time conceal from the world the cause of her act.

September 10, 1880 —————— (CCG)

FOUND DEAD. Col. Geo. B. Williamson, an old citizen of Waycross, was found dead in his office yesterday morning, supposed to have died on Monday. Col. Williamson had an incurable cancer on his face that had eaten through into his mouth. In this condition it is thought his death was produced by a dose of laudanum administered by his own hand. He was about seventy years of age.

December 2, 1880 (GWT)

INTO THE GULCH. Mr. E.S. Griffin's Fatal Fall.

Early on Thanksgiving morn intelligence was received in this city of the sudden and tragic death of Mr. E.S. Griffin, Jr., of Twiggs County. The news was a shock to his many friends in the city, with whom he had parted on the previous evening in the full flush of health.

The circumstances attendant upon the occurrence, as near as we can ascertain, are as follows: Mr. Griffin had been in the city making purchases and started home in a four-seated buggy, in which were two little negro girls and Mr. Bud Lingo.

The buggy was drawn by mules and contained quite a load besides. – All went smoothly until the party reached a point but a short distance from Jeffersonville. Night had overtaken them and driving became difficult. The lines were in the hands of Mr. Lingo, and unconsciously he drove the team out of the road and straight into a terrible gulch, whose bottom was twenty or twenty-five feet below the road level. Over into this pit went buggy, mules, men and girls in one confused heap. There was a minute's frightful struggle, from which emerged Mr. Lingo and one of the girls. Mr. Griffin was under the wreck.

One of the girls ran to the residence of Mr. Bullock for help, which soon arrived, and the body of the unfortunate man was lifted from the gulch dead. An examination showed several limbs to be broken, but whether his neck was also broken, it was impossible to tell. His head was badly bruised, and it is thought death ensued from the weight of the vehicle falling upon it. Neither the mules nor the wagon was seriously injured.

The funeral of Mr. Griffin occurred yesterday. He leaves a wife and seven children. His father was formerly sheriff of Twiggs County, was a delegate to the late Congressional Convention of this district, and a delegate to the late Gubernatorial Convention.

March 24, 1881 ————————————————— (DJ)

HORRIBLE DEATH. A Citizen of Calhoun County Blows Out His Own Brains with a Shot Gun!

We have learned the particulars of a most shocking case of selfdestruction, which took place in the North West portion of Calhoun county on last Saturday. Our informant is Rev. W.T. Everett, who was present at the inquest, and heard the testimony adduced before the coroner's jury. The unfortunate victim who came to his death by his own hand was Mr. James W. Bass, who for many years had been a prominent citizen of Calhoun county. On last Saturday morning, Mr. Bass took his shot gun and started to walk through his plantation, and to note what damage had been done to his fences by the storm which had prevailed in that section during Friday night. Mr. Bass was accompanied by one of his sons when he left his residence about seven o'clock that morning. After walking about the premises for several hours the son returned to the house, leaving his father along, who he supposed was trying to shoot birds in the field . . . at half past ten or eleven o'clock, the report of a gun was heard in the direction of the field. At dinner time Mr. Bass had not come to the house. . . . After waiting for half an hour, Mrs. Bass sent two children in quest of their father. When the children reached a cotton-house that stood in the field about a quarter of a mile from the dwelling, they were astounded to find their father dead, with all of the top of his head shot off, and his clothing on fire. . . . In one of his hands was held an iron ramrod which he had doubtless used to fire off the gun, by pressing it on the trigger. . . . His head was torn literally to pieces, and his brains scattered in every direction. His hat could not be found at all, and all his clothing down to his waist was burned off, and his face and body were terribly disfigured by the fire. . . . After his death was made known to his wife, she remembered that when he arose from his bed that morning, he had remarked that he would never sleep there again. . . . Mr. Bass has had several attacks of mental aberration for a year or two prior to his death. . . . It is said that his skull was fractured fourteen or fifteen years ago by a blow on the head, and it may be that he never fully recovered from the effects of the fracture. At the time of his death he was about fifty years of age and leaves a wife and several children . . .

April 12, 1881 ———————————————— (AtC)

Berrien County News. Last week we gave our readers in a special from Dixonia, an account of the robbing and burning of Mr. Dan Lott's store, in Coffee County, and the arrest of Willie Johns (an assumed name, no doubt) who was charged with the crime. Thursday last we learned the following additional particulars: Soon after his arrest, Johns was placed in (the) charge of five men who left Dixonia with him. The fourth or fifth day afterwards the prisoner's body was found at Indian Ford, on Seventeen Mile Creek. His head was literally shot to pieces and a large portion of his brain was found tightly clasped in his hands. The sight was a most horrible and sickening one. At the inquest two of the men who had charge of the prisoner when he left Dixonia, testified that they did not know who the firing party were, and a verdict was rendered that deceased came to his death at the hands of an unknown party or parties. A family living near Indian Ford say that they distinctly heard the report of five guns in the direction of the ford, one day last week, and supposed it was some hunting party. It is rumored that the guards were overpowered by a body of unknown men who seized Johns and after taking him to Indian Ford, shot him to death.

Johns came to this place from Florida about three months ago, and found employment as a farm hand with Mr. James Paulk, of Irwin County. About three weeks ago he stated to Mr. Paulk that he had to return to Florida to sell four lots of land he owned there. Three weeks ago today, he came to Alapaha and took the east bound train in the evening. He was considerable (*sic*) under the influence of whiskey.

Last Tuesday a detective was in town in search of Johns. He stated that he was the last of a gang of four who murdered a man at some point of the Central Railroad in 1877, and that he had traced him to this section. The detective had in his possession a photograph of Johns, and proceeded to Coffee County, where he will, no doubt, have the body disinterred, as there is a reward of four hundred dollars for him, dead or alive, offered at the time of the murder.

It would seem that just as the iron fingers of the law were about to close on Johns for the commission of a terrible crime, fate led him before the inexorable court of Judge Lynch, who found him guilty of another and a later crime, tried the case, found him guilty, passed sentence of death upon him and executed it, thus verifying the old saying that "the way of the transgressor is hard."

June 2, 1881

QUEER OCCURRENCE. We learn that a little negro child on the plantation of Dr. B. R. Rieves, of this county, came to its death one day last week under very peculiar circumstances. It seems that a cat had caught a garter-snake and carried it alive into the house where the child was sitting alone on the floor. The child, in its admiration for the snake, took it up in its hands, and was bitten by the reptile on the arm, and from the effects of the bite the child died, notwithstanding all the efforts that were made to afford relief.

June 9, 1881

A BOY GETS KILLED IN WRESTLING. The *Dublin Post* says: The chapter of Laurens County tragedies is getting to be a long one. On last Sunday Clarence Cross and Willie Dominy, two little boys about 10 years of age, were wrestling near Mr. Marshall Scarborough's place, four or five miles west of Dublin, when there resulted a very singular tragedy, which was no less than the death of Clarence. They fell on their sides (what is known as a dog fall) and Willie got up, leaving Clarence on the ground. Those standing by noticed that he did not stir, and approaching they found that he was dead. He died without a moan or struggle or any other indication that anything was the matter with him. This sad and singular catastrophe was witnessed by three grown men whose concurrent testimony is substantially as above and there can be no doubt of its truth.

The coroner's jury, after a careful investigation, returned a verdict of death in a friendly wrestle. The coroner took Dr. Hightower with him, who after as careful an examination as the circumstances would admit, thought he was killed by concussion over the heart, caused by a fall on his own arm, which the testimony showed was doubled against his heart when he fell.

June 16, 1881 ———————————— (DJ)

The *Walton County News* states that the little boy of Rev. J.C. Burton, of Social Circle, who swallowed a button some ten days ago, died last Thursday.

June 16, 1881 ———————————— (DJ)

A little son of Mr. Daniel Lott, of Coffee County, was found under a wash trough dead. The supposition is that the little fellow was playing in the trough when it turned over, catching him under it and smothering him.

June 30, 1881 ———————————— (ET)

CRUSHED TO DEATH. Mr. Thomas Boothe of Cochran was killed on Monday last by the falling of a two-story framed building in process of construction. He was struck by some falling timbers, and lived but a short time. Other workmen on the building received slight injuries.

We find the following additional particulars of the affair in the *Macon Telegraph* of yesterday: Cochran, Ga., June 28. We sent you yesterday a postal mentioning the blowing down of a building and wounding of four or five, which also has proven fatal in the case of Mr. Thomas Boothe, one of the contractors engaged in building the Daisy House. Mr.

Boothe, with three or four men, were at work on the building on top, putting on the sheeting, about 4:15 p.m., when a wind and rain storm struck it and crushed it to earth with the men among and under the timbers, after a fall of 28 or 30 feet. All the men crawled out with light cuts and bruised, except Mr. Boothe, who was fastened under the timbers, badly mangled and crushed, from the effects of which he died this morning about nine o'clock. From what we can learn, all the other men are able to be up, though suffering from cuts and bruises.

July 7, 1881 ——————————— (ET)

A STRANGE AND SUDDEN DEATH. One of the strangest and most sad deaths of which we have account occurred in the family of Mr. T.G. Ramsay of Montgomery County, a distance of about six miles from our town on Monday night last, the particulars of which, as we get them from Mr. R. are about as follows:

Miss Missouri Sikes, aged about 13 years, who had been adopted in the family of her aunt, Mrs. Ramsay, when but a child, heard on Monday afternoon of the death of her brother at the home of Mr. Frank Sikes of Houston County, which news so shocked her nervous system that she at once retired to her room. The family thinking it best not to disturb her in her lamentation, she was left alone in her room for about one half hour when Mr. Ramsay, hearing her muttering to herself, went to her bedside and asked her if she was asleep. She replied that she was dying, the meanwhile her whole frame giving evidence of the correctness of the assertion by the most fearful contortions. Mr. R., after failing to induce her to take something to relieve her, immediately applied such external remedies as best suited to the case and dispatched for Dr. Mobley, who came and pronounced the case beyond his medical skill, and between the hours of 12 and 1 her spirit took its flight from this world of sin and pollution back to the God who gave it. We condole with the family, who had learned to love her as their own, in their sore affliction.

−Wiregrass Watchman.

July 14, 1881 ———————————— (ET)

SERVED HIM RIGHT. The LaGrange correspondent of the *Columbus Times* says:

Reliable news reached this city this afternoon that is most horrible in the extreme. Last Tuesday a white man by the name of Waldroup, living in Heard County, committed a fiendish outrage upon the person of a most respectable white lady, several miles west of Franklin, the county site of Heard. Satisfying his hellish purpose, the villain then cut his victim's throat from ear to ear, and made his escape. However, he was caught and taken to Franklin yesterday and placed in jail. The next morning the jail was visited by sixty men, who demanded that Waldroup be turned over to them. He was taken out and carried to the spot where he committed the deed, and chained to a stake and burned alive.

September 29, 1881 ———————————— (DJ)

A BLOODY ENCOUNTER. ONE MAN KILLED, ONE BRAINED, ONE DISABLED AND ONE BADLY STABBED. A bloody tragedy occurred in Paulding county, six miles southwest of Powder Springs, on last Friday. An old feud, originating from a law suit about a fence, has existed between Mr. James F. Cook and Mr. William Mitchell for a number of years. Mitchell lives in Douglas county and Cook in Paulding county, the county line runs between their houses. On Friday last Mitchell's hogs, as was frequently the case, were found depredating in Cook's field. Cook sent Mitchell word to drive them out. Mitchell sent word back to drive them out himself. Cook got his army musket and went to the field to drive out Mitchell's hogs. He was confronted by Mr. Mitchell, his son and a hired white man named Notingham. Abusive words were indulged in freely, and Cook attempted to evade the trio with a view to returning to his house. The Mitchells had their knives drawn and Notingham had his hand on his pistol and started towards Cook as if to head him off. Cook warned Notingham not to approach him but he refused to halt. Cook raised his gun, took aim and fired, the load of buckshot stricking (*sic*) Notingham just below the heart, killing him instantly. Old man Mitchell rushed on to Cook with his knife, and was knocked down by Cook with the musket. Cook then covered Mitchell, when Mitchell's son ran up and stabbed Cook twice in the back. By this time Cook's step-son, Mr. Joe Mahaffey, heard the noise and appeared on the scene. He picked up the empty musket, knocked young Mitchell out of the way, disabling his arm. Mitchell by this time had turned on Cook and got on top, Mahaffey then hit the eldest Mitchell on the head with his musket, fracturing his skull, from which brains oozed. Mahaffey then carried Cook to his house, and as he lifted him up the steps, he discovered a knife sticking to the hilt in his back, which he pulled out. Cook is in critical condition and Mitchell it is said cannot recover. Notingham was buried next day, but his brother, Judge Notingham, of Houston County, came up on Sunday and had the body taken up and shipped to Macon, where his widowed mother resides. It is a sad affair and is to be deeply regretted.

October 6, 1881 ⎯⎯⎯⎯⎯⎯⎯ (DJ)

JAIL BURNED AND A PRISONER ROASTED ALIVE. – The *Atlanta Post* learns from parties just from Dawsonville, Dawson county, that on last Thursday morning, about 2 o'clock, the jail in that town was found to be on fire.

"It appears that on the previous evening a burly negro, charged with burglarizing Hamp Smith's store, was arrested and confined in the jail. The negroe's (*sic*) name was Billups, said to have been once owned by Col. C.A. Billups, of Madison. During the night the negro conceived the idea of burning out of jail, and so he fired the building. The flames ran up between the logs and frame work, attacking the roof and rapidly getting beyond control. Seeing this, Billups began screaming for help at the top of his voice, and soon aroused the town. Men turned out and endeavored to rescue the tortured wretch, but it was impossible to approach and open the door. The cries of the poor fellow are described as the most heartrending, but no relief could save him. He was literally roasted alive as the angry flames consumed the building. When the ruins were searched his head and limbs were entirely consumed, and only the shriveled, charred trunk of the man could be distinguished."

December 2, 1881 ⎯⎯⎯⎯⎯⎯⎯ (HJ)

A TERRIBLE DEATH. Wednesday morning last our entire community was horrified by the reception of the news that the dwelling house of Dr. Lucius C. Norwood at Whitesville was burned the night before and that he was consumed alive in it. The particulars, so far as we have been able to learn, are these: About one o'clock he and his wife were alarmed by the cry of fire. Awaking they discovered it to be their dwelling. It had caught from the stove room. It seems that this was the second time it had caught fire in the same place, and on the first occasion the Doctor had extinguished it by going into the second story and putting water on it from there. Hence his first thought upon being aroused was to go to the same place. It is supposed that when he reached the room, he was overpowered by the smoke and met a death too horrible to think of. Only a few charred bones were found when the fire retarded. The deceased was a well-known and highly respected citizen of the county, a man of generous (illegible), had many strong friends and enjoyed a lucrative practice. His widow has the sympathy of a host of friends in the sad hour of trial.

(Additional comments in the *Dawson Weekly Journal:* He was about forty-five years of age. During the war he did gallant service with the Twentieth Georgia Regiment.)

March 17, 1882 ——————————— (HJ)

MR. JOHN FLOURNOY, AN OLD AND RESPECTED CITIZEN IS DEAD. He with several others went from church to Mr. J.T. Goodman's last first Sunday where they all dined happily together. A part of the contents of a bottle of "Rough on Rats" had been placed in a jar where there was some lard. But through some mistake, the cook, an ignorant old negro woman, got hold of it and placed it in the victuals of which they all partook. All present were more or less poisoned. Mr. Flournoy being old and diseased could not survive the poisonous effect. The whole community regret the sad occurrence. May his ashes repose in peace.

April 6, 1882 — (DJ)

DEATH OF CHARLES A. MCDONALD. On last Friday night just after the concert was over at the college, our community was shocked by the report that Charley McDonald, a young lawyer of our city, was killed by a passing freight train. . . . They found him about one mile from the depot, in the direction of Brown's Station, lying upon the track between the rails, face downward. Upon examination his skull was found to have been crushed by the car wheel for a distance of about three inches. Otherwise his body was not touched, not mutilated in the least. There are very many in our town who believe that Charley sought his own destruction, therefore, it is claimed by some that it was a clear case of suicide. But by others it is thought that he was overcome by the influence of liquor, and in walking along the Railroad sank down in a state of unconsciousness and thus was run over and killed . . .

June 22, 1882 — (ECN)

On Saturday morning, June 17th, a terrible accident occurred at Kingston (Bartow County), on the Western and Atlantic Railroad, which resulted in the almost instantaneous death of Andrew J. West, the engineer, and George Bass, the fireman. The switches for the sidelings (*sic*) were left open and a train at almost lightening (*sic*) speed crashed into cars standing on the side track.

MR. HENRY GUEST COMES TO A HORRIBLE DEATH.
The sad news of the horrible death on Tuesday the 13th inst.,
of Mr. Henry Guest at the steam saw mills of Mr. J.F. Fuller,
four miles below Dublin, reached us on Thursday last. But as
we were not fully informed as to the particulars, we copy the
following from the *Dublin Gazette:*

"A most horrible accident causing death in twelve hours,
occurred at Fuller's mill about four miles from Dublin last
Tuesday. Mr. Henry Guest, a young man who had been working at the mill as a saw hand received his death in the following manner: Mr. Fuller has a mill for sawing raft timber. To
do this he has a large saw for squaring up and a small one
for butting. Mr. Guest was dragging off slabs from the large
saw, and to do this it was necessary to walk backward pulling
the timber with a hook. By some means the hold of the hook
gave way and poor Guest fell backward upon the small saw.
The saw first struck the left shoulder and then about half way
down the left side, reaching forward and cutting the abdomen open from bottom to top, entirely disemboweling him.
Three of the intestines were cut entirely in two, and in several places they were cut into, leaving orifices from an eighth
to an inch long. Drs. Harrison and Hightower were called in,
and the wounded man attended. The wound was sewed up
and opiates given to afford temporary ease. He lingered in
this condition perfectly rational, for about twelve hours and
then died.

Mr. Guest was born in Montgomery County, where his
mother and other family members still live. His father, Mr.
Benjamin Guest, having died in prison during the war, Henry
became an inmate in the family of Mr. Fuller when quite a
boy, and be it said to his credit he not only remained with

him till he was 21 years of age, which we believe was sometime in the early part of the present year, but so pleasant and agreeable was the relationship between them, that after his majority, he accepted a situation offered him at the mill where he continued faithfully to discharge his duty to the day of his death."

January 20, 1883 ——————— (TT)

FROM THE ALTAR TO THE GRAVE. A few days since the Rev. Elijah Blackshear was marrying a couple in the lower edge of Colquitt County, a Mr. James White and Miss Deliah Anderson; just as he pronounced them man and wife, the minister fell dead. It is supposed that he died from heart disease. Mr. Blackshear was something over 54 years old. Verily in this instance 'twas but one step from the altar to the grave.

February 1, 1883 ——————— (CT)

On Friday morning last, at the pauper farm near the town of Franklin, Heard County, Sanford Babb, an aged pauper, was found frozen to death. A coroner's jury investigated the case and arrived at a verdict that the deceased had come to his death by freezing for want of proper attention.

April 12, 1883 ——————— (ET)

A TERRIBLE DEATH. A LITTLE GIRL BITTEN BY A MAD DOG AND DIED IN THE GREATEST AGONY.
From the *Hawkinsville Dispatch*: On Friday night

last closed the terrible suffering of the little seven year old daughter of Mrs. Hill, who resides in the Sixth District of Dooly County, near the Pulaski Line. The child was bitten forty-three days before by a mad dog that came to Mrs. Hill's house. The child was bitten in the face, and the wound had nearly healed. Drs. Boatright and Johnson warned Mrs. Hill of the impending danger, and she was unusually careful and watchful.

On Wednesday of last week, she observed that the child acted strangely, and had an unnatural look in its eyes. She immediately sent for her brother, Mr. John Hoggsett, who came at once, and in order to test the child's disease he had a pan of water brought and put before it. At the sight of the water the child almost went into convulsions, and the poor mother was then convinced that her child was attacked with hydrophobia. The neighbors, in their sympathy, came, but the terrible agony of the child continued for two days. Two or three persons were constantly required to hold it in the bed and prevent its violence. The sight of water, or even the sound of water dropping upon the floor would throw it into convulsions. One of these paroxysms lasted three hours, and only terminated with complete physical exhaustion.

We conversed with several of the neighbors who came to Hawkinsville on Saturday, and they testified that they had never witnessed more excruciating agony than was endured by the child. It was very intelligent, and when its mother dis-covered that something was wrong, and sent for her brother, she was careful to keep from the child any knowledge of the object of the visit. The day before the little girl was bitten the same dog appeared upon the place of Mr. Robert T. Williams and bit a goose that hissed at it. The dog was driven away and the goose died.

Other dogs were bitten in the neighborhood. The dog

of Mr. A.J. Woods was bitten, and to guard against danger he contained the dog in a pen. Within the usual time the dog showed signs of hydrophobia and was promptly killed, though it was considered a very valuable animal.

May 24, 1883 ——————————— (CT)

Mr. H. Lawrence, a photographer who had a gallery at this place in 1881 and 1882, died at Birmingham, Alabama, on the 9th instant from poison while mixing chemicals. He was an Englishman and had been a sailor and traveled almost all over the world. He had just been married four months and leaves a young and affectionate wife.

June 7, 1883 ——————————— (CT)

Last week, on the plantation of Capt. John A. Coffee, nine miles from Hawkinsville, a negro boy accidentally broke his neck jumping head foremost into the creek, where he and several companions were taking a bath. Death was the result.

July 26, 1883 ——————————— (CT)

Mr. H.H. Loomis, one of the keepers of supplies of the East Tennessee, Virginia and Georgia Railroad at Atlanta, fell from the window of a hotel in Macon last week while asleep, and was killed.

October 10, 1883 — (HJ)

A little five year old daughter of Mr. Mitchell, who lives near Albany in Lee County, met a horrible death on Tuesday last. A loaded gun fell from the rack, sending the entire charge through the child's abdomen. While suffering the agonies of a dreadful death, she would beg for water, which, as fast as she drank it, ran out of the ghastly hole in her side.

November 15, 1883 — (CT)

Mr. W.J. Whitten, a train hand on the W. & A. Road, lost his life last week in uncoupling an engine from a freight train while it was running at the rate of six miles an hour. He fell on the track and was cut in half by five cars passing over him. His home was at Tunnel Hill.

December 6, 1883 — (BD)

Mr. Jeff Horn, an industrious young farmer, living in the lower portion of Thomas County, met with a fatal accident last Saturday morning. It seems that he was loading a wagon with cotton seed at his gin house, and attempted to jump from an elevation of some ten feet into the wagon. He slipped and fell, falling on his breast across the edge of the wagon bed. Death ensued in 15 or 20 minutes.

December 13, 1883 — (CT)

Two weeks ago a little son of squire W.M. Smith, of the 24th District, about nine or ten years old, was caught in the gearing of an old style cotton gin and horribly mangled. Every bone in his body was broken. The *Times* extends sympathy to the bereaved parents.

February 14, 1884 ——————— (CT)

On Saturday morning about 1 o'clock, the house of Mr. Asberry Vann, four miles above Kennesaw, was destroyed by fire. Vann was found burned to death in the smoking ruins. It seems Vann had been drinking, and abused and choked his wife. She left and went to her father's house some 200 yards off. Vann, in his drunken condition, put some pieces of railings in the open fire place, the ends protruding and resting on the floor. The fire was communicated to the floor this way.

February 21, 1884 ——————— (CT)

A FEARFUL DEATH. *Rome Courier*: Mr. John McCloud, of Desoto, brakeman on a freight train on the E.T.V. & G. Railroad, died at Dalton Friday night. He was on top of the freight car working the brake when the train passed under a low bridge and McCloud was knocked down between two cars. He fell across the track and was passed over by four cars and cut almost completely in half. He will be interred in Myrtle Hill Cemetery this morning. He was thirty years old and leaves a wife and three children.

February 21, 1884 ——————— (CT)

DIED. *Cartersville American*: Mr. Miles G. Dobbins, Jr. told us of an accident at the Dobbins Ore Mine a few miles east of town. The bank caved in at 2:30 o'clock yesterday, killing a negro named Jessie Mimms instantly and fatally wounding Taylor Buford, another negro man, whose recovery is considered impossible. Miles Dobbins was in the mine at the time and barely had time to escape before the dirt fell in.

June 19, 1884 ——————————— (DJ)

KILLED IN BED. *Hawkinsville Dispatch*: Mr. Joseph B. Dykes, at Cochran died on Saturday night last. He had retired to bed at the usual hour. About one o'clock his wife heard him struggling and breathing as if with great difficulty. She placed her hand upon his head and found it wet. Jumping out of bed she called Jimmie Clark and lighted a lamp. The light of the lamp revealed that the hand and arm of Mrs. Dykes were wet with blood. Among the first to reach the scene was Mr. B.B. Dykes, the aged father of the young man. Joe was dead in a few minutes, never having spoken.

The deceased had no enemies and was loved and esteemed by all his kindred. No reason for his death can be given, more than it was caused by a gun or pistol ball fired by some reckless person from the street. The ball had passed through a glass window and it appears Mr. Dykes had raised himself in bed just about that time. The ball entered the head just back of the left ear, and the brains came out of the wound.

The deceased was about twenty-nine years of age, and the youngest son of Mr. B.B. Dykes. He was a prominent member of the Baptist Church. . . . The grief of his widow and his aged father and brothers and sisters cannot be realized. Besides, he leaves two little children. The remains were buried on Monday at the family burial ground near Coley's Station.

June 26, 1884 ——————————— (CT)

FOUR MEN KILLED. *The Albany News*: Four men were killed Friday and several others were severely injured by the explosion of the boiler at the brickyard of Messrs. Hobbs, Fields, and Davis. Albert Miles, Manuel Grant and Mat Chapman were killed outright. Willis Watson, of Lee County, has a fearful wound in the head. Matt Hill, the engineer, was scalded and fearfully bruised, and died just as he reached his home.

June 26, 1884 ——————————— (ECN)

We learn that Mr. George W. Hamans, of Irwin County, died on the 7th inst. It will be remembered that Mr. Hamans had a difficulty with Mr. Jack Sumner in January last, and in the fight Mr. Hamans had his finger bitten. The wound refused to heal, and the system became poisoned from the foul blood. The doctors finally decided that Mr. Harman's (*sic*) life could only be saved by amputation, and the finger was removed from the hand. The poison had already gained too great a circulation in the blood, and Mr. Hamans continued to grow worse, and died as stated a few days ago.

An inquest was held, and evidence taken. The physician gave it as his opinion that death was caused from the bitten finger. A warrant was issued for Mr. Sumner, who was arrested, and he has probably given bond for his appearance at the fall term of Superior Court.

—Hawkinsville Dispatch.

October 9, 1884 ───────── (DJ)

A HORRIBLE ACCIDENT. Perry, Georgia, October 4: Yesterday morning at 9 o'clock, Mr. Roundtree Bryant met with a frightful accident, resulting in his death last night at 8 o'clock. While running the water gin of Mr. W. H. Houser, on Mossy Creek, seven miles from here, his entire left arm was drawn into the saws, horribly mangling it and fastening it so that it took a half hour to get him loose, which was done by taking the gin to pieces. Drs. Ross and Greene, of Fort Valley, were sent for and amputated the arm above the elbow, but the shock and previous loss of blood proved fatal. He leaves a wife and two children to mourn his death.

October 16, 1884 ───────── (BD)

AN OBITUARY NOTICE of the late James M. Wiggins in the *Swainsboro Itemiser* states that deceased led a life of poverty and toil, and that the property to which he was entitled through his mother was kept from him by his father. Wiggins finally went mad, and as there was not enough room for him in the asylum he was placed in the county jail, where he killed himself by beating his head against the wall. During his confinement he was never visited by his father and he was buried as a pauper.

November 25, 1884 ───────── (HJ)

A little son of Mr. Shackleford of Heard county was found dead in the lint room of his father's ginhouse the other night. He was not missed until supper time, when a search was instituted with the above result. It is supposed that in jumping into the cotton he struck his head against the wall and was stunned, and being unable to get out of the lint was suffocated.

December 18, 1884 ———————— (ECN)

We regret to hear of a sad accident that happened to a son of Mr. R.A. Lewis, on Sunday last. He was sent to a persimmon tree, by his mother, to get her some persimmons. While up the tree he stepped on a limb which gave way under him, and he fell to the ground. The fall gave him internal injuries which caused his death on Monday night. He was a lad of some ten or twelve years old, and was very sprightly.

February 12, 1885 ———————— (BD)

ANOTHER STARTLING SUICIDE occurred at Thomasville on Friday last. In a dilapidated old boarding house, kept by his mother, Eason B. Allen, an unmarried man, thirty-five years old, blew off half his head with a shot gun. His mother says she has feared his mind was a little off for the past few days. He went at noon to go on a train to Florida. The train had left, and he went immediately home to his room and emptied the contents of the gun into his head. He fell on a trunk in the corner of the room. His brains were scattered generally. Breathing continued for an hour after the shot was fired.

May 21, 1885 ——————————————— (CT)

Mr. J.P. Cole, of Spring Place, met a horrible death last Thursday. He slipped on rocks while on Cohutta Mountain, near the "Legal Tender Mine" of which he was one of the owners, and fell two hundred feet. He died at ten o'clock that night of severe internal injuries. He was a leading merchant, thirty-five years of age and leaves a wife and two small children.

December 4, 1885 ——————————— (GH)

DEATH OF MAJOR HALL. On last Sunday morning at five o'clock, Major Isaac R. Hall, a former citizen of Greene County, died at his home in Oglethorpe County. Mr. Hall had been in feeble health for some time. He was confined to his bed, and was gradually sinking. On last Thursday night, about ten o'clock, he got out of his bed near the fireplace. His brother, who was in another bed nearby heard him call out, "Pull me out! Pull me out!" His brother thought that he was talking in his sleep, but he rose and saw Major Hall lying upon his back in the fireplace.

He jumped from his bed and rushed to him. He was lying with his head far back in the fireplace against the chimney, his shoulders, neck and back upon a bed of hot coals. His brother raised Major Hall and found that he had been severely burned. A physician was sent for and Dr. Willingham, of Crawford, responded. The burns were dressed and the sufferer made as comfortable as possible. Despite all the attention given him, he continued to sink, and on Sunday morning, peacefully died.

The funeral took place at two o'clock Monday afternoon,

and was largely attended. The services were conducted by Rev. Henry Newton, of Union Point, and J.G. Gibson, of Crawford. Major Hall's death is deeply lamented. He was for a number of years Clerk of the Superior Court of Greene County, and was loved by all. Major Hall was about 90 years of age.

January 14, 1886 —————————— (CT)

A negro named George Kirkland, in Savannah, bet some friends one dollar he could drink a quart of whisky on Christmas morning. He drank the liquor and was found dead on Sunday, occasioned by alcohol on the brain and exposure.

January 14, 1886 —————————— (CT)

William Starr, the miller at High Shoals, in Walton County, wanted whisky so badly last Sunday that he drank two ounces of the alcoholic fluid used in patent smoothing irons. He was buried on Saturday.

March 11, 1886 —————————— (CT)

HOED TO DEATH. Buchanan, Georgia, March 3rd: Eight miles east of this place, yesterday at 8 o'clock in the morning, the hands saw George Elliot on his knee and Henry Norris standing over him with a drawn hoe, ready to strike a second time. In less time than it takes to write, Norris had beat Elliot's head into a jelly, his brains and skull being scattered about the ground. When asked why he did this, Norris said the deceased asked him for a chew of tobacco yesterday, and then threw it away. Some think that he is crazy.

April 22, 1886 ———————————————— (DJ)

Calhoun Times: Wednesday morning while Mrs. H.G. Findley at Fairmount was out looking after her work, her ten year old son, Colquitt, was taken with an apoplectic fit and she found him lying full length on a bed of burning embers. He has a frightful burn on one side of his face, one ear, his right hand and thigh. One eye and his tongue are also badly burned. His death is only a matter of time.

September 23, 1886 ———————————————— (CT)

Thomas M. Buckley and Cal M. Farris, both of Atlanta, were killed on the 15th instant at ten minutes past 6 o'clock, one half mile east of Chattanooga. Buckley was on the engine and Farris was the fireman. Coming around a bend, on a high embankment, the train struck a cow and went tumbling down the embankment, carrying both engineer and fireman with it. The baggage car and second class coach were derailed.

November 11, 1886 ———————————————— (ET)

SUICIDE AT VALDOSTA. – Valdosta, Ga., November 6 – At about 3 o'clock this afternoon, Taylor Hunt, of this place, was killed by the east bound way freight train. The train, having backed off the side track, was pulling up slowly at the warehouse for the purpose of discharging and loading freight. Hunt was standing close to the moving train on the Patterson street crossing, and threw himself between two of the box cars, apparently with the intention of committing suicide. Six truck wheels passed over his body, killing him instantly. Hunt was a middleaged man, and up to a short time before his death was engaged in the whisky business in this town. He has led a reckless and dissipated life for many years. He was never married, but leaves many relatives and friends here. No fault can be charged to the railroad company.

July 6, 1887 — (DCJ)

A HORRIBLE DEATH. As we prepare to go to press the sad news reaches us of the accidental killing on the morning of the 4th inst., of Mr. Simon L. Godwin, a young man in the employ of Messrs. Willcox and Powell, lumber manufacturers on the Ocmulgee River, some ten miles distant from Eastman.

From the best information obtainable it appears that the unfortunate man, while in the discharge of his duty as head block setter, let his foot slip, which precipitated him head foremost on the rapidly revolving saw, the fearful machine striking him on the head and passing downward severed his right arm and passed nearly directly through his body, tearing the flesh from the bones in a terrible manner and literally strewing the works around with brains and blood – a sight most awful to contemplate and worse to witness.

A coroner's jury was empaneled, and a verdict sustained the above facts as given by our informant. The deceased was a native of North Carolina, and we tender our sympathy to near and dear friends at his former home, to whom the intelligence of his terrible ending will be received with bitter pangs of regret.

September 14, 1887 ───────── (DCJ)

Miss McArthur, of Eastman, was thrown from a buggy Friday and instantly killed. Mr. Pierson, her escort, was dangerously injured. Miss McArthur, who was a niece of Mr. McArthur of the legislature, was engaged to be married to Mr. Pierson, and their wedding was to take place at the residence of Mr. Tup Holt, in Macon, within a few days. The young man's father, who is quite wealthy, had built the young couple an elegant residence, and furnished it with every modern convenience that would add to their comfort. They started Friday morning to drive to their new home in a buggy, and on the way the horse ran away. Miss McArthur was thrown out and instantly killed, and Mr. Pierson's shoulder was dislocated.

–Savannah Times.

January 18, 1888 ───────── (WGT)

POISONED BY A BRASS HARMONICA. From the *Albany News.* John Lamar Acree, the sixteen-year-old boy of Mr. J.L. Acree, of lower Lee County, died on last Thursday, after a lingering and painful illness, the result of blood poisoning from a brass harmonica. The harmonica was a Christmas purchase of the boy's and in blowing it the cankered brass poisoned his mouth and lungs.

Drs. Davis and McMillan were called in, but no physician's skill could arrest the deadly effects of the poison.

January 24, 1888 ——————————— (WGT)

CUT IN TWO. Horrible Death of a Child Near Milledgeville. Milledgeville, January 18. – A horrible accident is just reported on the Central railroad at a point a half mile from the city. A negro woman with her little four year old boy attempted to cross the track just as the train was approaching. She got safely over, but the engine knocked down the little fellow and his body was cut in halves. The particulars of the accident are meagrely (*sic*) reported, too meagrely to warrant the opinion as to the responsibility for carelessness.

February 1, 1888 ——————————— (MoM)

We learn from a dispatch to the *Atlanta Constitution*, that Hon. Joel H. Coney, member of the legislature from Laurens County, died on the morning of January 24th. He died from lockjaw, from a splinter in his hand. He was the wealthiest citizen of Laurens County . . .

March 21, 1888 ——————————— (MoM)

HORRIBLE ACCIDENT ON THE S.F. & W. RAILROAD. Twenty-Two Persons Killed, And Many Others Likely To Die.

The fast mail train from Savannah, on the Savannah Florida & Western R. R. fell from a high trestle at Hurrican (*sic*) Creek, a mile and a half from Blackshear, at 9:30 o'clock Saturday morning, entirely demolishing the train, and killing or wounding nearly all on board. Twenty-two persons were instantly killed, and many others are likely to die of their injuries. Among the killed were John H. Pate, of Hawkinsville, brother of Judge Pate; W.B. Geiger, salesman for Mohr Bros., Savannah; John T. Ray and daughter, Blackshear; C.A. Fulton, Master of Transportation of the Brunswick and Western railway; and many others. George Gould, son of Jay Gould of New York, was on the train, with his wife, and both were injured though slightly. The accident was caused by a broken truck under the baggage car, which caused the train to jump the track. The scene of the disaster was indescribably horrible. Thirty-four persons were wounded, seven of whom it is thought will die.

November 28, 1888 ——————— (DJ)

Edgar Perkins, a young man of Quitman County, was killed Saturday afternoon while packing cotton. He was standing on the platform of the screw and one of the leavers (*sic*) caught him on one of the upright posts, breaking his neck and crushing his head almost to a jelly.

March 21, 1889 ——————— (MoM)

STARVED HIMSELF TO DEATH. John L. Adams was put in jail in Macon sometime since on a charge of forgery. He refused to eat or take any nourishment whatever, and last week, at the end of a thirteen days' fast, nature gave way, and he died of starvation. He was a young man of good education and fair promise, and well connected.

March 21, 1889 —————————— (MoM)

Judge G.M.T. Ware, of the county court of Wayne, was run over and instantly killed by a passing train in Jesup on the 16th instant. He was one of Jesup's oldest and most prominent citizens, and highly respected there.

October 23, 1889 —————————— (DJ)

FIRE. One entire block of business houses is in ruins and two of Judge James Guerry's children, little Russell and Claude Guerry have been killed by falling walls. Judge Guerry was in Atlanta with a young son, Goode, at the time. L.A. Lowrey lost cotton, guano, bagging and ties, A.J. Carver lost his warehouse, W.F. Talbot the grocer lost $1,500.00, C.L. Mize lost books, confectionery, millinery, W.C. Kendrick the druggist lost $4,000.00, G.W. Eubanks lost general merchandise, F. Bethune's bar lost $5,000.00. T.H. Thurmond, the dentist, lost instruments and office fixtures, W.F. Locke lost a brick building, J.R. Janes' estate lost two brick stores and one office, H. Rogers lost a brick building, Dr. R.T. Hillman lost all office fixtures, books and instruments, N.W. Dozier lost 40 bales of cotton, W.C. Paschal lost 21 bales of cotton, W.R. Baldwin's News building was damaged, but insured. Mr. L.A. Lowrey says he will not engage in the warehouse business any more. Charlie Ridgeway, the colored boy who was so badly injured by the falling walls is still alive and it is thought that he will recover. Bill Talbot has received a letter from Smith & Gordon, his creditors in Macon, offering him goods and money to start in business again. Judge Homer Bell is using a crutch on account of having an ankle badly sprained at the fire. Bud Farrar lost about forty dollars by the burn. Russell and Claude Guerry were laid to rest Saturday afternoon, side by side, as they died.

November 6, 1889 ——————— (DJ)

DIED. Mrs. Sarah Jordan of Calhoun County, who was thrown from a buggy by a runaway horse, receiving serious injuries, departed this life at her home three miles from Leary last Tuesday night. Mrs. Jordan was recovering from her injuries when she was attacked with erysipelas in her face Tuesday afternoon, and died at half past ten o'clock that night from its effects. She was the mother of Messrs. Miles, Reuben and Tommie Jordan and Mrs. Barney Pace.

January 29, 1892 ——————— (TG)

HEARTRENDING TRAGEDY. Stephen Weston, of Westonia, Accidentally Kills One of His Sons.

In his newspaper career of more than twenty years the editor of the *Gazette* has never been called upon to chronicle a sadder tragedy than the one which occurred at Westonia, Coffee County, last Friday.

Mr. Stephen Weston has three sons, one a lad of seven years of age. On the day of the tragedy Mr. Weston was shooting birds with a Winchester rifle, had killed two and given them to two of his sons and leaving the seven-year-old without a bird. He asked his father to kill him one also; he consented, and father and son went to a small field, near their house, to fulfill the promise.

The lad went round the field to scare up some birds, which he had located while the father went up the fence row to hide himself from the birds and enable him to get as close to the birds as possible. One of the birds lighted on the fence just in front of Mr. Weston and he shot at it. The ball struck a lightwood post that was standing beyond but in line with the bird but a little quartering, passed through the sap part, glanced from the hard wood and passed through the boy's brain and killed him, notwithstanding he was standing almost at right angles from the post and not less than fifty yards away.

The grief stricken father is a nephew of Capt. S.R. Weston, of Albany, and a cousin of Mr. Jesse D. Weston, from whom we learned the details of the sad accident.

June 3, 1892 ——————————————— (TG)

A SAD DEATH. From Mr. Williams, partner of Rev. R.W. Huckabee of Sparks, who was in Tifton last Saturday night on route home from a visit to Albany, we secured the following facts relative to the sad death on Monday of last week of Jordan Dupree whose father, Mr. G.R. Dupree, lives in the vicinity of Afton postoffice, this county.

He attended school last summer and one day, during the noon respite, while at play with several of his schoolmates, chasing each other around the house, he suddenly collided with one of the girls engaged in the play with much force – both being knocked down. Developments showed that the girl had received little or no injury but that his skull was fractured just above the left eye.

Surgical aid was immediately summoned and every possible means used for his relief, but without avail. It was finally determined, about fourteen days before the young man's death that the piece of skull was pressing too severely against the brain and should be removed. To perform this operation Drs. Talley, of Valdosta, and R.J. Goodman, of Sparks, were called. They came and performed the operation, but it gave no relief, and he died in the greatest agony.

The young man's parents are nearly heartbroken with grief, and they have the sympathy of all their neighbors and friends in their hour of deep distress. *The Gazette* adds its sincere condolence.

August 5, 1892 ———————————— (TG)

Capt. W.C. Ashley met a violent death at his home in Irwinville last week. On Wednesday while having his dwelling prized, and while sitting on or holding to one of the poles used in prizing the house, some of the props slipped, upsetting the one Mr. Ashley was on. He was thrown several feet in the air, and when he came down his head struck a block fracturing the skull. He lingered till Thursday when he died.

—Douglas Breeze.

September 30, 1892 ———————————— (LR)

THE MOST HEARTRENDING ACCIDENT that has happened hereabouts for years, occurred near here yesterday afternoon. At about 3 o'clock, Mrs. Burney, accompanied by Dock Jarrett, left the home of her son, Mr. D.L. Burney, in Chambers county, Ala., on her way to town to take the evening train for her home in Texas. They had proceeded but about 1/3 of a mile from the house and were driving across the Hill crossing, 2 miles from town, when the North bound "Cannon Ball" train, under full speed, struck the buggy square in the center. Mrs. Burney was killed instantly, Mr. Jarrett severely and seriously injured, the mule killed outright and the buggy literally dashed to pieces. In Mr. Jarrett's case, the best is hoped, though the worst is feared. Dr. Cooper, surgeon of the road, was on board train, returning from the Opelika wreck, and carefully attended to the wounded man as soon as Conductor Bell could stop his train. Drs. J.W. Griggs, C.T. Pattillo and Hodges have since been attending Mr. Jarrett. Mrs. Burney was something over sixty years of age and was one of the best of women. . . . Her remains are to be interred in the West Point cemetery this (Wednesday) afternoon. Rev. W.R. Foote will conduct the burial service.

May 19, 1893   (DTJ)

Chas. Stubbs, a teamster in the employ of Mr. T.S. Willcox, was instantly killed Monday morning, by his team of oxen running away, cart turning over and wheel running over his head.

October 13, 1893   (DTJ)

THE MILL ROCKS BURSTED. (*sic*) At the grist mill of Mr. A.Y. McEachern, near Jacksonville, Ga., last Friday, the rocks bursted (*sic*) and Mr. McEachern was killed instantly. Two others, who were near, were seriously, if not fatally, injured and the fourth man had a leg broken.

February 16, 1894   (DTJ)

A FATAL ACCIDENT. A frightful accident occurred Saturday, nine miles north of Mount Vernon, in Montgomery

County, in which William Adams was killed and Riley Adams seriously wounded. Riley Adams owned a steam grist mill and had William employed to help him run it. At 10 o'clock the grist rocks burst, and fragments hit young Adams in the forehead, breaking his skull and killing him almost instantly. Another fragment hit Riley Adams, owner of the mill, in the breast, and made a serious, though it is not thought a fatal wound. It is not known what caused the rock to explode.

–Telfair Enterprise.

March 16, 1894 ———————————— (DTJ)

A little girl, aged about ten, of Mr. Wm. Furney, who lives near Cochran, was bitten on the neck by a mad dog on the first day of February, but the wound soon healed and nothing more was thought of the matter until last Friday, when the child was taken suddenly ill and on Saturday died in great agony. She would frequently call for water, at the sight of which she would turn away with horror and go into violent convulsions. The attending physician pronounced it a clear case of hydrophobia. *–Dispatch and News.*

November 6, 1894 ———————————— (DTJ)

A HORRIBLE DEATH. While playing around a hot tub of syrup on Thursday afternoon, the 15th inst., little Della Smith, the four-year-old daughter of Mr. and Mrs. J.H. Smith, near Mattie, by some means slipped and fell into same. The child lived in great agony, though without complaining, until Friday afternoon about sunset.

February 8, 1895 ——————————— (DTJ)

A FEARFUL ACCIDENT. Tragic Ending Of A Promising Young Life. While Out Hunting, Mr. J.N. Harper Is Killed By The Accidental Discharge Of His Gun.

Late on Thursday afternoon of last week (the 31st ult.) our little city was considerably shocked by the report that Mr. J.N. Harper had accidentally shot himself while out hunting, and shortly afterwards saddened by the intelligence that he was dead.

The sad affair occurred as follows: Mr. Harper and his brother-in-law, Mr. W.H. Cotter, had been out hunting and on their way back home stopped for a few moments at the farm of Mr. Cotter, a few miles from Eastman, and alighted. On getting back into the buggy, in some manner Mr. Harper's gun was jarred out and struck the wheel, causing the weapon to fire, and the entire load to take effect in Mr. Harper's right eye, tearing that side of his head almost completely away.

With all possible haste Dr. J.D. Herrman was summoned and responded immediately, but to no avail; he met a wagon out a mile or two containing the lifeless body of Mr. Harper. Death had been instantaneous. The body was carried to the residence of Mr. Cotter and remained until Saturday morning, when interred in Woodlawn Cemetery in the presence of many sorrowing relatives and friends – Rev. R.L. Wiggins performing the last rites. Funeral services were conducted at the Methodist church Saturday morning by Revs. R.L. Wiggins and J.C. Brewton in a most solemn and impressive manner.

January 3, 1896

A SAD FATE. Mr. Joe Hargraves a young man about 18 years old, formerly of Augusta, Ga., but who had been working at the steam mill of Messers.(*sic*) B.B. Gray & Bro., for the last two years, had the misfortune on Monday, December 23 to fall from the tram engine while it was in motion, and to have both legs mangled so badly that amputation was necessary. The operation was successful but he was so weak from the loss of blood that he died one hour after the operation.

A sad story is connected with this accident. When Hargraves was a child his father died, and his mother being too poor to support him, she put him in an orphans' home in Augusta. She afterwards went to Savannah, leaving her boy to grow up in the home. When he became large enough to support himself he left the home and went out into the world to make his way. He came to Pine [missing] eight months ago and Mr. Ben Gray gave him employment in his mill. After working a while he became a great favorite with every body, and his general proficiency won him a promotion as fireman on the tram engine. Two months ago he heard of his mother in Savannah and at once wrote to her. His letter was soon rewarded by a reply and a correspondence between them ensued. Just before Christmas he wrote his mother a letter that he would go to Savannah to spend Christmas with her and she in the mean time had sent him a Christmas box as a token of love for her long lost boy. He never knew that the box was in the express office awaiting his return from his trip on the tram, and his mother came to spend the Christmas with him, but he was dead.

January 3, 1896 (DTJ)

KILLED BY A LOCOMOTIVE. On Saturday, December the 20th, ult, little Johnnie Sapp, the son of Widow Tiny Sapp, was killed by a locomotive at Frazier.

It seems that Johnnie was playing at the station with a number of other children. The passenger train does not stop at Frazier and came through at a good speed, when Johnnie attempted to run across the track in front of the locomotive. He was too slow and the bumper of the pilot struck him on the neck, breaking it and throwing the little fellow to one side.

It will be remembered by those in a position to know, that the father of Johnnie was killed at Kramer by a locomotive of the same road in a similar manner six or seven years ago. Our deepest sympathy goes out to the bereaved mother.

March 20, 1896 (DB)

A LITTLE GIRL BURNED. About two weeks ago little Gussie, the four year old daughter of Mr. Fred Ricketson who lives near Pearson, was standing near a burning log heap when her clothes caught on fire, and before anyone could get to her she was burned so badly that it was evident that she could not live. After a season of intense suffering and a hard struggle for life, the dear little girl gave up the strife and passed away into the beyond. The grief stricken parents have our profoundest sympathy in their sore bereavement.

November 6, 1896 ——————— (DTJ)

RIGHT ARM TORN OFF. On Saturday, the 24th ult., Mr. Monroe Jump, a young gentleman of Rhine, happened to the misfortune of getting his hand caught in the gin at that place. His right arm was completely torn off and that night he died in great agony. Mr. Jump was a nephew of Coroner Jump of this county. The bereaved ones have our sympathy.

January 15, 1897 ——————— (DTJ)

HUBERT ROGERS IS KILLED. While Out Hunting Near Eastman Last Friday Morning. It was his own accident. In Attempting To Get Over A Fence With His Gun It Explodes With Fatal Results To The Lad.

On last Friday morning, the 8th inst., at about 8 o'clock, Homer and Hubert Rogers, two sons of Mr. and Mrs. Fletcher Rogers, an esteemed citizen of this city, went hunting and after reaching the woods became separated somewhat.

The rail fence around the farm of Mr. Wesley Rogers, near town is quite high. Coming to this fence, Hubert, the younger, commenced to climb it, first putting his gun between the rails and attempting to pull it through. The gun was in some manner shocked and exploded – the entire load of one barrel entering the right leg above the knee.

Hubert at once called loudly to his brother, Homer, who was some distance away. When Homer reached his brother, he found him upon the ground with his right leg broken all to pieces and bent under him. Aid was immediately summoned and the unfortunate lad was at once taken to the drug store of Dr. J.L. Estes, where, despite the combined efforts of that physician and Dr. J.B. Clark, he died at a quarter past

1 o'clock that afternoon – the shock was entirely too great to be withstood.

At 3 o'clock Saturday afternoon funeral services were conducted at the Methodist church by Rev. W.J. Robertson, after which the body was laid to rest in Woodlawn Cemetery in the presence of a large number of heartbroken relatives and sorrowing friends. Hubert was fifteen years of age. He was a quiet, gentle lad . . . and was much admired by all.

January 29, 1897 ———— (DTJ) —

HE DRANK TOO MUCH BOOZE. We learn that a Mr. Cox, who came to this county a few years ago from North Carolina, and was employed at the sawmill of Mr. W.L. Powell, came to an untimely death on Saturday night of last week. It seems that Mr. Cox, in company with a number of other young men, were on their way to a social gathering in the neighborhood. There was a jug of whiskey in the party, and Mr. Cox continued to take copious draughts of the juice, despite the entreaties of his companions not to imbibe so freely.

Cox continued to drink, however, and was soon unable to travel. His friends then placed him in an old vacant house by the roadside and continued on their way, intending to arouse the unfortunate man upon their return from the entertainment. Upon their return, they found Cox cold in death – having died from excessive drinking, or was frozen to death as the liquor lost its stimulating effects.

April 23, 1898 ——————————— (DB)

Odum, Ga., April 19. Last Saturday afternoon Mrs. Elizabeth Aspinwall was thrown out of a wagon by a mule and received injuries from which she died three hours later. Mrs. Aspinwall was helpless, being in her 74th year. The mule became frightened at a passing ox team and made a break to run throwing Mrs. Aspinwall from the wagon and breaking both her legs and her shoulder. The wagon ran over Mrs. Clary and her baby also seriously, but not fatally injuring them.

June 17, 1898 ——————————— (DTJ)

THROWN BY A MULE AND KILLED. On Thursday, 9th inst. Mr. Talbot Lindsey, son of Mr. J.R. Lindsey, residing in the edge of Laurens County, was killed by a mule. It was noon and the young man was watering the mule at the trough when the animal got frightened at a chicken flying from the bushes nearby and jumped, throwing the rider to the ground. It seems that in falling the boy unfortunately got tangled up in some manner in the reins of the bridle which threw him under the frightened animal's front feet, causing him to get trampled to death.

July 1, 1898 ——————————— (DTJ)

MRS. CARNES BURNED TO DEATH. A Lamp Exploded and Ignited Her Clothing – Horrible Particulars.

Eastman received a shock on last Saturday night at 9:30 o'clock which will remain fresh in the memory of our citizens for many years to come. As was her custom, (Mr. Wynne being a merchant and being at the store late on Saturday nights) Mrs. S. Carnes went over to the home of her daughter, Mrs. W. Wynne, to sit until bed time. There were two lamps burning in the hall and Mrs. Carnes decided to extinguish one. She chose the large hall lamp, and turning the wick low, blew into the chimney. Immediately there was an explosion and Mrs. Carnes was covered with burning oil and her clothing burst into flames.

Even in this terrible moment thinking of the little grandchildren and the house, Mrs. Carnes ran into the yard. Alf Kelsey, a colored boy who lived near, saw the horrible condition of affairs, and rushing over with a pail of water threw it upon Mrs. Carnes, but as that did no good, Mrs. Wynne and Kelsey tore the clothing from Mrs. Carnes – burning their hands terribly. When the flames had been extinguished Mrs. Carnes was found to be in a terrible condition. Her face was burned almost beyond recognition and her body was literally baked.

July 28, 1898 — (HDN)

On last Friday morning Robert Prickett, a white man, while down in the well of Willie Clements near Jacksonville, for the purpose of cleaning it out or digging it deeper, was overcome by gas and died before he could be rescued from the well. Help was gotten as soon as possible and his body finally brought up to the surface, but life was extinct and resuscitation beyond the question. Mr. Prickett leaves a wife and four children together with many relatives to mourn their great loss.

–Telfair Enterprise.

July 29, 1898 — (TG)

KILLED BY A TRAIN. Ashburn, Ga., July 23. Last night as the early morning train was going into Sycamore it ran over and killed Mr. J.B. Oliver. The ponderous engine cut off both arms and legs and otherwise mangling his body. Mr. Oliver was on the track trying to light a piece of paper with which to wave down the train. It was coming at such a rapid rate that he could not get out of the way. Mr. Oliver lived at Arabi and leaves a wife and three children. He had a small policy of life insurance. This morning his remains were carried to Arabi on the shoofly for burial. [Ed. Note: The shoofly was the name of the train.]

August 13, 1898 — (DB)

BOILER EXPLOSION. On Thursday morning, the 13th instant, the boiler of Mr. John McGovern's saw mill bursted (*sic*) and killed Mr. James Cannon and David Hursey, son of Mr. W.T. Hursey outright and seriously wounded John Hursey, son of Mr. John J. Hursey, have not learned extent of injuries as yet. This is a sad affair, and the families and relatives of the dead and wounded have the sympathy of the entire community.

December 9, 1898 — (DTJ)

Roscoe, the 16 year-old son of Mr. J.M. Pratt, of Pratt, Ga., was instantly killed on Wednesday of last week, by being caught between the lever and capsill of a cane mill. His neck was broken twice, his head crushed and jaw bone broken.

December 23, 1898 —————— (DTJ)

SHOT **A LITTLE BROTHER**. One day last week at Montezuma, Ga., Howard Beverly shot accidentally and killed his little brother, Willie Beverly. Howard had just been killing hogs and was cleaning his pistol, and in unbreaching it fired and struck Willie, who was in front. He lived only five minutes. Howard tried to kill himself, being so overwhelmed with grief.

March 16, 1899 —————— (DTJ)

A MOST HORRIBLE DEATH. Mr. John Holland, Of Laurens County, Is Burned To Death.

Maureen, Ga., March 8, 1899 – A Mr. John Holland, while on his way from his home near Bluewater Church, in Laurens County, to Williams' Shingle Mill, near Musgrove, at which place he worked, met a terrible and tragic death on Monday morning last.

It seems that Mr. Holland, becoming cold on the road, stopped to rest and warm, whereupon he set fire to a turpentine box, which was on a tree that had partly blown down, but had lodged upon a stump. It is supposed that he lay down by the fire and went to sleep, and while he slept the tree burned off of the stump, falling across the small of Mr. Holland's back, and pinning him to the earth, where he was compelled to remain and endure the agonizing tortures of the most terrible death mortal man ever experience.

When found his clothing was burned entirely from his body, and some of his bones were burned to ashes. His flesh was baked in a terrible manner, and every indication pointed to the fact that he had suffered indescribably agonies before death relieved him. It is not known how long he remained under the tree, but it is supposed that the accident happened about sunup and his body was found at 9 o'clock. The coroner's jury returned a verdict that he came to his death as above stated.

March 18, 1899 ———————— (DB)

TWO FATAL ACCIDENTS. A log train of the Southern Pine Company, running out from Offerman, in Pierce County, ran off the track over a trestle Monday morning completely wrecking the train and instantly killing Will Holly, a laborer.

Legree Avant, a brother of Dr. A.L.R. Avant, of Patterson, was seriously injured and will probably die. Three Negroes also were more or less seriously hurt.

March 18, 1899 ———————— (DB)

James, the 14 year old son of D.J.Walker at Patterson, was thrown from his horse and instantly killed late Sunday afternoon. Young Walker was riding a spirited young horse in company with some companions, and it is supposed they were racing when the accident occurred. The young man was thrown violently against a stump, striking head first. His neck was broken and his head severely cut.

June 10, 1899 ———————— (DB)

HE WOULD DIE FIRST. At Buena Vista, a negro prisoner in the jail there took his own life in the presence of the jailer, rather than go to the chain gang, to serve a sentence of twelve months. The negro was Jessie Jones, convicted at the last term of Marion court upon the charge of selling whiskey. He was given one year in the chain gang and when the train from Americus reached Buena Vista Friday morning the jailer went to Jones' cell and told him to get ready, that he had come to carry him to the chain gang; Jones made no reply for a moment, regarding the officer in sullen silence as the door was being unlocked. "I'll never go to the penitentiary", he screamed out. "Farewell wife." Instantly Jones whipped a keen razor from his pocket and cut his throat before the jailer could enter the cell and stop him. The negro staggered a moment and then fell to the floor, the blood pouring in (missing) from the horrible wound.

August 3, 1899 ———————————— (DTJ)

DIED FROM HIS INJURIES. McRae, Ga., July 29. Mr. Pate Wood of this place died yesterday evening of injuries received last Tuesday evening at the bridge on Turnpike Creek. He was driving a pair of horses to a heavy wagon and they became unmanageable while crossing the bridge, both of the horses and wagon fell off the bridge and Mr. Wood fell with them, one of the horses falling on him, producing internal injuries from which he died. Mr. Wood was a young man and was one of the first to enlist from this place in the first Georgia Regiment.

October 19, 1899 ——————————— (DTJ)

SUICIDE AT BREWTON, GA. Monday night at Brewton, eight miles from Dublin, Mr. Charles L. Orr, a merchant of that place, committed suicide by taking strychnine. The fatal dose was taken at the supper table, Orr telling his wife that it was medicine. He then lay down on the bed and began playing with one of his children. In a few minutes convulsions set in and a physician was summoned, but Mr. Orr soon died. He acknowledged that he took strychnine with suicidal intent. Ill health is supposed to have been the cause of the deed. Mr. Orr was a brother-in-law of Mrs. Geo. Elbert, of Eastman, and formerly lived in Washington County.

October 19, 1899 ———————— (DTJ)

Joseph Bullard was found dead in the road near R.L. Collins' place last Wednesday morning. He had started home from town very much under the influence of whiskey, and it is thought that his mule threw him and then stepped on him. His skull was crushed and it was thought at first that there had been foul play, but Coroner Overstreet held an inquest and the jury decided that his death was accidental. He leaves a wife and five children.

–Baxley Banner.

October 21, 1899 ———————— (DB)

IS IT MURDER OR SUICIDE? Decomposed Body of White Man With Bullet Hole in His Skull Found Near Town. "Yesterday morning about nine o'clock Mr. Joe McQuaig, who lives on the hill near the old nursery noticed a drove of buzzards collected in his pasture, about half a mile from his dwelling. Thinking that some of his cattle had been killed, he went to investigate and was horrified to find the decomposed body of a human being. A bullet hole in the center of the forehead showed how he had met his death. Laying (*sic*) on the ground near the body was a revolver with two chambers containing empty cartridges. An umbrella and a black valise was (*sic*) also lying near by. Two empty beer bottles, a half pint flask which had contained laudanum and a small laudanum bottle were seen a few feet away.

Mr. McQuaig believed the body was that of a negro, as the head was in such a decomposed condition no hair could be found. He returned home and sent word to Coroner Grimes.

News of the find was soon circulated and hundreds visited the scene. Coroner Grimes arrived and empaneled a jury early in the afternoon. Upon investigation the body was found to be that of a white man. Some little trouble was caused in the investigation on account of the disturbance of the body by parties who arrived early on the scene. The finding of an empty pocket book near by, caused the suspicion that robbery and murder had been committed, but it was learned shortly that the pocket book had been extracted from a pocket by an early visitor.

The trigger of the revolver was found to be down on a loaded cartridge. No one committing suicide could have done this, so the murder theory was again brought up. It was then learned that the trigger had been tampered with by some one in the crowd.

What at first appeared to be as fracture in the back of the skull was later discovered to be the bursting of seams in the skull, probably caused by the heat of the sun.

A letter found in his pocket was written August 5th at Roseboro, North Carolina, by John F. Hall and addressed to B.H. Vinson, Douglas, Georgia. It was received in Douglas on August 24th and forwarded to Waycross, August 26th. Another letter, dated October 5th, was addressed to W.H.

Wright, Waycross, Georgia. This letter had not been completed.

In the satchel was a suit of clothes and a pair of overalls. By marks on the overalls, the supposition is that Vinson was a brick mason.

The coroner's jury brought in a verdict that Vinson had come to his death by hands unknown. Many people stick to the murder theory. They claim that no one would have selected such a place to commit suicide. The body was lying partly in soft mud in a thick clump of bushes, probably fifty yards from an unused road and near a thick swamp. The remains of the man were buried this morning on a small knoll about sixty feet from where the body was found."

We publish the above from the *Waycross Herald* of last Monday for the benefit of those interested, and because we believe it to be a full and complete statement of this deplorable affair. The writer went to Waycross on the same train with Mr. Vinson in the early part of the present month, and pointed out to him the boarding house of Mr. T.B. Benton, with whom he expected to board in the event that he secured employment with the Plant System. That is the last we ever saw or heard of him until last Monday morning in Waycross we were shown the letter spoken of above. Mr. Vinson was well known here, and was as clever a man generally as we ever met. What could have led to his suicide, if the theory is correct, is beyond conjecture, and if he was foully dealt with, it is hoped that no stone will be left unturned that will lead to the discovery of the fiends that took his life.

November 30, 1899 ———————— (DTJ)

David W. Perdue and Daniel W. Pope, of near Lovett, Ga., were found dead in their bed in Savannah one morning last week, at which place they were attending the reunion. The room was full of gas and one of the gas jets was turned on. It is supposed that they "blew out the light" and death resulted from asphyxiation.

December 26, 1899 ———————— (AtC)

ENGINE RUNS OVER NEGRO MAN. Coroner's Jury Decides the Road Was Not To Blame. Sandersville, Ga., December 25. Alex Carswell, colored, while under the influence of whisky, was run over and instantly killed by an engine on the Sandersville railroad here last Saturday night. The engine was in charge of Engineer O.M. Wood, and was drilling cars in the freight yards of the railroad when the accident occurred. The negro was very old and when last seen on Saturday night was beastly drunk. It is thought he started home and when he reached the point where the accident occurred he laid down across the track in a small culvert, and the flagman on the back end of the train did not see him, and that after the front trucks of the car had passed over his body he raised up and was caught under the wheels. His body was badly mangled. The verdict of the coroner's jury exonerates the road from blame.

December 27, 1899 ——————————— (AtC)

USED HIS PISTOL CARELESSLY. Farmer Hardy Meets Instant Death Before His Mother's Eyes. Chipley, Ga., December 26. T.W. Hardy, a young farmer, was accidentally killed at the home of his mother, four miles north of this place, late yesterday afternoon. He was stooping over splitting some kindling wood, when his pistol fell from his breast pocket; the hammer striking a log, the weapon was discharged, the ball entering just above the breast bone. He was about thirty-two years of age, and leaves a widow and one child.

December 27, 1899 ——————————— (AtC)

WAS JUST AS DEADLY AS A GUN. Negro Meets His Death Trying to Make a Christmas Noise. Zebulon, Ga., December 26. Four miles below here Tom Thomas bored a hole in a stump yesterday. He filled the hole with powder and after igniting a fuse drove a peg into the opening, making the old stump a Christmas cannon. When all was ready, Thomas applied a match to the fuse and waited for the explosion. The fire reached the powder and the plug was forced out like a bullet from a gun. Thomas was standing in line with the hole. The plug struck him in the chest and tore its way entirely through his body, causing instant death. No load from a gun could have been more deadly in its effect.

December 29, 1899 —————— (AB)

CANNON CRACKER Causes Death of Young George Poer in West Point.

West Point, Ga., Dec. 28. – One of the saddest accidents that has occurred here was the one that befell young George Poer on Christmas morning.

While discharging fireworks, he lit a cannon cracker, but it seemed that it went out. He turned it towards him and blew to see if a spark still remained when the cracker exploded in his hand, shattering it to pieces and blowing some of the heavy paper into his throat and windpipe.

Physicians were immediately summoned and did all in their power to save him, but despite their efforts he succumbed. He was only thirteen years old and the youngest son of Mr. George W. Poer, one of West Point's most prominent citizens. He was a prime favorite among both old and young and stood at the head of his class at school.

March 14, 1901 —————— (AbC)

A GHASTLY FIND. The Headless Body of an Unknown White Man Found in the Ocmulgee River. Lumber City, Ga., March 6, 1901.

On last night the body of an unknown white man was found on the lower part of Oaky Bluff Ocmulgee river, where it had drifted during the recent high water. This morning the following citizens, J.M. Wall, J.J. Mobley, J.C. Clements, A.B. Clements, J.E. Clements, Thomas Bush, I.J. Lowery, L.F. Hinson and little Bruce Smith, met there to examine and bury the body. We were unanimous in the opinion that he was murdered, and that the weapon used was an axe. The head was not found. Three wounds in the lower chest and abdomen show most clearly that an axe was used. The body must have been in the river from six to eight weeks and was clothed in a navy blue suit and heavy shoes. Nothing could be found to identify him in any way.

March 21, 1901 ————————————— (AbC)

MAY BE BODY OF YOUNG EVANS. Laurens County Man Thinks the Headless Trunk May be the Body of His Son. Dublin, Ga., March 16. – Mr. W.J. Evans, who lives in the western part of the county, was in the city yesterday and stated that he was fearful that the headless body found recently in the Ocmulgee river was that of his twenty-year-old son who recently disappeared from his home in Pulaski County, near the river.

Mr. Evans states that when last seen his son wore a blue suit of clothes and had on a heavy pair of shoes. The body which was found in the river was dressed in this fashion. Mr. Evans is quite sure that the body is that of his son, and has dispatched another son to Lumber City to see if it is possible to identify the body.

Young Evans was married about two years ago to a Miss Coley, of Pulaski County. He and his wife could not agree and about five weeks ago Evans disappeared. His father made inquiries of his wife as to his whereabouts and was informed by her that she did not know or care where he was. In a short time thereafter she left for Texas where she is at present.

July 5, 1901 (DTJ)

A LITTLE CHILD'S NECK BROKEN. While sitting on the piazza in his little rocking chair last Sunday morning, the little two-years-old son of Mr. and Mrs. W.L. Holder, who live eight miles east of Cordele, became overbalanced and fell to the ground, a distance of about four feet, breaking his neck. The parents were at the cow pen milking and the grandmother, who was near at hand, rushed to the child, picked it up and gave the alarm. The father hurried to the house and took the little one in his arms, but after a few gasps the child was dead. The little body was interred Monday in the Noles Cemetery.

November 26, 1902 (VN)

WILD ELEPHANT KILLS TRAINER. Becomes Unruly in Valdosta and Crushes Life Out of Trainer – Captured Near the City and is Killed.

While riding the big elephant, Gypsy, which belongs to the Harris Nickel Plate show, through the streets of Valdosta Saturday night, the keeper, who was drunk, fell from the elephant's head and was instantly crushed to death by the great beast kneeling on him. Someone saw the tragedy and gave the alarm. Town people and showmen started out to capture the elephant which had become infuriated and wild with excitement.

Guns and pistols were secured and the crowd followed the animal down the streets to Pine Park, into which it entered. Several shots were fired at it, some of which took effect.

With a mighty effort the five-ton beast tore down the inclosure surrounding the park and started for the open country, the crowd following. The chase was kept up until Sunday morning, when the elephant was overtaken about six miles from town and killed by a single shot from a Krag-Jorgenson rifle, the bullet passing entirely through the head. Large crowds went out to see the carcass of the dead beast which was left lying in the middle of the road. An effort will be made to stuff the hide.

March 14, 1903 —————————— (VN)

KILLED BY A TRAIN. Young Man Horribly Mangled By a Freight Train in Cordele on Thursday night. The 19-year-old son of Conductor Young, of the A. & B., was killed in Cordele Thursday night by falling under a moving train. He had just been given a freight conductor's position on the road and had made his first trip on an extra freight and upon entering the yards in Cordele, stumbled and fell through between the cars, eight of which passed over his body, grinding it into a mass of bones and flesh. The pieces were picked up in a sheet and carried to the house of his parents.

March 20, 1903 —————————— (MCC)

A HORRIBLE DEATH. Joe Jones, a colored porter in the employ of the Central of Georgia Railway Co., met a horrible death at the depot at Oglethorpe Thursday morning.

Jones was on the northbound passenger train and had changed the switch for it to take the sidetrack for the south-bound train to pass. After changing the switch he jumped upon the pilot of the engine to make as coupling with a freight car that was in the way ahead, and in so doing slipped and fell upon his back across the track. Neither the engineer nor fireman saw him, and the engine went ahead, dragging him fifteen feet to a side bar where his body hung, the engine and one car grinding him to death, cutting the body to pieces. All this time the engineer never suspected anything wrong until Mr. W.J. Griffin, of Oglethorpe, who was standing nearby and saw the negro fall, ran to the engine and gave the alarm. The mangled remains were gathered up from the bloody track and taken to Macon.

Jones was one of the best porters on the road. He has been passing here several years and had many friends. He was always kind and courteous, and leaves a wife and seven little children.

July 16, 1903 ———————————— (DTJ)

STUMP FELL ON HIM. George Inman was instantly killed by a falling stump near Camps on Turnpike creek in Telfair County, where he had been fishing and had set fire to a black gum stump, or broken off tree about fifteen feet high, and then fallen asleep near it. He and his brother, Ben Inman, had been fishing all night until toward day, when George lay down to take a nap. His brother had gone down to the creek a short distance, but heard the stump fall and heard his brother groan. Hastening to the spot, he found the stump across his brother's body. George's neck had been broken.

July 16, 1903 ———————————— (DTJ)

DEATH OF JOEL HORNE. We have received news of the death of Mr. Joel Horne, of near Dubois, which occurred on Friday afternoon under very unusual circumstances.

Mr. Horne was visiting at the home of Mr. Tucker, a near

neighbor. While there he ate some watermelon, after which he became slightly sick. To relieve his sickness Mr. Tucker offered him some brandy, which he drank a small quantity, and in company with his wife, immediately started for home. Before going very far he informed Mrs. Horne that he was very sick and began having convulsions. Mrs. Horne called for assistance and Messrs. Cothran and Tucker promptly responded. When they reached Mr. Horne he was then in the throes of death and died in a very short time. His death occurred in his buggy.

July 23, 1903 ———————————— (DTJ)

RICHARD TUCKER MEETS DEATH IN STRANGE MANNER. Supposed to Have Been Poisoned by His Wife and Farm Hand. Both now in Eastman jail. Stomach of Dead Man Has Been Sent to State Chemist in Atlanta to be Examined for Strychnine Poison.

A terrible sequel to the death of Mr. Joel Horne, an account of which was published in this paper last week, developed Tuesday night in the sudden death of Mr. Richard Tucker, who died under similar unusual circumstances.

It will be remembered that Mr. Horne died from the effects of a drink of brandy and a small piece of watermelon given him at the Tucker home, but no official investigation was made of the cause of his death. Tuesday night, however, Mr. Tucker died very suddenly after having taken a capsule of what was supposed to be quinine, and this led the neighbors to believe that their deaths resulted from foul play. Accordingly, Sheriff J.C. Rogers was notified. He left early Wednesday morning for the Tucker home, and returned to Eastman about noon, bringing with him Bob Cawthorn, a white man, about 35 years old, who has been living with Mr. Tucker since January as a farm hand, and placed him in jail upon suspicion that he poisoned the dead man. Sheriff Rogers, accompanied by Drs. J.B. Clark and J.D. Herrman returned to the Tucker home Wednesday afternoon, when the stomach of Mr. Tucker was taken out by Drs. Clark and Herrman, and Mrs. Tucker was arrested by Sheriff Rogers upon suspicion that she was implicated with Cawthorn in the commission of the crime.

Dr. Clark went to Atlanta Wednesday night, carrying with him the stomach of the dead man. He will have the contents of the stomach analyzed by the state chemist, and it is confidently expected that the results will show that Mr. Tucker's death was produced by strychnine poison.

The evidence against Cawthorn and Mrs. Tucker is all circumstantial, but very strong. Mrs. Tucker says that on the afternoon preceding her husband's death she and her husband were away from home. In their absence Cawthorn had her little daughter to fill some capsules with quinine, the filled capsules being placed in the box with the empty ones. After supper Cawthorn pretended to be very sick with colic, and made up a fire in the stove to heat some water. She and her husband assisted him all they could, applying hot cloths to his abdomen, administering tea, etc. Cawthorn claimed to be considerably better and lay down on the porch by the window, which was open. He then told Mr. Tucker, who had been complaining that he had felt badly for several days, that he (Tucker) had better take a capsule of quinine. Tucker said he didn't think he needed it, but Cawthorn insisted and handed him a capsule, which Tucker took with a swallow of water. About thirty minutes later he was seized with terrible pains and asked who filled those capsules. He was told that his little daughter filled them. He then asked if there was anything on the place they could be filled with except quinine. His wife replied no. However, she says there was a package of strychnine in the house that was bought last year, but that it was no good. Sheriff Rogers now has that package of strychnine. Mrs. Tucker says she believes that Cawthorn poisoned her husband, thinking that he could get the crop. She denies that any improper relations existed between herself and Cawthorn.

Cawthorn denies giving Tucker the capsule and says Mrs. Tucker administered it. He acknowledges buying a quarter's worth of strychnine from Dr. Kimberly, but says that Tucker sent for it to poison dogs with and that he delivered it to Tucker, but does not know whether it was ever used. Cawthorn further acknowledges that Mrs. Tucker was very friendly with him and that he kissed her every time he left the house when her husband was away.

The supposition is that Cawthorn and Mrs. Tucker were very intimate and that Tucker was put out of the way on this account. It is also thought that the brandy given Mr. Horne by Tucker had been poisoned for the purpose of killing Tucker. Cawthorn came to this county last September from Butts County and worked awhile with Mr. W.H. Smith, from whom it is said that he stole a pistol, and for which the grand jury found a bill of indictment against him. It is said that he came from a splendid family, but has always been considered the black sheep of the flock. He is a man of unusual intelligence and has a manner of recklessness and adventure.

Mrs. Tucker is 31 years old and is fairly good looking. She is a daughter of Ephran Harrison, deceased, who is well known to the citizens of Dodge, having moved here from Fulton County 20 years ago. She says she has no relatives in this county except two half sisters and a stepmother.

There is nothing in her appearance to indicate a vicious or brutal temperament, and her reputation has been splendid up to this time, so far as we have been able to learn. She has three children. Her husband, Mr. Richard Tucker was a native of Butts County, but married Mrs. Tucker, who is his second wife, in this county. He was a prosperous farmer and is said to have been an honest, upright man, a splendid neighbor and of a very pleasant, courteous disposition. His body was buried at the Empire Cemetery Wednesday afternoon. He was 44 years old.

The Tucker home is situated two miles northwest of Dubois and twelve miles from Eastman. A preliminary trial will be held as soon as the state chemist announces the result of his analysis of the contents of the stomach, and we may be able to give our readers a more definite account of the affair next week.

September 18 1903 ——————— (MCC)

Mr. Isdol was killed at Ricks' saw mill last Monday. There was no eye witness to the killing, but he was hauling logs with an ox team, and in dragging the logs it is supposed he went to get on the tongue and his foot slipped throwing him under the wheel, tearing his face from his head, and spilling his brains upon the ground. The tram pulled on further and when they found him he was wedged under the log. He left his family destitute as they were dependent upon his daily labor.

November 21, 1903 ——————— (VN)

WAS CUT TO PIECES IN A COTTON GIN.

Lafayette, Ga., Nov. 19 – Sam Andrews, a 16-year-old boy, met a horrible death here today, being literally ground in pieces. He was feeding at a cotton gin when he in some way fell into the hopper and it was several minutes before he was discovered, and the body was horrible (*sic*) mutilated.

December 3, 1903 —————————— (DTJ)

MR. JNO. W. LOVETT KILLED BY AN ACCIDENT. Mr. Jno. W. Lovett of Atlanta, supervisor of bridges and trestles of the Atlanta division of the Southern railway, died at a hospital in Chattanooga Sunday morning at 4 o'clock as a result of an accident with which he met on Wednesday, November 25th, near Apperson, Tenn., twenty miles this side of Chattanooga. Mr. Lovett was making an inspection of the road on a lever car and had knowledge that a train was behind him, but had no idea of meeting one ahead. He was making good speed to keep out of the way of the train behind, when, while turning a sharp curve, the lever car collided with a freight train in front. Mr. Lovett was knocked from the car and received injuries from which he died on Sunday morning. Several of his ribs were broken and crushed into his body and he was otherwise bruised and injured. It is said that he never regained consciousness after the accident. His body reached Eastman Tuesday on the 12:30 train, and was met at the depot by the Eastman relatives and friends of the deceased and an escort from the Eastman Lodge of Free and Accepted Masons, all of whom accompanied the body to Woodlawn Cemetery, where it was interred with Masonic honors.

Mr. Lovett lacked only a few days of being fifty-one years of age. He was born and reared near Dublin in Laurens County and had been married twice. His second wife was Mrs. Anna Pournelle, a daughter of Mr. and Mrs. J.T. Rawlins of Eastman ... Mrs. J.C. Rawlins of Eastman is a sister, and Messrs. Frank,

Thomas and Richard Lovett of Towns, Fitzgerald and Atlanta are brothers to the deceased.

December 16, 1903 — (VN)

J.E. SIMERLY KILLED BY A FREIGHT TRAIN AT ALBANY. Albany, Ga., Dec. 11. J.E. Simerly of Poulan, was killed here last night by being crushed under the wheels of a freight car.

He was a prominent citizen of Poulan, and had been in Albany for a day or two on business. He had been drinking freely, and while on his way to the depot to take a train for home, lay down under a freight car which was standing on a north street side track. A switch engine backed onto the car and pushed it upon Simerly while he was asleep. His head was completely severed from his body, and one arm and one hand were cut off. The body was not discovered until about four hours later. Simerly leaves a widow and three children. The body was taken to Pike County for interment.

February 18, 1904 — (DTJ)

YOUNG TOM ROGERS ACCIDENTALLY KILLED. A very sad accident occurred at the saw mill of T.M. Rogers & Son, across Gum Swamp, about dark on Tuesday afternoon, that resulted in the death of Mr. Tom Rogers, the 21yearold son of Mr. Cullen Rogers.

Mr. Clem Rogers, a cousin of the young man killed, had been hunting. When he returned several boys were in the room, and in a playful manner two or three of them caught hold of the gun. It is said that one of the young men was smoking, and that the lighted cigar dropped on the hand of one of the boys, causing him to jerk his hand backward. In doing this the gun was struck against the door-facing, causing its contents to be discharged. The whole load took effect in the lower abdomen and groin of Mr. Tom Rogers, who was standing nearby and he died in about five minutes.

It is said that all of the young men who were present are heart-broken over the sad affair. Mr. Rogers' body was buried at the Mullis burying ground, about two miles from Eastman, Wednesday afternoon.

April 13, 1904 ——————————— (VN)

MAN KILLS SELF IN PRESENCE OF FAMILY. Turner Pearson, Formerly of Atlanta, Commits Suicide at His Home In Devereaux, Ga.

Milledgeville, Ga., April 11 – Turner Pearson committed suicide yesterday morning at 10 o'clock at the house of his father-in-law, S.M. Devereaux, at Devereaux, Ga. He walked into a room where his wife and other ladies were getting ready to go to church, saying no one cared for him and he was going to kill himself.

He went to a bureau drawer, took out a revolver and shot himself twice in the left temple. The first shot glanced. The ladies all ran screaming from the room. He died about 1 o'clock. He leaves a wife and one child. He lived here a few years ago but recently was employed by the Atlanta Milling Company. He came here from Atlanta about ten days ago. No cause is assigned for the deed. He was about 35 years old.

May 14, 1904 ———————————

MAN IS GROUND TO DEATH UNDER WHEELS OF TRAIN.

Hawkinsville, Ga., May 12 – Wilbur Morgan, a young man employed at the cotton mills, was thrown under the wheels of the Southern train in the yards here last night and literally cut to pieces. His body was mangled almost beyond recognition and both legs cut off.

It is not known exactly how the accident occurred but it is thought that he had stepped from the train while moving and was struck by a car standing on the siding. The body was carried to Ways' undertaking parlors and will probably be carried to Ashburn for interment.

May 21, 1904 ——————————— (VN)

THE FIRST CIGAR SMOKED COST THAT BOY HIS LIFE. Philadelphia, May 18. A coroner's inquest on the death of 10-year-old William Black who on Sunday smoked his first cigar, has shown that the lad died in convulsions at a hospital after having been given an emetic which brought to light the stump of a cigar. The boy recovered consciousness shortly before he died and said he had swallowed it accidentally while attempting to smoke for the first time.

August 17, 1904 — (VN)

BOILER EXPLOSION KILLS THREE PERSONS.
Negroe's (*sic*) Eyes Blown From Head. J.F. Arnold, Proprietor of the Mill, Had Just Arrived on Scene and Was Killed.

Senoia, Ga., Aug. 15. – At 3 o'clock this afternoon, the boiler at the saw mill of J.F. Arnold, about 5 miles from this place, exploded, killing three persons. Following is the list of the dead and injured:

> J.F. Arnold, dead
> Buford Arnold, dead,
> Will Arnold, colored, dead
> Alfred Shipp, leg broken
> Unknown negro, eyes blown out.

J.F. Arnold owned the mill and was one of the wealthiest and most popular men in the county. He was out on his farm after dinner and went to the saw mill to see how work was progressing, arriving there just at the time of the explosion.

The three other men were employees of the mill. The cause of the explosion is not known, but it is thought it was owing to the lack of water in the boiler.

October 1, 1904 — (VN)

PRINTER MET HORRIBLE DEATH IN VALDOSTA.
Valdosta, Ga. Sept. 29 – R.C. Claiborne, a well-known printer, whose home is understood to be in Savannah, met a horrible death here at 8 o'clock tonight.

Claiborne was under the influence of whiskey and going into the engine room of the Valdosta Ice and Manufacturing Company, was struck and instantly killed by one of the large fly wheels. The man was seen whirling around the wheel by the engineer, and before the machinery could be stopped, his body was crushed into an almost shapeless mass.

Coroner Solomon held an inquest over the body tonight, and the jury returned a verdict of suicide. Claiborne had been here only two days.

December 17, 1904 —————————— (VN)

BODY HURLED INTO ETERNITY. Boiler Bursts at Everett's Shingle Mills. W.D. Lupo, of Kerns, Met Sudden Death by The Explosion of the Boiler – Was Hurled About Fifty Feet.

The life of Mr. W.D. Lupo, a prominent farmer and citizen of the Kerns community, was suddenly hurled into eternity Wednesday afternoon about two thirty o'clock by the explosion of a boiler at the A.E. Everett shingle mill about four miles from this city. Mr. Lupo had just rode (*sic*) up on his horse, hitched and walked up to the boiler to warm. He had been there only a few seconds when the explosion took place. Mr. Lupo's body was blown possibly fifty feet away, knocking down a small pine tree and tearing every piece of his clothing from his body and one of his shoes. Death was instantaneous.

He was the only person very near the boiler at the time of the explosion and therefore, fortunately, he was the only one hurt. Mr. Lupo was about 50 years old, and leaves several relatives and friends to mourn his sad death. His last remains were placed in the Lupo burying grounds, near Kerns, Thursday.

December 24, 1904 ————————

HANDLING MONEY CAUSED DEATH OF R.H. BLANDFORD. Supposed That he Contracted Small Pox While Selling Tickets.

Columbus, Ga., Dec. 22 – Captain Robert H. Blandford, 49 years of age, son of the late Judge Mark H. Blandford, of the Georgia supreme court, died at his home, in Wynton (*sic*), today after an illness of ten days, of smallpox of the worst type. There have been hundreds of mild cases in Columbus during the past few years, but only three or four deaths, and this is the first person of prominence here to succumb to the disease. Captain Blandford was ticket agent at the union depot here and came in contact with hundreds of people daily, and, it is supposed, that it was in this way that he contracted the disease. One theory was that he handled infected money received in payment for tickets. He had never been vaccinated. Captain Blandford had been in the employ of the Central of Georgia railway for many years, in various capacities, working his way up from the freight department. . . . The funeral occurred this afternoon, being private. A family survives him.

December 24, 1904 ———————— (VN)

ENGINE CUT HIS HEAD OFF. Ed Bonaparte, colored, employed as a section hand on the Seaboard Air Line Railway, was run down and killed by Seaboard engine No. 501 at Jacksonville. The engine wheels passed over the man's body, completely severing his head and horribly mangling him about the shoulders and arms.

February 17, 1905 ———————— (VN)

SPLIT IN HALF BY SAW. Negro Meets Horrible Death While Working at Saw Mill.

Valdosta, Ga., Feb. 14 – Oscar Mitchell, a negro man employed at the saw mill of S.J.A. Copeland, at Dasher Station, met a horrible death this afternoon, his body being split open by the circular saw.

Mitchell was at work pulling timbers away from the rapidly revolving saw, when a piece slipped and threw him headforemost on the saw. In an instant his body was split in halves, and horribly mutilated otherwise.

The first intimation many of the other workers had of the accident was when they turned and saw his divided body lying by the saw with one of his legs also cut off.

March 21, 1905 ———————— (VN)

BODY SCATTERED ALONG ROAD. Mangled Body of Unknown Man Found on Railroad Track.

West Point, Ga., March 20. – The mangled remains of an unknown white man were found yesterday morning scattered along the railroad track from the car shed to a distance of 200 yards. He is supposed to have attempted to board the outgoing freight train that passed here at 3 o'clock a.m.

The train, after some shifting, as it left the shed, was moving with great speed in order to make the incline a short distance ahead, and the unfortunate man was thrown under the wheels and was dashed into eternity in a second. His body was so horribly mangled that from the parts gathered it was impossible to identify him.

He was evidently very stout and wore black suit of clothes,

but not a card or paper of any kind has been found. His face was entirely destroyed so that his identity is likely to remain enveloped in mystery.

March 31, 1905 ——————————— (NN)

OLD NEGRO KILLED ON RAILROAD. John Dollar, an aged negro living on Hon. J.H. McCollum's plantation at Coweta, was killed last Saturday afternoon about five o'clock by the southbound A & W.P. fast passenger train. He was crossing the track and, being deaf to some extent, probably did not hear the train coming. He was knocked from the track and instantly killed.

John Dollar was near 80 years of age and was a faithful and reliable negro. He was Mr. McCollum's blacksmith and was an expert workman, despite his advanced age.

June 2, 1905 ——————————— (MCC)

DIED WHILE PRAYING. Late Monday afternoon Clayton Bird,(*sic*) a well known young farmer, entered a saloon at Americus and called for a glass of water. Then bidding the barkeeper farewell he deliberately swallowed 46 grains of morphine and immediately began to pray.

Within fifteen minutes physicians were at work upon him, but despite their efforts Byrd (*sic*) died in two hours without regaining consciousness. He was much esteemed and no cause is assigned for his act. He leaves a young wife and child and was a prosperous young farmer.

June 20, 1905

KILLED AT TELEPHONE. A.T. Reader Meets Sudden and Awful Death at Talbotton, Ga.

While standing at a telephone, in his office, in Talbotton, Ga., last Friday afternoon, A.T. Reader, of Sylvester, Colo., was killed by a stroke of lightning, that tore his body into pieces. No one was in the room at the time he received the stroke and when found by a servant, both legs were split in half from the ankles up and his arms were almost completely severed from his body.

Mr. Reader had been in Talbotton for some time, super-intending the construction of telephone lines in that section of the state. He was well known in Atlanta, being the neph-ew of A.B. Trueston, civil engineer for the Southern railroad. The body was brought to Atlanta yesterday morning, and taken to the undertaking parlors of H.M. Patterson, where it will remain until the arrival of relatives from Colorado. It is probable that the body will be carried to the former home of the deceased for interrment (*sic*).

—Atlanta Constitution.

July 21, 1905

A HORRIBLE DEATH FROM BITE OF CAT. Samuel Cook, of Macon, Aged 15, Dies of Hydrophobia. Picked up Strange Cat in Public Road and, While Petting it the Cat Bit the Boy on His Thumb.

A dispatch from Macon, dated July 19th, says: Samuel Cook, a farmer living near Cross Keys, outside the city lim-its, on the east side of the river, died a most horrible death Wednesday morning after suffering about eight hours from rabbies (*sic*), supposed to have been caused by a cat bite. Early this morning the boy complained and asked that a physician be summoned to relieve him of a peculiar suffering which he was unable to explain. He soon afterwards asked for a drink of water, and as soon as he had touched his lips, he became wild and was beyond the control of his parents during the remainder of the time. Nearly a dozen physicians were called in, and the general opinion was that the young man was suffering from hydrophobia, and every effort was made to relieve him, but with no avail. He died this afternoon after a day's suffering, the horrors of which are indescribable . . .

July 21, 1905 ————————————— (NN)

NEGRO BOY KILLED. A negro boy, a son of John Langford, aged about 15 years, was killed at Arnall, six miles from Newnan on the Central Railroad, last Saturday morning by a passing freight train. It is believed he was asleep on the track.

September 12, 1905 ————————— (VN)

HARRY DAVIS RUN OVER AT CORDELE. He Undertook to Couple the Cars While in Motion and Was Instantly Killed.

Cordele, Ga., Sept. 10 – Harry Davis, aged 19 years, a graduate of Emory College and son of wealthy parents at Lumber City, was run over an instantly killed by a through freight on the Atlantic & Birmingham railroad here at 5:30 o'clock this morning.

The accident happened in the yards of the road at the

intersection of Sixth street and Tenth avenue. As nearly as the facts can be ascertained, the train was just ready to pull out when young Davis noticed that one of the air brake couplings had become disconnected. He called to a trainman to have the engineer stop, the train having just begun to move off, until he could make the coupling. His foot was caught by the wheel. He slid along until he struck a joint in the rail. There his foot hung, and the wheel passed along his right leg, grinding it to pulp. When the wheel reached his abdomen the body switched around in some way and the body was severed. His remains were scattered along the track for seventy or more feet. Death must have been instantaneous.

Davis was a son of T.H. Davis, of Lumber City. He was also a cousin of J.B. Wooten, of Cordele. Mr. Wooten notified the lad's parents and had the remains prepared for burial and shipped on the afternoon train.

Records found in the dead man's clothing show that he went to work for the Atlantic & Birmingham as a flagman on May 25. He had been out after the injury of his foot on the same line for only a few days. The first accident occurred at Fitzgerald. Mr. Wooten immediately employed counsel, but it was decided that no inquest would be necessary.

December 21, 1905 ———————— (DTJ)

SCAFFOLDING BROKE, TWO PAINTERS KILLED.

Fitzgerald, Ga., December 15 – Fred Elder, of Chicago, and Vard Dickerson, whose home is here, were killed today by the breaking of the scaffolding from which they were painting a residence. Dickerson's neck was broken, death resulting instantly. Elder lived seven hours dying from internal injuries.

January 4, 1906 ————————————

SUDDEN DEATH OF A YOUNG LADY. On Monday of last week in the suburbs of Ailey a most shocking tragedy occurred in which a young woman 18 years of age lost her life. The girl, Miss Blanche Pitts, daughter of Mrs. Eliza Pitts, had the top of her head blown off by a gun in the hands of her brother, a boy six years old.

The little fellow had been slapped for taking an orange away from a smaller child, and, seizing a gun from another boy standing near, fired at his sister who stood combing her hair preparatory to making a visit. Dr. Palmer was called, but found her brains running out, and she died in three hours.

February 15, 1906 ————————————

THREE MEN MEET HORRIBLE DEATH IN BURNING JAIL. Fire Started On the Inside of the Building and Was Not Discovered In Time to Save Them From Death. Charred bodies taken from the burning calaboose. Messrs. D.A. Cooper, Elbert Mullis and John Hart Burned to Death In the Eastman Guardhouse Last Friday Night.

One of the most fearfully horrible catastrophes within the conception of the human mind took place in Eastman Friday night about 9 o'clock, when the Eastman calaboose was destroyed by fire and Messrs. D.A. Cooper, Elbert Mullis and John Hart perished in the flames. They were all highly esteemed citizens and the terrible affair has caused a dark gloom over the entire town and county.

McDonald Brother's show gave two performances here Monday, one in the afternoon and one at night. Liquor seemed to be plentiful and easily obtained, and during the afternoon a number of citizens appeared in a partially drunken condition. About night Policeman Burnham found it necessary to arrest Messrs. Elbert Mullis and John Hart. Both gave bond and efforts were made to get them to return to their homes. They, however, failed to do this. Mr. Mullis was found later lying on the street and Mr. Hart was found at the show ground. They were again arrested and this time were placed in the town calaboose to remain until they became sober. Previously Mr. D.A. Cooper had been arrested for drunkenness and locked up for a like purpose.

Mr. John Hart was the last man incarcerated, and policeman Burnham says that at this time Messrs. Mullis and Cooper were asleep, and that when he left the guard house Hart was trying to wake them up. About forty minutes later the fire was discovered, and it is supposed that Hart originated the fire by striking matches in an effort to see who his companions were. There was nothing in the cell except a mattress, some bed clothes and a zinc water bucket partially filled with water. It is probable that the mattress caught fire first, from which the flames spread to the walls.

Some negroes living near the calaboose heard the cries of the doomed men, but it being nothing unusual for men confined there to yell and whoop, paid no attention to it. The fire was first discovered by Dr. J.B. Clark, who had gone to his lot to hitch his horse to his buggy, preparatory to making a visit to a patient in the country. He heard the cries of the men and saw the reflection of the fire on the outside window. He hastened to the scene, called some of the negroes living nearby to his assistance, and did everything possible to rescue the unfortunate men. Mr. Doc Day and others also soon came on the scene and Policeman Burnham was hurriedly sent for and responded immediately, he being found at the show ground. Before his arrival efforts were made with axes and blacksmith tools to break the outside door down, which was accomplished, but in the meantime the fire was raging within, and when Policeman Burnham arrived and opened the cell door the flames and smoke leaped into his face and drove him from the building.

The alarm of fire had been sounded and hundreds of people flocked to the guard house. The fire hose was quickly attached to the waterworks and the fire was extinguished before the building was completely destroyed, the walls being left standing. The roof was burned completely away and the walls were badly charred.

At the coroner's inquest Saturday a verdict was rendered to the effect that the deceased came to their death by burning, the origin of the fire being unknown.

Dr. Clark informs us that all the men were probably dead before the outside door was broken in, as their cries ceased before this was accomplished, that Mr. Mullis evidently survived longer than the others, his voice being recognized last. When the body of Mr. Mullis was reached the zinc water bucket was over his head, he evidently having thrust his head into the bucket of water to protect it from the flames.

When the unfortunate men were reached practically all of the flesh had been burned from their limbs and they could not have been recognized except by the size of their frames. The bodies were taken in charge of by Undertaker J.W. Peacock and prepared for burial. The remains of Mr. Mullis were taken to his home about seven miles in the country Saturday morning and interred in the family burying ground.

Relatives of Mr. Hart, who formerly lived at Central Point, but who had recently moved just across the line into Pulaski County, came for his body Saturday morning and carried it home for burial. The remains of Mr. Cooper, who was a resident of Eastman, were interred at Little Ocmulgee church, five miles from town, Saturday afternoon. Rev. M.H. Massey conducted the services at the burial of both Messrs. Mullis and Cooper.

Mr. Cooper was about sixty years of age and leaves a wife and a large family of sons and daughters. He was a highly intelligent, well educated, honorable gentleman, and for many years taught school in Dodge and Laurens counties. He was reared in North Carolina . . . Mr. Mullis was about fifty years of age and leaves a large family. He was a brother-in-law to Mr. W.F. Harrell of Eastman, and a member of one of the largest families in the county . . . Mr. Hart was a younger man, probably 35 years of age, and leaves a wife and one child. He is said to have been a model citizen aside for his weakness for drink, which weakness resulted in the death and his companions of Friday night, drunkenness and disorderly conduct being the only charge against any of them.

March 16, 1906 ——————————— (NN)

CHILD KILLED PLAYING WITH GUN. Whitesburg, Ga., March 13. John Treadwell's twin boys, 5 years old, had been playing with an old gun barrel by blowing their breath through it to hear the noise as it came out at the tube. It had been taken away from them and hidden.

When the boys were alone they climbed up on the bed, took down their father's loaded gun and, it is supposed, was (*sic*) blowing in it when the weapon was discharged and one of the boys killed. The whole load entered at his mouth, passed through his head at the top. He died instantly.

July 19, 1906 ─────────────────── (DTJ)

HEAVY TIMBERS FALL UPON DIXON.

Dublin, Ga., July 15. – Information has reached the city of the accidental killing of Jack Dixon at the sawmill of Mr. Tilden Hall, treasurer-elect of Laurens County. Mr. Dixon was at the mill engaged in piling some lumber. He went under the pile to fix a plank which had gotten out of place. The entire pile fell on him, breaking his neck, breaking his backbone in two places, crushing his chest, and otherwise mangling him most horribly. His death was instantaneous.

As soon as possible the lumber was removed from his body. His remains were interred at Grove church. He is survived by a wife and two children.

September 13, 1906 ─────────── (DTJ)

MISTAKEN FOR DEER AND FATALLY SHOT. While Out Hunting in Thick Brush His Companion Fired Buckshot Into Him.

McRae, Ga., September 6. – A hunting party of prominent people of McRae and vicinity wounded a deer near Wooten's Mill twenty miles south of here yesterday afternoon. In their excited efforts to drive him from a pond full of thick brush where he had taken refuge, F.E. Boyd passed near W.A. Cook, who mistook him in the bushes for the deer, and fired a load of seventeen buckshot into him, all taking effect. Dr. Burch was called at once and Dr. Born, of McRae, was later called. Information says the wounds will prove fatal. Boyd has a wife and several children. W.A. Cook is a son of Hon. J.F. Cook.

December 7, 1906 ———————————

ENGINEER KILLED IN CENTRAL WRECK. A disastrous wreck occurred about 4:30 o'clock Wednesday morning at Raymond, six miles from Newnan on the Central Railway, instantly killing Engineer L.J. Norton, and seriously injuring a negro fireman, Charley Johnson.

An extra freight running west encountered a switch left open and derailed the train, overturning the engine and six cars. Engineer Norton was found pinioned under the debris with his neck broken, both feet crushed and horribly bruised about the body.

The negro fireman sustained a broken hip and painful bruises. A negro brakeman was slightly injured. The remains of Norton were brought here and prepared for burial before sending to his home in Cedartown.

If Engineer Norton had remained on his engine he would not have been killed, as it remained upright on the ties. He jumped, however, after reversing the throttle lever, and landed in the path of one of the overturning cars. The car was heavily loaded with lumber and the engineer was instantly crushed to death.

December 28, 1906 ———————————

KILLED IN GIN AT SHARPSBURG. H.B. North, Well-Known Citizen, Killed in Machinery of Cole's Gin.

Mr. H.B. North, one of the best citizens of Coweta county, met a horrible death in the machinery of J.R. Cole & Co's gin at Sharpsburg last Saturday. He had been superintendent of the gin for years, and was one of the best known residents of the community.

Mr. North went under the gin floor to mend a belt, and as

he was alone it is not known just how he came to his death. It is supposed, however, that his clothing caught on a set screw in a shaft, as he was throwing the belt on a pulley. The machinery was running at the time and Mr. North was crushed between the shaft and the timbers of the building and almost instantly killed. Some person on the floor of the gin, hearing the noise below, rushed down and found his mangled body lying on the ground, where he had fallen, after being hurled away from the shaft.

Mr. North was a son of Mr. N.A. North and leaves numerous relatives in this city and county. He was probably 45 years of age and a bachelor. He was a model citizen, and his untimely death caused much regret among a large circle of friends.

January 18, 1907 ——————— (NN)

J.G. PUCKETT KILLED ON A.& W.P. Young Flagman Fell Under Freight Train at Moreland Last Saturday Night.

J.G. Puckett, a young flagman on the Atlanta & West Point Railway, was killed at Moreland last Saturday night by falling under a moving freight train. He was instantly killed, his body being cut to pieces by the revolving wheels.

It was at first reported that Puckett was knocked under the train by a couple of white boys stealing a ride. The investigation of the coroner's jury did not confirm this rumor. Coroner Broadwater went down to Moreland at an early hour Sunday morning and empaneled a jury consisting of P.A. Carmichal, J.P. Cureton, Henry Keith, A.S. Robertson, J.A. Reynolds, and E.J. Haynes. The investigation showed that Puckett's death resulted from an accident. He found two white boys, who gave their names as James Smith and Wade O'Callaghan, stealing a ride on his train and when the train stopped at Moreland he called the marshal and assisted in placing the boys under arrest. The train started to pull out and in trying to swing onto the moving train, Puckett lost his footing and fell under the cars.

Young Puckett was born and reared near Moreland. He bore an excellent reputation and was steadily working his way up as a railroad employee. He had just been promoted to be a conductor and was making his last run as a flagman. His tragic death is greatly deplored by everybody.

The boys, Smith and O'Callaghan, who were the indirect cause of Puckett's death, live in Atlanta and belong to good families, it is said. They are young fellows 17 or 18 years of age. After being arrested they were jailed here and on Tuesday were brought to trial before Judge A.D. Freeman. On pleas of guilty of stealing a ride on a train, they were fined $5 and costs each, making the escapade cost each of them about $30. They communicated with their relatives in Atlanta, who immediately furnished money to pay their fines and they were released.

April 23, 1907 — (HDN)

Comer McWilliams, sawyer for W.A. McWilliams, whose mill is located near C.C. Williams and within two miles of Dubois, was accidentally killed last Thursday. Mr. McWilliams was operating the saw when a piece of lumber struck him in the side, causing internal injuries from which he died in about two hours . . . He is survived by his wife and one child.

JNO. W. GRIFFIN MANGLED TO DEATH BY TRAIN. Horrible Accident in Eastman This Morning Results In Death Of Prominent Young Man. Body dragged 200 Yards. – Both Feet Amputated and Limbs Torn Into Shreds, The Right Thigh Being Jerked From Its Socket.

One of the most horrible accidents of which the human mind can conceive occurred in Eastman this morning about 1:30 o'clock, which resulted about four hours later in the death of John W. Griffin, Jr., a brother of Col. C.W. Griffin of this city and Mrs. J.G. Girrardeau of Abbeville.

Up to about two weeks ago Mr. Griffin had been working with his cousin, Mr. J.L. Wooten, in the naval stores business near Americus, since which time he had been visiting his sister in Abbeville. On Wednesday afternoon he accompanied Mr. Charlie Harrell from Abbeville to Eastman, they driving through the country and reaching Eastman about 1 o'clock this morning, Mr. Griffin having come through for the purpose of going to Macon on the Southern train that passes here about 1:30 o'clock. They drove to the Southern depot, where Mr. Griffin got out of the buggy, after which Mr. Harrell went to his home on College street.

For some reason, when the train reached Eastman, Mr. Griffin did not get on the regular passenger coach; in fact he did not get on the train at all until it pulled out from the station. He caught on to the rear step of the sleeper next to the rear coach of the train, and this was the last seen of him until about 4 o'clock, when he was discovered by Mrs. D.M. Bush, who had risen to see her husband off to his mill about five miles below town. She went to her front door, and as she did so was seen by Mr. Griffin, who whistled to attract her attention. Mr. Griffin was lying on the right hand side of the railroad track, looking north, just in front of the residence of Depot Agent W.A. Burk, who resides just above the Bush residence.

Mrs. Bush saw immediately that something was wrong and Mr. Burk was hurriedly called. He went at once to the young man's rescue, but before he could extract him from his position he was obliged to leave him and run up the railroad to flag down freight train No. 52, which was approaching. Mr. Burk then soon had Drs. Herrman, Wilkins and other citizens on the scene, and the young man was carried to the office of Dr. Herrman, where he died about 8:45 o'clock.

Both of Mr. Griffin's feet were cut off just above his ankles and were found about 75 yards above the depot on the right hand side of the track. From this point signs show that his body was drug (*sic*) on the inside of the right hand rail a distance of about 200 yards, during which time his legs were terribly mangled, his right leg being torn from its socket and cut off just below the body. This part of Mr. Griffin's leg has not yet been found. His left leg was broken to pieces and mashed into the frog of the railroad where the oil mill side track comes into the main line, at which point his body was found. There were also many bruises on his body and head. As soon as the physicians saw his condition they recognized at once that there was no chance for him to live; in fact it is very remarkable that he lived as long as he did. How it was that Mr. Griffin boarded the train on the left side and his body was drug (*sic*) 200 yards on the right side of the track and thrown out on that side is unexplained except by the theory that he found the door to the sleeping car locked and attempted to step to the next car slipping in under and between the two, but over and above the air brakes, and holding on to some object until he slid to the other side of the train and had his feet amputated by the wheels on the right side. Mr. Griffin's hands were badly blistered, and this fact would seem to bear out the theory stated. Freight No. 53, going north, passed up the road about an hour behind the passenger, and this train was also compelled to have passed over the limb of Mr. Griffin wedged in the switch.

Mr. Griffin was conscious to the extent of recognizing his friends and acquaintances in Eastman, but was never able to give any intelligent statement of the accident.

October 10, 1907 ───────────── (DTJ)

CAUGHT IN COTTON GIN, LOST HIS LIFE AS RESULT. W.R. Pharis Mangled in Purvis Gin. Lived Several Hours. Two Hours Getting Body Out of the Machine.

The first ginning accident of the season occurred Friday about noon at the Purvis gin in Lowery district. Mr. W.R. Pharis, age about 52 years, was caught in the gin and lost his life.

From what we can learn the gin was a hand feed machine, which Mr. Pharis was operating. In some manner, just how, cannot be learned, Mr. Pharis' right arm was drawn into the machine together with his shoulder and head. Fully two hours was required by those present to get the body from the gin, which literally had to be taken to pieces. The right arm was literally cut into small pieces, two ribs were sawed in two, and the neck and face were badly lacerated by the saws.

Mr. Pharis was rendered unconscious from the shock almost at the outset, and never regained consciousness, although he lived until 8 o'clock Friday night. The funeral was held Saturday morning, attended by a large number of friends and relatives.

—Dublin Times.

MORRIS KAUSMAN INSTANTLY KILLED. Fell From Top of Court House, Striking His Head Against Stone Steps and Causing Almost Instant Death.

Morris Kausman, while working on the Court House Tuesday afternoon, fell and was almost instantly killed. His head which struck the stone steps of the east entrance, was horribly crushed and received as gash five inches long. In the descent his head grazed one of the large stone columns, leaving marks of blood.

The body was carried to J.W. Peacock's undertaking parlor and shrouded. Early Wednesday morning it was shipped to Savannah for burial. An inquest held Tuesday night resulted in a verdict by the jury that Mr. Kausman met his death by accident. He carried life and accident insurance to the amount of several thousand dollars.

Mr. Kausman was a Polish Jew. He came to Eastman from Savannah, where a brother, sister and other relatives live, something less than two weeks ago, to assist in adjusting the copper work on the Court House. He was 42 years of age and his aged mother whom he had not seen in several years, lives in Poland. Shortly before his death he was heard to remark that he was going back to Poland to see his mother, just as soon as his work here was finished. This would have been within the next two or three weeks.

December 5, 1907 ──────── (DTJ)

CARBOLIC ACID CAUSED DEATH. Tax Receiver Davis, of Crisp County, Took Drink Through Mistake.

Cordele, Ga., November 30 – The entire population of

the city was made sad at an early hour this morning when it was learned that J.M. Davis, tax collector of Crisp County, was dead.

Sadder still was the fact that the deceased came to his death from a drink of carbolic acid taken through mistake for medicine. The unfortunate man was suffering from an operation which had been made on him a week or two ago and when the physician called last night to dress the wound he requested his patient to take a stimulant. He went to another room for the stimulant and there, by a fatal mistake, took the deadly acid instead and died in twenty minutes. Davis was one of the city's most prominent citizens and was ex-postmaster.

The funeral took place this afternoon, conducted by Rev. F. W. Cramer, and the remains were interred by the Masonic Order.

March 14, 1908 ———————— (DE)

DRANK WOOD ALCOHOL. A correspondent writing from Baxley last Sunday says: Reports reached here tonight to the effect that Andrew Wilson, Watson Norris, Middleton Overstreet and Troy Roberson of Appling county were poisoned at Brunswick today.

Wilson is dead and Norris and Roberson are reported to be in a dying condition. The four men carried a raft of timber to Darien and from there the party went to Brunswick where they secured a bottle of wood alcohol, supposed to have been whiskey.

The unfortunate young men are well known in Appling where they were born and reared.

July 24, 1908 —————————————— (HDN)

LIVED WEEK WITH BROKEN NECK. A.B. Young Died At Macon After Injuring Himself in Telfair County While Diving.

Macon, July 18 – A.B. Young, a prominent citizen of Telfair County, residing in Eastman, died in the hospital here today from a broken spinal column which he sustained one week ago while in bathing with a number of friends at his home. He jumped head-foremost into the lake where the party were swimming and struck bottom, inflicting the fracture that resulted fatally.

He lived a sufficient length of time after the accident for the physicians to have hopes of saving his life. The neck was found to be badly fractured. He is survived by a family of ten children and is well known throughout a wide community.

October 6, 1908 —————————————— (HDN)

VIENNA MAN IS KILLED. M.A. Sheppard, Oil Mill Superintendent, Beaten to Pulp When Caught by Revolving Pulley.

Vienna, Ga., October 3 – M.A. Sheppard, night superintendent of the Vienna Cotton Oil Company, was caught on a pulley in the gin room this morning and crushed to death. Every bone was broken, and one arm torn from the body. He leaves a mother and sister in Unadilla. The interment will take place there.

October 30, 1908 ——————— (HDN)

BY FALL OF PLATFORM. Superintendent of Cotton Mills Killed at Eastman.

Eastman, Ga., October 27 – This morning, between 8 and 9 o'clock, an accident occurred at the Eastman Cotton Mills. While Will Hurt, Cleve Holder and Tom Dye were trucking a bale of cotton from the warehouse to the line room, the platform fell from an elevation of about ten feet.

Superintendent T.J. Bolin was standing on the platform and the four men fell with the cotton and trucks, killing Bolin almost instantly, and injuring the others more or less seriously.

December 22, 1908 ——————— (HDN)

SWALLOWED A FLY; DIED IN TWO HOURS.

Quitman, Ga., December 18 – News was received here this morning of the death of Mrs. J.W. Crawford under most unusual circumstances. Yesterday morning while preparing breakfast Mrs. Crawford was talking, when a fly flew into her mouth and before realizing what had happened she swallowed the insect.

She at once became ill and her husband gave her a glass of salty warm water as an emetic. This had the desired effect of removing the fly from her stomach, but she had a violent headache as a result of the experience and in less than two hours she died, almost without warning.

E.L. WALKER SHOT TO DEATH. While Quail Shooting Prominent Lawyer is Accidentally Killed by His Friend, Ben J. Dixon.

Blackshear, Ga., December 18 – Col. E. Lawton Walker, a prominent attorney, recently elected to succeed John W. Bennet as solicitor general of the Brunswick circuit, was shot and killed accidentally by Ben J. Dixon, a special friend, near Walkersville, in this county, while quail shooting Thursday afternoon.

The load of bird shot took effect behind Colonel Walker's right ear, and he expired without speaking, in the arms of his first cousin, Willie Walker.

Colonel Walker leaves a wife and three little children. Col. Walker was elected three times to the Georgia lower house and twice to the senate. He was a brother of J. Randall Walker, the present representative from Lowndes County. His father and mother, Mr. and Mrs. D.J. Walker, reside at Paterson. He married the daughter of Hon. E.S. McGehee, of Blackshear. Col. Walker was 40 years of age. He was a member of the well known law firm of Estes & Walker, of Blackshear. He was a Mason, K. of P., and an Odd Fellow.

FARTHER (*sic*) **MISTAKEN FOR BURGLAR.**

McRae, Ga., June 7 – News has just reached here that Henry E. Morris, a farmer, about six miles out, was mistaken last night for a burglar by his young son and was shot with a shotgun loaded with buckshot. Mr. Morris is an old man and is hard of hearing and when halted by his son did not make any response. The young man, believing that he was a burglar, shot him.

July 3, 1909 ——————————————— (DE)

FATAL RESULTS FROM EATING WATER MELON.
Little Willie Clement the eleven year old son of Mr. and Mrs. Berry Clement who live about seven miles from town, died last Saturday afternoon and was buried at Arno church on Sunday morning following. He was apparently in good health on Thursday, when he and his cousin Miss Lota Stevens, of this place, ate a water melon that had been in the sun all day, and the little fellow was suddenly taken with pains in the stomach which continued without relief until his death.

Miss Lota Stevens was also taken violently ill on Friday . . . her mother who was with her, put her in a buggy and hurried to her home in Douglas where a physician could be secured and relief obtained, and the young lady . . . will soon be in her usual health.

July 24, 1909 ——————————————— (DE)

RALPH SEDELMEYER MEETS HORRIBLE DEATH.
Fitzgerald, Ga., July 19 – At 9:30 this morning Ralph Sedelmeyer, the only son of Jacob Sedelmeyer, was instantly electrocuted by a live electric light wire while on the top of a building that he was helping to move. The wire, which were (*sic*) carrying a current of 2,280 volts, caught on the chimney of the house, and the young man caught hold of them with his hand to lift them over the obstruction.

He fell on the three wires and was held there until pulled off by one of the men who was working with him.

August 21, 1909 ———————————— (DE)

Fitzgerald, Ga., While helping move a piano today Mr. Eugene Keefer was instantly killed by the falling out of the wagon on him. Keefer fell out first and as he lay on his back the piano struck him on the chest, crushing him. He leaves a widow, four sons and two daughters . . .

August 24, 1909 ———————————— (HDN)

KILLED AT SHINGLE MILL. D.W. McCartney Fell On Saw Last Monday and Was Cut Almost In Two.

Mr. D.W. McCartney, a sawyer at the shingle mill of C. Parker & Bro., about nine miles east of Hawkinsville, met with a horrible death last Monday morning as the result of an accident. He was standing on a piece of bark at the mill when his foot slipped, causing him to fall on the saw and before he could be removed and the machinery stopped he was cut almost in two and died a few moments later in great agony.

Mr. McCartney was about 20 years old and formerly lived at Findley, Ga., to which place the remains were shipped for interment.

October 9, 1909 ———————————— (DE)

A.P. PERHAM, JR., KILLED DURING ELECTRIC STORM.

Waycross, Ga., Oct. 6 – A.P. Perham, Jr., editor of the *Waycross Herald*, was instantly killed in an electric storm of violence, that swept over this place today, destroying telephone and telegraph wires and throwing live wires about the streets.

A number of horses, some of them fine animals, met instant death in coming in contact with the wires, while danger was rife.

That no immediate death except Mr. Perham's occurred is regarded as surprising. Mr. Perham was on the street near the office of the Southern Express Company, when a live wire, dangling from a pole struck him. He dropped to the street dead.

December 18, 1909 ———————— (DE)

LITTLE GIRL KILLED AT CAIRO.

Cairo, Ga., Dec. 12 – At an early hour this morning while sitting at the table eating breakfast, the little daughter of Mr. and Mrs. A.D. Brinson was instantly killed when a pistol ball crashed through her brain.

An uncle of the little girl was sitting in an adjoining room and was examining a pistol, when it accidentally discharged, the bullet passing through the wall between the two rooms and hitting the little girl in the head. She fell forward in her plate dead.

The little victim was 5 years old and was a bright little girl.

The accident was singular and very horrible. Members of the family were sitting at the table with the little girl at the time of the accident.

Almost instantaneous with the report of the gun the ball passed through the wall and struck the little girl. The ball passed through her head and into an adjoining wall.

May 10, 1910   (HDN)

BOY KILLED BY PLAYMATE. He Was Son of State School Commissioner Pound.

Milledgeville, Ga., May 7 – Today at noon Jere M. Pound, son of State School commissioner Pound, was accidentally shot to death by a playmate. With a playful remark the boy pointed the gun at his schoolmate and pulled the trigger. Young Pound's side was torn off and the backbone severed, causing death instantly. The boy who did the shooting is in a critical condition. Both were in the sophomore class, Georgia Military College, here. Pound was just 15 years of age, but had many friends among older people. Commissioner Pound was at home and soon on the scene, but was not allowed to view his child for some time. . . . The funeral will be held at Barnesville Sunday afternoon.

July 30, 1910   (HDN)

FOOLED WITH PISTOL AND KILLS HIS FRIEND. The Sad, Old Story Bobs Up Again In The Death Of Ollie Hubbard.

Eastman, Ga., July 27 – News reached here this afternoon of the accidental killing of Ollie Hubbard by Earnest Horne. It seems that these men had just purchased two improved Smith and Wesson pistols. Horne's pistol cylinder revolved to the right, while Hubbard's revolved to the left. Hubbard said jokingly to Mrs. Horne, after putting the muzzle of the pistol to his breast, to pull the trigger. She asked him to put the weapon up. Hubbard then turned and told Horne to pull the trigger since his wife would not.

Horne, after seeing no cartridges in the cylinder on

the side from which he thought the cylinder should revolve, pulled the trigger, the gun firing and killing Hubbard instantly. The bullet passed entirely through Hubbard's body, and struck Dewey Horne, a 10-year-old boy, who was standing behind him. Young Horne isn't fatally hurt. Both men were the best of friends and have been for years. Hubbard is survived by a young wife, having been married but a few months.

September 20, 1910 ——————— (HDN)

DOUGLAS MAYOR KILLED. AUTO HIT BY TRAIN. F.L. Sweat Meets Tragic Death At Railroad Crossing – Auto Owner Hurt.

Douglas, Ga., September 16 – Hon. F.L. Sweat was killed here today at noon at Cherry street crossing by the northbound Georgia and Florida passenger train. He was in an automobile with T.S. Price, who was also seriously but not fatally injured.

The car was struck by the pilot of the engine and almost totally demolished. Mr. Sweat was mayor of the city, a director of the Georgia and Florida railroad and interested in many large business enterprises.

September 20, 1910 ——————— (HDN)

DIED IN DENTIST'S CHAIR. J.E. Kitchens of Vidalia Meets Unusual Death.

Vidalia, Ga., September 16 – J.E. Kitchens, of Vidalia, met death at Lyons yesterday in a peculiar manner. He had gone to Lyons to have some dental work done. The dentist used gas in order to extract a tooth and Kitchens succumbed to the influence of the anaesthetic and died in the chair. Kitchens was a yard master here for the Macon, Dublin and Savannah Railroad and had been connected with the road for several years. He was 25 years of age, unmarried, and son of Allen Kitchens, of Ohoopee.

September 20, 1910 ———————— (VN)

INSTANTLY KILLED AT A SAW MILL. Jim Brown, a Young Negro Fell Across Saws at Lupo's Mill Thursday And Was Cut To Pieces.

Jim Brown, a young negro man employed at the saw mill of S.N. Lupo on the Jordan Bros. plantation six miles southwest of Lilly, met instant death last Thursday about 1 o'clock. From information furnished the News, it seems that the negro jumped up on the carriage when his left foot was caught in the saws and cut off. The force of this jerked his body across on the saws which resulted in his body being almost cut in twain, only being held together by a small piece of skin.

Mr. Lupo was sawing at the time and his clothing was badly smeared up with blood from the horrible accident which happened almost in the twinkling of an eye.

December 7, 1910 ———————— (AB)

MET DEATH. In Horrible Manner – Mr. Cody, Produce Trader, was Killed by Falling Blacksmith Shop.

Mr. J.B. Cody, an elderly man, a chicken and produce dealer by trade, met his death in an especially horrible manner Monday night near Clarkesboro on the Gainesville Midland Railway. Driving his team through Jackson county buying chickens and eggs he was overtaken about 9 o'clock by the rain and wind storm and drove into the yard and under the blacksmith shelter on the place of Mr. John Seegars to protect himself and horse from the severe weather. He had hardly gotten under cover before a strong gust of wind struck the building and it collapsed. The horse, spring wagon, and driver were caught under the debris. A beam of the roof struck Mr. Cody on the back of the head and from indications his death was instantaneous. The horse was pinned to the ground and injured. The groans of the horse aroused Mr. Seegars' family who went to their barn to see if any of the stock were sick. Finding their animals all right they were returning to the house when the moans again attracted their attention. They made further search and discovered the wounded animal piteously moaning from the pain with heavy loads of timber upon him. While extricating the horse they made the horrible discovery of the man, dead evidently for some time.

September 24, 1912 ——————— (VN)

TWO KILLED IN SEABOARD WRECK. Engineer Finch and Flagman Die in Collision – Fireman Fatally Injured.

Americus, Sept. 22 – Two killed outright, one fatally injured and several trainmen more or less hurt was the result of a head-on collision between two Seaboard railroad trains at Stewart's Mill, 8 miles west of Americus.

The dead are:

Engineer Robert Finch, of freight train No. 19, Americus to Montgomery.

John Colbert, colored flagman on train No. 19.

Fireman Thomas Stanley, white, of No. 19, had his left leg

crushed and badly mutilated, besides being scalded on the body. His injuries are regarded as necessary fatal. He was carried to the hospital here. Several of the colored crew of the two trains are more or less injured, but none of these fatally.

Engineer Finch's watch stopped at 6:25 o'clock. He was 25 years old and was to have been married shortly. Fireman Stanley resides in Americus and has a family.

June 5, 1913 ———————————— (AbC)

POSTMASTER WIMBERLY DIES OF POISONING. Which It Is Believed Was Intended For Another – City Greatly Shocked – Investigation Made.

Mr. Leon P. Wimberly, for sixteen years postmaster of Abbeville, died Tuesday morning at 4:30 o'clock from accidental poisoning.

Sunday morning Mr. Wimberly went to the postoffice to attend to his duties as postmaster. On arriving there he found a package at the parcel post window with three ordinary two cent stamps on it and without an address. Upon examination it appeared to have had an address but it had been lost off. Mr. Wimberly made an inquiry trying to find out the sender, but being unable to do so, he in the presence of Mr. J.R. Monroe, opened the package which proved to be a half pint flask apparently filled with whiskey, bearing a well known brand. Mr. Wimberly started home and on the way met two of his nephews, Messrs. J.L. and Wimberly McLeod, who accompanied him home. Arriving there Mr. Wimberly made a lemonade and dashed it with a small quantity of the whiskey of which he and Mr. Wimberly McLeod partook, the latter going to his home several blocks away.

Soon afterward both became deathly sick and physicians

were summoned and the symptoms denoted poisoning. Dr. George attended McLeod, and in a few minutes caused vomiting which emptied his stomach of the poison and he soon recovered, having eaten a hearty breakfast, which the doctor says caused him to throw off the poison.

Mr. Wimberly called Dr. Heiser at once and owing to the fact that he had not eaten any breakfast the treatment did not have the desired effect. Dr. Googe was called in and they did everything they could to relieve him; and about 3 p.m. Mr. Wimberly lapsed into unconsciousness from which he never rallied. He died Tuesday morning at 4:30 o'clock.

That it was intended that Mr. Wimberly should get the poison is not generally believed, as he was beloved by all and did not have a known enemy. What the nature of the poison is cannot be known until the chemist makes his report, but some express the belief that it is bichloride of mercury.

Funeral services were held at the Methodist church Wednesday morning at ten o'clock by Rev. A.B. Hall, pastor of the Baptist church, after which the interment was at Stubbs cemetery by the Knights of Pythias, of which he was a beloved member.

Deceased leaves a wife and three small girls, one son, Leon P. Wimberly Jr., of Cordele, his mother, Mrs. Julia Wimberly, of Hawkinsville, one brother, Mr. Will Wimberly of Macon, and three sisters, Mrs. Geo. F. McLeod and Mrs. J.J. Barfield, of this city and Mrs. T.B. Ragan of Hawkinsville, and a large number of friends to mourn his sad demise.

March 31, 1914 ———————————— (HDN)

W.H. THORNTON, CORDELE, MANGLED BENEATH TRAIN. Former Chief of Police Killed As He Tries to Cross the Tracks.

Cordele, Ga., March 28 – Mr. W.H. Thornton, a prominent citizen and former chief of police of Cordele, was run over and instantly killed by southbound passenger train of the Georgia Southern and Florida railroad at 2 o'clock this afternoon at the union passenger station in this city. Mr. Thornton was caught beneath the pilot of the engine just before the train came to a stop at the station and his body was severely gashed and both of his legs were cut off before the train came to a standstill.

It is said that Mr. Thornton crossed over the platform of passenger train standing at the station to go to his place of business and as he alighted from the train to the ground the train from the south was approaching and caught him under the pilot. Engineer F.E. Long, in charge of the train, makes the statement that he did not know the accident had happened until he had stopped his train. The body was dragged about thirty feet. Mr. Thornton leaves a wife and two daughters.

April 28, 1914 ———————————— (HDN)

AUTOMOBILE DEALER KILLED NEAR MACON. Cordele Man's Skull Crushed When Auto Overturned. Three Others Injured.

Macon, Ga., April 26 – Harry Jacobs, an automobile dealer of Cordele, was killed outright, and three other well-known Cordele men were injured early this morning when the automobile in which they were traveling from Cordele to Atlanta, overturned at D_____, Ga., fourteen miles south of Macon. The injured men are A.J. Little, cashier for the Seaboard; E.C. Purcell, employed by the implement house, and J.A. Smith, a wholesale hide dealer; Charles Greer, prominent farmer. The other men in the car escaped injury.

The accident was due to a tire blowing which caused the speeding car to turn turtle. Jacobs was caught under the tool box of the machine, his skull being crushed. The other three injured men were pinioned beneath the car. Green (*sic*) was thrown free of the wreckage.

Jacobs was 34 years of age and for several years was employed by the Seaboard Air Lines Railroad at Americus, where he married Miss Lizzie Hays. Besides his widow he leaves four children. The body will be taken to Americus for interment.

October 29, 1914 ——————————— (AbC)

MR. J.F. FUTCH MEETS WITH INSTANT DEATH.
Mr. J.F. Futch, a prominent citizen of Telfair County, who resided about two miles from Milan, was instantly killed on the public road midway between Milan and Chauncey on Monday afternoon, when his automobile became entangled in a telephone wire, and the pole at the side of the road, to which the wire was attached, broke off about a foot above the ground, and fell across Mr. Futch's head with terrific force, crushing his skull and killing him instantly.

Mr. Futch, accompanied by Mr. Dillard Lucas, was en-route from Milan to Chauncey, and . . . passed under a drooping telephone wire, which a little further along the road in the direction they were traveling, lay on the ground parallel with the road, rising gradually to the height of the next pole. It is supposed that Mr. Futch discovered that the wire had become attached to the car, and threw out his clutch, cut off the gasoline and applied the brakes, but by this time the strain on the wire had become so strong that the pole to which it was attached popped off and was jerked with fearful force across the side and back of Mr. Futch's head, Mr. Futch evidently being in a leaning position at the time. . . . The automobile, which is a large Cadillac, stopped within a very short distance from the point of the accident, and was not injured . . .

Mr. Futch was 46 years old, and leaves a wife and five children. . . . Mr. Futch's funeral was conducted in the Methodist church at Rhine Tuesday afternoon . . . after which the body was interred in the Rhine Cemetery . . .

—Eastman Times-Journal.

November 26, 1914 ———— (HHJ)

A DEATH AT HENDERSON. On last Friday evening at six o'clock this community was shocked to learn of the accidental death of Charlie Jim Davis, oldest child of Mr. And Mrs. J. W. Davis, who was struck such a blow by part of a falling tree, which he was helping to saw as to cause death three hours later.

On the day before he was at school, one of the brightest and happiest of the number, with prospects of a long and useful life. How soon the death summons came and shadowed the promising future of this bright boy . . .

March 17, 1915 — (HDN)

BLOWS WIFE'S HEAD OFF. John (*sic*) Morrison Was Unloading Gun When It Accidentally Discharged.

Scotland, March 11 – Mrs. Robert (*sic*) Morrison was instantly killed last night about 8 o'clock at Erick, her head being blown off when a shot gun in the hands of her husband was being unloaded after a hunting expedition. Mrs. Morrison was 19 years old, and had been married about three years, her husband being 21. They had no children. There were no witnesses to the fatal accident. Mr. Morrison is almost prostrate with grief. [Ed. Note: It is unclear what Mr. Morrison's given name was; he is called John in the headline and then Robert in the text of the article.]

April 7, 1915 — (HDN)

LITTLE BOY KILLED AT GRIST MILL. Thomas Martin Caught in Shafting and Hurled Instantly to Death. Thomas Martin, the nine-year-old son of Mr. and Mrs. W.A. Martin, met with a horrible death last Saturday morning at the grist mill of Mr. T.J. Martin, three and one-half miles northeast of the city. Little Thomas, with two other small boys, was in the engine room watching the machinery, when his clothes got caught in the shafting and he was hurled to death instantly, his body being mangled in a horrible manner. . . . The remains were interred in the Martin cemetery Sunday afternoon at three o'clock, the funeral services being conducted by the Baptist and Methodist pastors of Cochran.

MRS. A.B. FLOYD KILLED AT FITZGERALD. By a Switch Engine As She Stepped On Track At a Street Corner. News of the tragic death of Mrs. A.B. Floyd, in Fitzgerald, Wednesday morning, was learned here over the telephone a short time afterward. According to the information at hand, Mrs. Floyd, en route to the home of a relative for a visit, stopped at a street and railroad crossing while a long freight train pulled by. After it had passed she stepped forward and on a parallel track on which was a switch engine going in an opposite direction to that of the freight train.

The noise of the train had prevented Mrs. Floyd hearing the approach of the switch engine, and as she stepped on the track, she was struck a death-dealing blow, her neck being broken and internal injuries sustained. . . . The body was brought to the old family burying ground at Pope's church near Finleyson, Thursday, for funeral and interment.

—Fitzgerald Leader

COOKED TO DEATH IN VAT OF HOT ROSIN. Waycross Man Meets Terrible Death at a Turpentine Still — Body is Coated With Rosin.

Waycross, June 15. – W.H. Bennett, Turpentine operator, fell head first into a vat of boiling rosin at a still here today and was cooked to death. A coroner's inquest was held this afternoon and the jury agreed that Mr. Bennett must have suffered a stroke of apoplexy when he was near the vat, plunging to his death when stricken.

A negro helper pulled Mr. Bennett from the vat, but too late to save his life.

The upper half of the man's body was covered by a coating of rosin from one to three inches thick and the flesh on the face was cooked to the bone. The deceased was 56 and had made his home here for years. His wife and eight children survive.

November 3, 1915 (HDN)

J.B. CURRY CRUSHED TO DEATH AT ASHBURN. He Was Coupling Two Cars When Run Over By An H. & F.S. Freight Train.

Mr. Josh B. Curry, aged 26 years, a flagman on the Hawkinsville & Florida Southern railroad, was crushed to death at Ashburn Friday while attempting to couple freight cars on the oil mill siding when he fell through a pair of scales and was run over by the train. The accident occurred about noon and the unfortunate man, though mangled in a horrible manner with both legs cut off, lived about an hour . . .

The body was brought to Hawkinsville Friday evening and carried to his home on Houston street, and the funeral was held from the Baptist church Sunday morning at 9:30 o'clock . . . the interment was made in Orange Hill Cemetery.

April 20, 1916 (ECN)

A SHOCKING TRAGEDY. Curry West, 14 year old son of Mrs. T.E. West, accidentally shot himself and died instantly Tuesday morning about nine o'clock.

The fatal accident occurred out on Little river, where the lad went with a party of boys to spend the day fishing. Young

West had a twenty-two calibre rifle, and while they were all fixing their fishing tackle he took a bullet from his rifle and cut off the end of it, making a sinker for his line. The same shell was placed back in the rifle and he attempted to hang the gun up on a tree. It fell from the limbs of the tree, the barrel falling against his bosom and the trigger striking an object that caused it to fire. The bullet which he had just cut in half entered the lower part of his chest and pierced his heart.

"I am shot" the young man cried to the boys close by, and they came immediately to him, but he never spoke further. His body was lifted into the automobile and with all haste he was brought to Moultrie where he might receive medical attention. But somewhere en route he died. When the car came into Moultrie the body was lifeless . . .

May 31, 1916 ———————————————— (HDN)

BOZEMAN KILLED WHEN AUTO TURNS OVER.
Petty Escapes, But Negro Is Seriously Injured and is Expected to Die.

Jeffersonville, May 28 – Losing control of his Ford automobile as he sought to speed past a buggy on the road between here and Danville this afternoon, "Dud" Bozeman, of the latter place, was instantly killed when the machine turned turtle and rolled over two or three times.

A negro riding in the car was so badly injured that he is expected to die but Frank Petty, who sat beside Mr. Bozeman, marvelously escaped injury. The victim, who was driving, was instantly killed, his neck being broken and his skull crushed. . . . The dead man was about 45 years old and is survived by his wife and several children.

May 31, 1916 ——————————————— (HDN)

YOUNG MAN DROWNED IN THE OCMULGEE.

A young man by the name of Peek, who is said to have lived near Abbeville, was drowned in the Ocmulgee river a short distance below Henley's landing Tuesday morning. He is said to have gone to the river fishing, and is supposed to have fallen in while in the throes of an epileptic fit, to which he was subjected. His body, which was lying in shallow water with his knees protruding above the surface, was discovered by Mr. Dave Dowdy and companion, supposedly an hour or two after he had fallen into the water. The body was carried to Rhine, where an inquest was held by Judge George W. Ryals the verdict of the jury being that death was caused by drowning. It is said that there was not a bruise or scratch of any nature on the body.

—Eastman TimesJournal

June 1, 1916 ——————————————— (AbC)

BIG CARP DROWNS NEGRO IN OCMULGEE. Negro Is Found In River With Fishing Line Wrapped Around Leg and 46 Pound Fish On Line.

News reached Abbeville today of the drowning of an old negro by the name of Wilcox, near Mossy Log landing on the Ocmulgee river several miles below this place. The old man, who was about 80 years old, went carp fishing and as he had not returned the next morning his family went to the place where he usually fished and saw the pole sticking out of the water across the river. Getting a boat they went to the pole and upon pulling it up found the old man with the line wrapped around his legs. Upon trying to pull the line out of the water it was found to be hung in an old tree top which finally gave way and they brought up a carp which weighed 46 pounds. The supposition is that the fish pulled the old man in the river and he became tangled in the line and was drowned.

August 31, 1916 ──────────── (AbC)

J.M. WALKER DROWNED IN TANK OF GASOLINE.

Thomasville, Ga., August 27 – To be drowned in a tank of gasoline was the unusual fate of Joel M. Walker, agent in Monticello, Fla., for the Standard Oil Company, a few days ago. Mr. Walker, it is supposed, was taking the measurement of the tank when he fell in and was drowned. The tank was an 8,000 gallon one and it would have been impossible for anyone to get out alone. It was some hours before he was missed and when found had been dead some time.

November 22, 1916 ──────────── (HDN)

THREE KILLED BY TRAIN AT FITZGERALD. Will J. Royal, Jr., Miss Minnie Royal and Miss Taylor Victims of Auto Accident.

Fitzgerald, November 18 – William J. Royal and sister, Miss Minnie Royal, and Miss Mary A. Taylor, a school teacher of Americus, were instantly killed, Miss Irene McGough, of Lilly, suffered fractures of her limbs and the Rev. B.C. Pritchett, of Mystic, was injured abdominally when a mixed train of freight cars and empty passenger coaches of the Ocilla Southern struck Royal's Overland automobile at the Central avenue crossing of the Ocilla Southern this afternoon at 4:30 o'clock.

A flagman, it is said, signaled the automobile to stop.

Royal put on his brakes and stopped on the track as the train crashed into the tonneau. The party had been in town shopping and were returning to Royal's home in Ambrose. Miss McGough and Mr. Pritchett are at a Fitzgerald hospital and both are doing as nicely as could be expected . . .

January 3, 1917 ———————— (HDN)

SHOCKED TO DEATH WHILE UNDER TENT. Clyde Beard, Operator of a Merry-Go-Round, Killed By Electricity at Eastman.

Eastman, December 27 – Clyde Beard, 18-year-old son of W.J. Beard, of Martinsville, N.C., who has been operating a merry-go-round in Eastman for the past week, was shocked to death by electricity this morning at 5:30 o'clock under the tent that shelters the merry-go-round. Young Beard, with another young man, slept under the tent. Just how he met his death no one knows, but it is supposed that a live wire came in contact with the metal frame of the merry-go-round, and that when he arose from his cot he came into contact with parts of the metal frame, a large volume of electricity passing through his body.

The other young man was also severely shocked but scrambled from under the tent and fell unconscious outside. He soon revived but was unable to tell how either of them received the injury. The body of young Beard, accompanied by his father, was taken to Eller, N.C. for interment.

January 10, 1917 ———————— (HDN)

KILLED DURING COON HUNT. J.J. Christian, Well-Known Laurens County Man, Meets With Accident.

Dudley, January 6 – J.J. Christian was killed while on

a coon hunt. A limb of a tree he chopped down fell on him and broke his neck. The decedent lived on R.F.D. No. 2 from Dudley and was a successful country merchant and farmer. He was 35 years old and well known in Laurens County.

January 17, 1917 ————————— (HDN)

MRS. WHITSON MEETS WITH HORRIBLE DEATH.
Many of our citizens will remember Mrs. Mary T. Whitson, the well-known newspaper correspondent who visited Hawkinsville a few weeks ago and furnished a complimentary writeup of some of our leading business men and county officers for the *Dispatch and News*. On Tuesday of last week Mrs. Whitson was crushed to death when a freight elevator descended upon her as she stood in the shaft in the rear of 81 North Prior street in Atlanta, Ga. Mrs. Whitson was 70 years old and a pioneer resident of Atlanta.

February 15, 1917 ————————— (AbC)

MANGLED BODY ON RAILROAD TRACK.
The mangled body of Mr. Sam McCranie, of Milan, was found on the railroad track in front of the Studstill Hotel, in that place, on Sunday morning, the condition of the body indicating that death had taken place several hours previously, and his skull was badly crushed and mangled; his feet were also cut off, and one of his arms had been crushed. The balance of the body was practically intact. It is supposed that Mr. McCranie was run over by a westbound freight train that passed through Milan about 3 o'clock Sunday morning.

Coroner G.C. Rogers, of this county, was sent for, and an inquest was held Sunday afternoon. At the inquest evidence was developed that Mr. McCranie was drinking Saturday night, and that his brother, Mr. Dave McCranie, who is a policeman at Milan, had taken a pistol away from him during the early part of the night; also that the dead man had afterward borrowed another pistol from Mr. George Lowery. This pistol, containing five empty shells, was found on his person Sunday morning. Evidence was given that a number of pistol shots had been heard during the night in the vicinity of where the body was found. Mr. McCranie was last seen alive, according to the testimony, about 1 o'clock Saturday night.

A verdict was rendered by the coroner's jury to the effect that Mr. McCranie came to his death by being run over by the Seaboard train above referred to. Prominent citizens of Milan, however, expressed the opinion that Mr. McCranie had been killed and his body then placed on the track, and in support of this opinion cited the fact that practically no blood was found on the railroad track where the body was found, or along the track over which the body had been dragged by the train. Mr. McCranie was about 35 years of age and leaves a wife and two children.

–Eastman TimesJournal.

March 14, 1917 ———————————— (HDN)

UNADILLA WOMAN DIES FROM HEADACHE TABLETS.

Unadilla, Ga., March 7 – Mrs. Floy Hudson, twenty-two years old, of Snow, four miles west of here, died in a drug store an hour after taking two strychnine tablets for the headache.

Mrs. Hudson came to Unadilla Monday morning about 10 o'clock to consult a doctor. She took the two tablets, according to her statement, before she died about 12 o'clock. Her statements were broken but it was gleaned from them that she had a headache and did not think the tablets would hurt her. When she was about fourteen years old she married Louis Hudson, well known farmer of Snow but they have not been living together in a number of months.

August 15, 1917 ——————— (HDN)

MRS. E.H. BACON MEETS TRAGIC DEATH.

Mrs. E.H. Bacon, one of Eastman's most prominent and greatly beloved women, was instantly killed and her body horribly mangled at 11:45 on Saturday morning last by a local freight train No. 97, southbound, in charge of Conductor Dave Simpson and Engineer Burgess.

The accident occurred at the railroad crossing just south of the Southern depot, and in the heart of the business section of the city. The engineer was switching cars, and had pulled down on the eastern side tract (*sic*) for the switch to be turned so as to run a car back in on the side tract (*sic*) extending toward the W. & T. line. Mrs. Bacon, who was driving a horse, evidently thought the train had pulled on down the road, and was not expecting it to back into the side tract (*sic*) connected with the W. & T. She, therefore, drove onto the track just in time to be struck by the rear car attached to the engine, which was a coal car. The buggy she occupied was completely demolished.

The negro brakeman, Millard Cullers, who was attending the switch, seeing the danger that threatened Mrs. Bacon, ran to the rear of the train, threw on the air brakes, and grabbed the rear wheels of Mrs. Bacon's buggy, making a desperate effort to throw it around and clear the track, but was unable to accomplish his purpose. His arm and shoulder were struck by the car and were badly bruised. The desperate effort of this negro to save Mrs. Bacon's life, in which he really risked his own, is a worthy act that has been the subject of the highest praise.

Mrs. Bacon was the widow of the late Dr. E.H. Bacon, who was for many years a prominent citizen of Eastman. She was born in Allendale, S.C. in 1849, and was 68 years old at the time of her death. She was a daughter of Mr. and Mrs. Thomas Willingham. Soon after the Civil War her parents moved to Albany, Ga., and it was while a resident there that Mrs. Bacon attended Monroe Female College, now Bessie Tift, named for Mrs. Bacon's sister, from which she graduated with first honor . . .

−Eastman Times-Journal.

August 2, 1917 ———————— (AbC)

WORRY OVER DRAFT COSTS TWO LIVES. Young Farmer Kills Wife and Then Suicides – Was Despondent Over the Conscription Law.

Nashville, Ga., July 31 – William Tyson, an industrious young farmer living near Sparks, Ga., shot and instantly killed his wife and then killed himself near Alapaha early this afternoon. They leave four children. Tyson, it is understood, had grown despondent over the conscription law and decided to end it all by taking the life of his wife and himself.

November 1, 1917 ━━━━━━━━━ (AbC)

TWO KILLED WHEN TRAIN HITS AUTO. Tragedy Occurs at Odum – Curry Aspinwall and Baby Meet Death.

Jesup, Ga., October 17 – Two lives were lost at Odum this morning when the Kansas City Special of the Southern Railway hit a Ford car. The dead are: Curry Aspinwall and a two-year-old child. Mr. Aspinwall was teaching Randall Westberry how to run a new Ford automobile. They had Mrs. Lewis and her baby with them, sitting in the back of the car.

Mr. Aspinwall and Mr. Westberry were so intent upon driving the machine that they paid no attention to the fact that they were approaching the track of the Southern railway. As the automobile rolled across the railroad track the locomotive smashed into the rear of the machine. Mr. Aspinwall was hurled against a tree and killed instantly. The baby was thrown under the wheels of the rapidly moving train and both its little legs were cut off. It died a few minutes later.

Mrs. Lewis was thrown out and painfully bruised and cut but her injured (*sic*) are not thought to have been of a serious nature. Mr. Westberry was at the steering wheel and was not thrown out, though he was badly bruised.

November 28, 1917 ━━━━━━━ (HDN)

TEACHER IS KILLED BY FALLING TREE. J.A. Garrard Dies From Injuries Received While Cutting Wood Near Abbeville.

Abbeville, Ga., – From injuries received yesterday while out cutting down trees near the home of W.S. Bush, his father-in-law, J.A. Garrard, a school teacher, died last night eight miles northwest of Abbeville. Mr. Garrard was caught under a falling tree, his skull being fractured. . . . According to information received here, the tree that Mr. Garrard was cutting struck another tree in falling and was thrown in a direction the teacher did not anticipate it would take.

July 1, 1920 ————————————— (AbC)

MR. S.T. CHANDLER, OF MILLEDGEVILLE, FALLS FROM HOUSE; HIS NECK BROKEN.

Milledgeville, Ga., June 30 – Mr. Samuel T. Chandler, one of the most widely-known young men in Baldwin county, and a member of one of the prominent families of this section, fell from the roof of a two-story residence Tuesday evening shortly before 7 o'clock and broke his neck, dying instantly.

At the time the accident happened Mr. Chandler was assisting in the painting of the roof of his mother-in-laws summer home, about six miles out from Milledgeville. When he fell he had just reached the eaves of the two-story residence, his foot slipping, and he fell head first to the ground, a distance of some thirty feet.

September 30, 1920 ————————— (AbC)

TWO DIED WHEN A.B.& A. TRAINS MEET. Disaster Follows Wreck of North-Bound Passenger Train in Collision With Freight Saturday.

A.B.&A. passenger train No. 16, northbound, last Saturday morning met a special freight train near Manchester, Ga., in a head on collision with the result that beside inestimable property damage to the trains, R.L. Foster, of Woodland, section foreman, and Mack Gunn, of this city, fireman, were instantly killed, and other members of the crews and passengers in the colored coach were more or less severely injured.

Engineer William Swain, of this city, pilot of the freight special, entirely exonerated the other members of his crew and shouldered the entire blame for the accident. According to his statement, he failed to take account of the time lost in repairing a hot box, and thought he had plenty of time to make the next siding. This wreck was probably the worst in the history of the road from the standpoint of both life and property lost.

Besides the two dead, Engineer E.W. Carney, of this city, Mail Clerk McElroy, of Manchester, and a chinaman of Macon, were severely wounded, while strong hopes are held for their recovery and Harry Riddick, passenger conductor, and three negro passengers were hurt.

−Fitzgerald Herald.

ACKNOWLEDGMENTS

I am grateful to the University of Georgia Main Library in Athens, and the Georgia Archives in Morrow, GA, for their collections of newspapers on microfilm available to the public. I originally found many of the items in this book at UGA in their newspapers on microfilm. This extensive collection includes microfilms of every available Georgia newspaper, and researchers can use their facilities free of charge. I made copies of many death reports from newspapers such as the Vienna News, LaGrange Reporter, and Hamilton Visitor while doing genealogy research at UGA.

At the Georgia Archives, I copied many of the items in this book from published collections of newspaper abstracts from various cities and counties. In an effort to conform to copyright laws, I then looked up as many of the articles as possible in the original newspapers on the Georgia Archives website, and have tried to reproduce exactly the spelling, punctuation, capitalization, bold type, and italics used in the original newspaper article.

With the onset of the COVID-19 virus pandemic, it was no

longer advisable to use the newspaper microfilms at the university of Georgia, so I used the Georgia Archives website (www.georgiaarchives.org) exclusively. Some of the items I wished to use were from published books about newspapers not available on this website, namely:

Dodge County Newspaper Clippings, by Tad Evans, 1991

Greene County, Georgia, Newspaper Clippings, by Tad Evans, 1995

Pulaski County, Georgia, Newspaper Clippings, by Tad Evans, 2000

Wilcox County Georgia, Newspaper Clippings, by Tad Evans, 2010

Terrell County, Georgia, Newspaper Clippings, by Elizabeth Evans Kilbourne, 1996

Gordon County, Georgia, Newspaper Clippings, by Elizabeth Evans Kilbourne, 1997

I am grateful to Ms. Elizabeth Evans Kilbourne of Savannah, Georgia, for giving me permission to quote items from her books listed above, as well as those of her late father, Tad Evans. Ms. Kilbourne, Mr. Kenneth L. Thomas, Jr., and Ms. Eve B. Mayes all read the manuscript and offered helpful criticism and suggestions. I am especially grateful to Ms. Mayes for indexing and numbering the pages in this manuscript.

CAUSES OF DEATHS

ACCIDENTS:

Alcohol/Drug Overuse:4, 37, 37-38,62-63,79,97,100,103, 117-118,124-125,126,177,202,218,271-272,287-288.

Animals:
- Alligator: 160-161.
- Bear: 58.
- Bull: 157.
- Elephant: 232-233.
- Horse: 96-97,177.
- Mule: 46, 90, 91,112, 127,140-141,158, 166, 219, 225.
- Rabid Dog/Cat: 192-194, 213, 248-249.
- Snake: 58, 108, 127, 154, 183.

Blunt Force Trauma: 17, 25, 47, 49-51, 77, 82-83, 84, 118-121, 132, 136, 153, 163-164, 179-180, 183-184, 195, 210-211, 211, 212, 212-213, 234, 258, 277-278, 278.

Burns: 5, 20-21, 23, 26, 26-27, 29, 44-45, 45, 68, 72, 75, 79, 79-80, 86, 92, 104, 106, 123, 125-126, 142-143, 150-151, 158, 159, 165-166, 171-174, 176, 188, 188-189, 196, 201-202, 203, 213, 216, 219-220, 222-223, 251-254, 280-281.

Chemicals/Dynamite/Fireworks: 14, 40-41, 131, 229, 230.

Crushing: 12, 59-61, 73, 101-102, 123, 146, 162, 166-167, 184-185, 196-197, 256-257, 264.

Drowning: 3, 3-4, 7-8, 44, 59, 74-75, 76, 87, 100-101, 108, 116-117, 128, 128-129, 162-163, 165, 167, 283, 283-284, 284.

Electrocution: 267, 268-269, 285.

Falling Object: 71, 77, 82, 88, 104, 124, 130, 133, 134, 139, 161-162, 170, 208-209, 255, 268, 285-286, 290-291.

Falls: 2, 20-21, 32, 46, 49, 69-70, 70-71, 71, 121, 149, 149-150, 165, 168, 171, 194, 200, 201, 262, 291.

Firearms:40, 41-42, 42-43, 55-56, 56-57, 66-67, 73, 107, 110-111, 117, 123, 130-131, 138, 145, 145-146, 148-149, 155-156, 168, 170-171, 195, 197, 209-210. 214, 217-218, 222, 229, 240-241, 251, 254, 255, 266, 266-267, 269, 270, 270-271, 279, 281-282.

Freezing: 25, 157-158, 192, 218.

Hanging/Strangling/Broken Neck: 38, 69, 162, 164, 194, 232, 264.

Infection: 85, 198, 206, 245.

Lightning: 12, 68-69, 80-81, 99, 102-103, 163, 248.

Loss of Blood: 9-10, 81-82, 199, 215.

Machinery: 29, 53, 54, 78, 79, 100, 124, 131, 147, 155, 195-196, 207, 217, 221, 238-239, 243-244, 261, 279.

Moving vehicles:

Automobile Wreck: 276-277, 282.

Run over by: Fire Engine: 76.

Stagecoach: 10.

Train: 8, 11-12, 15, 18-19, 35-36, 37, 53, 55, 71, 75-76, 78, 85-86, 98, 107, 108, 113-115, 134, 147-148, 168, 169-170, 190, 195, 196, 206, 208, 221, 228, 233, 233-234, 240, 242, 245, 246-247, 249,

MURDERS

NATURAL DEATHS:

Apoplexy/sudden death: 31-32, 73-74, 89-90, 139, 192, 280-281.
Cancer/abnormal growth: 2, 89.
Sunstroke: 45-46, 77.
Other/unknown:39-40, 134-135, 150, 153, 154, 156, 174, 185-186.

SUICIDES:

Burning: 4-5.
Cutting throat:106-107, 223-224.
Drowning: 5, 11, 32, 167.
Drugs/Poison: 26-27, 28, 33, 121, 123, 137, 177-178, 178-179, 224-225, 247.
Hanging: 14-15, 93-95, 104.
Jumping: 48, 152; in front of train: 164, 203-204.
Shooting: 30, 57-58, 105-106, 175-176, 180-181, 200, 241, 289.
Starvation: 45, 207.
Unknown/Other: 84, 90, 199, 243-244.

INDEX

Atlantic & Birmingham rail
   road, 249,250
Attaway
   Ab., 42
Augusta and Savannah
   Railroad, 30
Augusta, Richmond County,
   GA, 20, 27, 30, 54, 77,
   79, 85, 107, 215
Auraria, Lumpkin County,
   GA, 148
Austin
   Mr., 25
Avant
   Dr. A.L.R., 223
   Legree, 223
B.B. Gray & Bro., 215
Babb
   Sanford, 192
Bacon
   Dr. E.H., 289
   Mrs. E.H., 288-289
Badger
   Mattie, 151
Bailey
   Col., 6
   Mr., 85
Bailey's mills, 6
Bainbridge, Decatur County,
   GA, 49, 117, 127, 132,
   167
Bainbridge Independents,
   117

Baker County, GA, 12, 141,
   156
Baker's creek bridge, 134
Baldwin
   W.R., 208
Baldwin County, GA, 2, 25,
   118-119, 206, 270, 291
Baltimore, MD, 172
Bank of Augusta, 20
Banks County, GA, 97-98,
   104, 137, 164
Bankston
   Mrs.William R., 26
Barfield
   Mrs. J.J., 275
Barnesville, Pike (now
   Lamar) County, GA,
   270
Barrow
   Charles, 64
Bartow County, GA, 69, 71,
   104, 157, 190
Bass
   George, 190
   James W., 180-181
Baswildebald
   Charles, 93-95
Bates
   Rowell, 53
Bavaria, 94
Baxley. Appling County, GA,
   169-170, 225, 263

Brown
 Green, 31
 H.M., 126
 Jim, 272
 Robert, 62
Brown's Station, Terrell
 County, GA, 190
Brunson
 Mr., 145
Brunswick and Albany
 Railroad, 109
Brunswick and Western rail
 road, 207
Brunswick, Glynn County,
 GA, 77, 126, 263
Bruster
 John, 38
Bryan County, GA, 82
Bryant
 Jackson, 27
 Roundtree, 199
Buchanan
 Johnnie, 116-117
Buchanan, Haralson County,
 GA, 202
Buchannan
 Conrad, 117
Buckley
 Thomas M., 203
Buena Vista, Marion County,
 GA, 139, 223-224
Buford
 Taylor, 197

Buford, Gwinnett County,
 GA, 73
Bull Street, Savannah, GA,
 70
Bullard
 Joseph, 225
Bulloch County, GA, 101
Bullock
 Mr., 179
Buntin
 Charles, 97
 Rev. William, 97
Burch
 Dr., 255
Burdett
 Dr. William, 73-74
Burgess
 Engineer, 288
Burk
 W.A., 260
Burke County, GA, 32, 50
Burney
 D.L., 211
 Mrs., 211-212
Burnham
 Policeman, 252-253
Burrus
 Jacob, 52
Burton
 Rev. J.C., 184
Bush
 Dr. E.B., 135
 John, 64

Dorough
    Thomas T., 147
Dorse
    Mr., 34
Dorsey
    Mrs., 120
Dossen
    Susan, 174
Dossett
    Hampton, 42
Dougherty County, GA, 89,
    96, 163, 177, 198
Douglas
    William, 53
Douglas County, GA, 187
Douglas, Coffee County, GA,
    226, 267, 271
Douglass
    William, 109
Dowdy
    Dave, 283
Downing
    Jeff, 160-161
Doyle
    Rev. Father, 167
Dozier
    N.W., 208
Drake
    Dr., 118
Dry Creek, 116
Dublin, Laurens County, GA,
    148, 183, 191, 224,
    231, 239, 255

Dubois, Dodge County, GA,
    174, 234, 258, 261
Dudley, Laurens County,
    GA, 286
Dumas
    Obadiah, 29
Dunaway
    Frank, 166-167
Duncan
    John, 168
Dupree
    G.R., 210
    Jordan, 210
DuPree Hall, Athens, GA,
    165
Dutton
    Thomas A., 123
Dye
    Tom, 265
Dykes
    B.B., 197
    Joseph B., 197
Eagle and Phoenix, Augusta,
    GA, 77
Eagle Tavern, Sparta, GA, 2
Early County, GA, 55, 79, 135
Early Street, Columbus, GA,
    63
East Pass, FL, 121
East Point, Fulton County,
    GA, 24, 35-36
East Tennessee and Georgia
    Railroad, 71, 194, 196

Floyd Springs, Floyd County,
GA, 104
Fogarty
Dr., 66
Fokes
Joel, 144
Folsom Mill, 162
Foote
Rev. W.R., 212
Forbes
Dr. Joseph, 112
Forester
G.W., 116
Forsyth County, GA, 5
Forsyth, Monroe County,
GA, 29
Fort
Dr. Tomlinson, 4
Fort Gaines, Clay County,
GA, 19, 61
Fort Jackson, Chatham
County, GA, 50
Fort Pulaski, GA, Chatham
County, 49-50
Fort Valley, Houston (now
Peach) County, GA,
91, 121, 158, 199
Foster
R.L., 291
Robert, 75
Franklin
Max, 164

Franklin Lodge of Odd
Fellows, 54
Franklin, Heard County, GA,
9, 186, 192
Frazier, Pulaski County, GA,
216
Freeman
Jacob, 17
Judge A.D., 258
Friar
Joshua, 81
Frog Pond place, 163
Frost
Samuel J., 129-130
Frozier
Fanny, 72
Fuller
J.F., 191
Fuller's mill, 191
Fulton
C.A., 207
Fulton County, GA, 237
Furney
William, 213
Futch
J.F., 277-278
Gaff
Samuel, 89
Gaffney
Dr., 154
Gainesville Midland Railway,
272

Griffin
> Col. C.W., 259
> E.S., Jr., 179-180
> John W., Jr., 259-261
> Mr., 107
> W.J., 234

Griffis
> J.B., 166-167

Griggs
> Dr. J.W., 212

Grimes
> Coroner, 226

Groover
> J.R., 122

Grove church, 255

Grovenstein
> John, 83

Guerry
> Claude, 208-209
> Goode, 208
> Judge James, 208
> Russell, 208-209

Guest
> Benjamin, 191
> Henry, 191

Gum Swamp, 240

Gunn
> Mack, 291

Gunnells
> Mrs., 177-178
> Woodson L., 177

Gunter
> George, 155

Gwinnett County, GA, 63, 73, 78, 88, 124

Gypsy, the elephant, 232

Hail
> Dr. N.B., 104

Hal, 43

Hall
> Emma, 79
> Ira J., 79
> John F., 226
> Maj. Isaac R., 201-202
> Rev. A.B., 275
> Russel, 73
> Tilden, 255

Hamans
> George W., 198

Hamilton
> John, 102

Hammond
> Col. A.W., 24
> Mrs. Abbie, 172-174

Hampton, Henry County, GA, 106

Hancock
> James, 24

Hancock County, GA, 26, 42, 78, 118-120, 241

Hardeman
> Dr. L.G., 147

Hardy
> T.W., 229

Hargraves
> Joe, 215

Hargroves
    William H., 18
Harmony Grove, Jackson
    County, GA, 147
Harper
    Capt. William H., 40
    Green, 86
    J.N., 214
Harrell
    Charlie, 259
    John, 43-44
    W.F., 254
Harris
    Dick, 176
    Dr., 159
    J.C., 175
    Martin, 159
Harris Camp-meeting, 7
Harris County, GA, 4, 7-8,
    48, 100, 118, 188-189
Harris Guards, 52
Harris Nickel Plate show,
    232
Harrison
    Dr., 191
    Ephran, 237
    Frank, 177
Harrison's Mill, 145
Hart
    John, 251-254
Harvill
    Thomas, 73
Havana, Cuba, 13

Hawkinsville & Florida
    Southern railroad,
    281
Hawkinsville, Pulaski
    County, GA, 44, 66,
    149-150, 193, 194,
    206, 242, 268, 275,
    281, 286
Hayes
    John E., 62
Haynes
    E.J., 257
Hays
    Lizzie, 277
Heard County, GA, 9, 154,
    186, 192, 199
Heard's Store, Dawson
    County, GA, 122
Heiser
    Dr., 275
Helfrich
    S., 94
Henderson, Houston
    County, GA, 278
Henley's landing, 283
Henry County, GA, 21, 106
Herrman
    Dr., 260
    Dr. J.D., 214, 236
Hicks
    Henry, 47
High Shoals, Walton County,
    GA, 202

Hubbard
 Ollie, 270-271
Hubbert
 Mr., 121
Hubert
 John, 121
Huckabee
 Rev. R.W., 210
Hudson
 Louis, 288
 Mrs. Floy, 287-288
 W.D., 133
Hudspeth House,
 Hawkinsville, GA, 149
Hughes
 Mrs., 101
Hulsey
 Mrs., 64
 Mrs. John, 148
 Terrel, 138
 Thomas, 148
Hunt
 Taylor, 203
Hunter
 Mrs. A.E., 29
Hurricane Creek, 206
Hursey
 David, 221
 John, 221
 John J., 221
 W.T., 221
Hurt
 Will, 265

Indian attack, 6
Indian Ford, 181-182
Inman
 Ben, 234
 George, 234
Irvin
 Alex, 128
 John, 39
Irwin County, GA, 146, 168,
 182, 198, 221, 271
Irwinville, Irwin County, GA,
 211
Isdol
 Mr., 238
Isham, 39
Ivey estate, 156
J. Davis' mill Pond, 163
J.R. Cole & Co's gin, 256
Jack, 43
Jackson
 Rev. James, 11
 Rev. Mr., 38
 William A., 62
Jackson County, GA, 147-
 148, 272-273
Jackson County, WV., 124
Jackson Street, Columbus,
 GA, 63
Jackson, Butts County, GA,
 26
Jacksonville, FL, 39, 245
Jacksonville, Telfair County,
 GA, 43, 102, 212, 220

Jacobs
 Harry, 276-277
 Lizzie Hays, 277
James
 William A., 156
Janes
 J.R., estate, 208
Jarmon
 Capt. James, 39
Jarrett
 Dock, 211-212
Jasper County, GA, 3, 79
Jaugstetter
 boys, 41
 John, 41
Jay
 Thomas, 165
Jefferson County, FL, 6
Jefferson County, GA, 57
Jeffersonville, Twiggs
 County, GA, 179, 282
Jenkins
 Gov., 57
Jernigan
 James, 139
 W.G., 62
 W.H., 62
Jesup, Wayne County, GA,
 208, 290
Joe, 39, 52
John, 54
Johns
 Willie, 181

Johnson
 Charley, 256
 Dr., 193
 Dr. Thad, 173
 John, 33
 Mr., 104
 Mrs. Tabitha S., 65
 Mrs. Thomas, 119
 Nancy, 63-65
 Thomas, 119
Johnson County, GA, 101
Jones
 Frank, 83
 Jessie, 224
 Joe, 233-234
 Miles, Esq., 83
 Mr., 169
 Mrs. Lewis, 121
 Ophelia, 64
 Walter, 4
 Wellington, 88
Jones County, GA, 24, 46,
 118, 145
Jones' saw mill, 67
Jordan
 Miles, 209
 Mrs. Sarah, 209
 Reuben, 209
 Thomas, 131
 Tommie, 209
Jordan Bros. plantation, 272
Judge
 Charley, 111-112

Landon
Mr., 52
Lane
Joseph T., 175
Langford
John, 249
Langley and Robinson, 131
Larrimore
D.W., 45
Mrs., 45
Laurens County, GA, 5, 183,
191, 206, 219, 222,
224-225, 231, 239,
254, 255, 285-286
Lawrence
H., 194
Lawson
Henry, 78
Leary, Calhoun County, GA,
130, 142, 209
Lee County, AL, 87
Lee County, GA, 195, 198,
205
Leftwich
Rev. J.T., 115
Legal Tender Mine, 201
Leitch's mills, 168-169
Lester
Rev, R,B,, 46
Wade H., Esq., 45
Leverett
Nancy, 64
Nancy Jane, 65

Levy County, FL, 58
Lewis
Mrs., 290
R.A., 200
William McBride, 5
Lexington, Oglethorpe
County, GA, 167
Liberty County, GA, 59
Lighthouse, 77, 121
Lilly, Dooly County, GA, 272,
284
Lindsey
J.R., 219
Talbot, 219
Lingo
Bud, 179
Lipscombe
Nathan, 61
Little
A.J., 277
Little Ocmulgee church,
253-254
Little River, GA, 100,
281-282
Lively
George W., 48-49
Locke
W.F., 208
London, England, 44
Long
F.E., 276
John, 99

McWhorter
  Frederick, 44
McWilliams
  Comer, 258
  Mr., 166
  W.A., 258
Mechanicsville, Lee County,
  AL, 87
Mercer University, 91
Merry-Go-Round, 285
Methodist Episcopal Church,
  38, 165, 278
Middleton
  James, 62
Milan, Telfair County, GA,
  277, 286-287
Miles
  Albert, 198
Milledgeville, Baldwin
  County, GA, 32, 50-
  51, 135, 206, 270, 291
Millen
  Robert, 171
Millen, Burke (now Jenkins)
  County, GA, 30
Miller
  Henry, 89-90
  Mrs., 90
  Pierce, 137
Miller County, GA, 135
Mimms
  Jesse, 197

Mims
  Seab., 91
Mitchell
  Col. W.D., 138
  Francis, 152
  Mr., 195
  Oscar, 246
  William, 187
Mize
  C.L., 208
Mobley
  Dr., 186
  J.J., 230
Mobley Mill, 132
Mohr Bros., Savannah, 207
Molene
  Daniel, 99
Monroe
  J.R., 274
Monroe County, GA, 29, 38,
  86, 118
Monroe Female College, 289
Montezuma, Macon County,
  GA, 222
Montgomery County, GA,
  185, 191, 212-213, 251
Montgomery, AL, 13, 117,
  175, 273
Monticello, FL, 284
Monticello, Jasper County,
  GA, 3, 79
Moore
  Douglas C., 52

New York state, 57

New York City, NY, 150, 207

Newnan, Coweta County,
GA, 249, 256

Newson
Andrew, 62

Newton
Rev. Henry, 202

Newton County, GA, 14, 86

Newton, Baker County, GA,
12

Nobles
Clarinda, 38

Noles Cemetery, 232

Norcross, Gwinnett County,
GA, 124

Norfolk County, VA, 13

Norris
Henry, 202
W.N., 99
Watson, 263

North
H.B., 256-257
N.A., 257

North Carolina, 204, 218,
254

North Port, AL, 47

Northeastern railroad,
147-148

Northey
L.M., 30

Norton
Hiram, 5

L.J., 256

Norwood
Dr. Lucius C., 188-189

Notingham
Judge, 187
Mr., 187

O'Brien
M., 149

O'Callaghan
Wade, 257-258

Oakey Woods Place, 99

Oaky Bluff, 230

Oats
Marion, 107

Ocean Pond, 161

Ocmulgee River, 204, 230,
231, 283

Oconee freight engine, 41

Oconee River, 140

Oconee Swamp, 140

Odd Fellows, 54, 95, 266

Odum
C.H., 147
R.J., 174

Odum, Wayne County, GA,
219, 290

Offerman, Pierce County,
GA, 223

Oglethorpe County, GA, 48,
140-141, 201

Oglethorpe, Macon County,
GA, 37-38, 233-234

Atkinson) County,
GA, 216
Pease
J.W., 52
Peek
Mr., 283
Pennington
Mr., 72
Perdue
David W., 228
Perham
A.P., Jr., 268-269
Perkins
Edgar, 207
Marshall, 50
Perrine
Mrs., 6
Perry, Houston County, GA,
199
Persons
Dr. R.T., 121
Rev. G.W., 121
Peters
R.L., 62
Petty
Frank, 282
Pharis
W.R., 261
Philadelphia, PA, 92, 242
Philips
John, 64
Phillips
Nimrod, 2

Pickens County, GA, 122
Pierce
G.F., 14
J.L., 14
Pierce County, GA, 206, 223
Pierson
Mr., 205
Pike
Josie, 87
Pike County, GA, 177, 240
Pine Park, Valdosta, GA, 232
Pittman
John, 101-102
Pitts
Blanche, 251
Mrs. Eliza, 251
Plains of Dura, 31
Plains, Sumter County, GA,
31
Platt
C.A., 54
Player
Mr., 150
Pleasant Hour bar room, 37
Poer
George, 230
George W., 230
Poland, 262
Polhill
Rev. Joseph, 32
Ponder
Coroner, 176

Pope
Daniel W., 228
Pope's church, 280
Port Royal, 128
Poulan, Worth County, GA, 240
Pound
Jere M., 270
School Commisioner, 270
Pournelle
Mrs. Anna, 239
Powder Springs, Cobb County, GA, 162, 186
Powell
W.L., 218
Powell's Station, Washington County, GA, 90
Pownall
Dr. A.P., 74
Mary J. Wilson, 74
Pratt
J.M., 221
Roscoe, 221
Pratt, GA, 221
Presley
Mr., 16
Mrs., 16-17
Price
T.S., 271
Prickett
Robert, 220

Primitive Baptist Church, 125, 152
Pritchett
Rev. B.C., 284-285
Procter
William B., 91-92
Providence Church, 152
Prussia, 71
Pucket
Clifford, 88
Puckett
J.G., 257-258
Puckett's Chapel, GA, 97
Pulaski County, GA, 149-150, 184, 194, 197, 213, 216, 231, 242, 253, 268, 279
Pulaski House, Savannah, GA, 51
Purcell
E.C., 277
Purvis Gin, 261
Putnam County, GA, 45, 58
Quillian
Clem, 81
Quincy, FL, 131
Quinn
Dr. Terry, 37
Quitman County, GA, 106, 207
Quitman, Brooks County, GA, 88-89, 176, 265

Rivers
    John, 58
Roberson
    Troy, 263
Roberts
    Luke, 151
Robertson
    A.S., 257
    Rev. W.J., 218
Robinson, 133
    Deputy Sheriff, 23
    Samuel C., 133
Rogers
    Clem, 240
    Coroner G.C., 286
    Cullen, 240
    Fletcher, 217
    H., 208
    Homer, 217
    Hubert, 217-218
    Sheriff J.C., 235-236
    T.M., 240
    Tom, 240-241
    Wesley, 217
Rolling Mill, 95
Rome, Floyd County,
    GA, 145
Rosdale Garden, 114
Rose Hill Cemetery, Macon,
    GA, 54
Roseboro, NC, 226
Ross
    Dr., 199

James C., Esq., 59
Rounsaville
    Charlie, 145
    J.W., 145
Rowe
    John, 91
Royal
    Minnie, 284
    Will J., Jr., 284-285
    William J., 284-285
Rutledge, Morgan County,
    GA, 105
Ryals
    Judge George W., 283
Salt Creek, 128
Sand Hill, KY, 74
Sand Hills, GA, 20
Sandersville, Washington
    County, GA, 147, 228
Sapp
    Johnnie, 216
    Tiny, 216
Saunders
    John, 42
Savannah Florida & Western
    Railroad, 206
Savannah House, Columbus,
    GA, 63-64
Savannah, Chatham County,
    GA, 31, 62, 69, 70-71,
    72, 76, 110, 123, 128,
    144, 156, 202, 206-
    207, 215, 228, 262

J.N., Jr., 40
Jefferson, 43
Mary A., 284
Taylor County, GA, 158, 168
Tebeauville, Ware County, GA, 109
Teel
Elizabeth, 87
Susan, 87
Telfair County, GA, 43-44, 66, 102-103, 174, 220, 224, 230, 234, 255, 261, 264, 266, 277-278
Terrell County, GA, 33, 56, 89, 130, 190, 208-209
Texas, 211, 231
Texas district, Heard County, GA, 154
Theus
B.T., 31
Thomas
Kenneth L., Jr., 294
Robert, 8
Tom, 229
W.H., 99
Thomas County, GA, 112, 116, 134, 138, 162, 195, 200, 284
Thomasville, Thomas County, GA, 76, 162, 200, 284

Thompson
Benjamin, 76
Thornton
W.H., 276
Thurmond
T.H., 208
Thweatt
Pvt., 52
Tibbs
Charles H., 55
Tifton, Berrien (after 1905 Tift) County, GA, 210
Tinsley
Martin, 130
T.D., 59-60
Tishomingo County, MS, 72
Tobeesaufky swamp, 23
Tornado, 118-121
Towell
John, 39
Towne
Franklin P., 129
Towns, Telfair County, GA, 240
Tozier
John, 10
Travellers Rest, Dooly (now Macon) County, GA, 38
Treadwell
John, 254
twins, 254

Vienna Cotton Oil Company, 264

Vienna, Dooly County, GA, 264

Vineville, Macon, Bibb County, GA, 60-61

Vining Station, Cobb County, GA, 41

Vinson

B.H., 226-227

W. & T. line, 288

Wade

John T., 175

William, 70-71

Walden

William, 62

Waldroup

Mr., 186

Walker

Col. E. Lawton, 266

D.J., 223, 266

J. Randall, 266

James, 223

Joel M., 284

William, 7

Willie, 266

Walkersville, Pierce County, GA, 266

Wall

J.M., 230

Wallace

Campbell, 57

Walnut Creek, 3

Walters

Mr., 160

Walton County, GA, 184, 202

War of 1812 soldier, 49

Ward's Station, Randolph County, GA, 165

Ware

Judge G.M.T., 208

Ware County, GA, 35, 178, 268-269

Warren County, GA, 90, 120

Warthen

Mr., 147

Washington

Charles W., 3

George, 140

Washington, DC, 77

Washington County, GA, 90, 101, 147, 161, 225, 228

Watson

Willis, 198

Waycross, Ware County, GA, 178, 226-227, 268-269, 280-281

Wayne County, GA, 1, 208, 219, 290

Ways' undertaking parlors, 242

Webb

Mr., 55

Webster County, GA, 177

Wells

Edward, 74

Welsh
    Mrs. John, 123
West
    Andrew J., 190
    Curry, 281-282
    Mrs. T.E., 281
    Sylvanus, 48
West Point cemetery, 212
West Point, Troup County,
    GA, 80, 92, 108, 212,
    230, 246
Westberry
    Randall, 290
Western & Atlantic Railroad,
    12, 41, 57, 133, 164,
    190, 195
Westmoreland
    Dr. Willis, 173
Weston
    Capt. S.R., 210
    Jesse D., 210
    Stephen, 209-210
Westonia, Coffee County,
    GA, 209
White
    Ben, 92
    Deliah Anderson, 192
    James, 192
    Joseph, 76
    Mr., 73
    Rev. R.E., 155
    Tim, 142
    William, 124

Whitehall crossing, Atlanta,
    GA, 113-114
Whitehead
    D.A., 159
Whitesburg, Carroll County,
    GA, 99, 254
Whitesville, Harris County,
    GA, 188
Whitfield
    M.S., 108
Whitfield & Blackburn, 47
Whitfield County, GA, 71, 81,
    84
Whitson
    Mrs. Mary T., 286
Whitten
    W.J., 195
Wiggins
    Aylesbury, 161-162
    James M., 199
    Rev. R.L., 214
Wightman
    William F., 28
Wilcox
    James Y., 43
    Joseph, 102-103
    Mr., 283
    Rebecca, 102
    S.W., 116
    Thomas, 68
Wilcox County, GA, 150, 216,
    274-275, 283,
    290-291

Wilkes County, GA, 96, 102, 155

Wilkins
    Dr., 260

Willcox
    T.S., 212
    William, 43

Willcox and Powell, lumber, 204

Williams
    Arad, 121
    C.C., 258
    Charles J., 52
    Joseph, 2
    Joseph B., 43-44
    Mr., 210
    R.M., 139
    Robert, 139
    Robert T., 193
    W.E., 154

Williams' Shingle Mill, 222

Williamson
    Col. George B., 178

Williford
    Samuel, 104

Willingham
    Dr., 201
    Thomas, 289

Willis
    Dennis, 144

Willson
    S.P., 125

Wilson
    Andrew, 263
    George, 79
    Mary J., 74
    Stewart, 81

Wimberly
    Dr., 34
    Leon P., 274-275
    Leon P., Jr., 275
    Mrs. Julia, 275
    Will, 275

Wiseman
    J.W., Esq., 56
    John, 56

Withlacoochee River, 165

Wolf Creek, 56

Wood
    George, 105
    Henry, 25
    John W., 105
    O.M., 228
    Pate, 224
    Robert A., 64
    Thomas, 105

Woodall
    Mrs. Mary, 78
    William, 78

Woodland, Talbot County, GA, 291

Woodlawn Cemetery, Eastman, GA, 214, 218, 239

Woods
		A.J., 194
Woodstock, Cherokee
		County, GA, 68
Wooten
		J.B., 250
		J.L., 259
Wooten's Mill, 255
Worcester, MA, 129
Worth County, GA, 97, 111,
		153
Wright
		David, 23
		Mrs., 120
		W.H., 226-227
Wyatt
		William, 21
Wynne
		Mr., 220
		Mrs. W., 220
Wynnton, Columbus,
		Muscogee County,
		GA, 245
Yates
		James, 1
Yellow Creek, 122
Yellow River, 86
Young
		A.B., 264
		Mr., 233
		Conductor, 233
		M.E.J., 134
		Uncle Jenks, 134

W.H., Esq., 22
Zebulon, Pike County, GA,
		229